Anne Hooper's sex Q&A

Anne Hooper's sex Q&A

LONDON, NEW YORK, MUNICH,
MELBOURNE and DELHI

Senior Managing Art Editor Lynne Brown
Managing Editor Stephanie Farrow
Senior Art Editor Karen Ward
Project Editor Kesta Desmond
Project Art Editor Tracy Miles
DTP Karen Constanti
Production Sarah Dodd

Photographers
Luc Beziat
Patricia Morris
James Muldowney

First published in Great Britain in 2001
by Dorling Kindersley Limited,
80 Strand, London WC2R 0RL

A Penguin Company

A CIP catalogue record for this book is available from the British Library.

ISBN 0-7513-3875

Produced by Colourscan, Singapore
Printed and bound in Singapore by Star Standard

see our complete catalogue at
www.dk.com

contents

introduction

Such is the strength of human optimism that men and women fight hard to save their sex lives when something goes wrong. Sex is one of nature's rewards and sensuality is particularly valued as a buffer or comfort zone. Being the enduring creatures that we are, we do our utmost to address our sexual problems and dilemmas and try to put them right. That is where this book comes in. It comprises a series of the most frequently asked questions on the gritty subject of loving relationships. It covers many life stages – from dating to pregnancy to middle and old age – and does its best to offer sexy starting points to help you improve your sexual relationship.

We live in difficult times – sexually speaking. There's a pandemic of AIDS raging and stress-related sex problems have gone to the top of the list in sex therapy clinics. If you are single, it may be hard to make new friends in the big cities and depressing not to have a partner to cuddle ns

up to. If you are married, your partner may not want as much as sex as you do or, alternatively, he/she may want it, but with someone else. Some sex problems are caused by ill health or aging, some turn out to be innate,

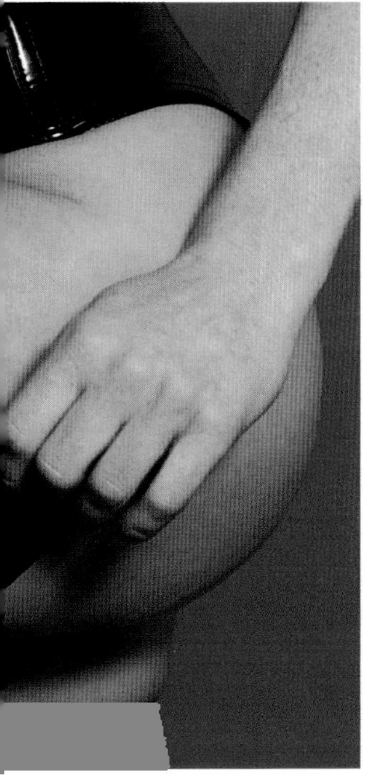

and some result from inexperience, ignorance, or misunderstanding. And our sex life is the one area that we really don't want to go wrong – we all need to feel sexually confident. Sex lies at the core of our personalities and is a crucial part of how we define ourselves.

Sex Q&A is is inspired by the many questions that my readers have asked me over the past few years. The answers tackle all the subjects that you most want to know about. I sincerely hope that they prove useful to you. If you want to ask some more questions, you can write to me at: anne@annehooper.com. Good luck with your sex life.

Anne Hooper

sex in relationships

Long-term relationships provide the setting for many people's sex lives. Sex tends to be most intense at the start of a relationship and then it settles down into a pattern and frequency that – hopefully – suits both partners.

action in bed

What do most couples do in bed?

Most couples start off with foreplay in which they both concentrate on arousing each other. Foreplay focuses on erogenous zones such as the lips, neck, breasts, nipples and genitals and it includes a personal combination of stroking, hugging, caressing, massage, kissing, mutual masturbation and oral sex. Intercourse most popularly happens in the missionary position or in variations of this. Many couples also enjoy sex from the rear and woman-on-top positions.

How long should sex last from foreplay to orgasm?

How long is a piece of string? The answer depends on the sexual responses of the lovers, their physical fitness and stamina, and on how much or little they know about prolonging lovemaking. Some men and women enjoy fast sex in which they climax almost immediately. Others relish taking a long time over lovemaking. Part of the getting-to-know-you period in a relationship involves working out what a couple's particular needs are.

In sex therapy, it is generally thought that genital excitement for the man needs to be sustained for at least 15 minutes to give the woman a chance to become properly aroused.

Of course, different women have different sexual timing: some can go from start to climax in three minutes; others take three-quarters of an hour or more. It's a sensible idea to allow for at least an hour of lovemaking even if you don't need so long. Why create a time limit?

How can I make my partner as aroused as possible?

Try to get inside each other's minds. See if you can work out what fires his or her sexual imagination and share your sexual fantasies. And take some risks – if you've always fancied doing something, but thought it too outrageous, voice it. You don't actually have to do it – you're just aiming to be sexy and provocative. Don't rush things – take time building up to sex so that when you arrive in bed, you're desperate to make love. Even then you can prolong the experience – let your hands roam around your lover's body, whipping up a storm of goosebumps.

I want to introduce more variety into my sex life. Are there any special techniques that I can try with my partner?
There are many. Take a look at the suggestions for sex games in Chapter 5 and, in the meantime, try out some of these ideas:

- Give a thought to how you undress – do you rush through it, ending up with just your socks on or do you peel off your clothes to reveal some sexy underwear? Try performing a special striptease for your partner.
- Turn your bedroom into an exotic sex temple. Use candles, incense, scented oils, cushions, pillows, silky fabrics, sexy music and flowers to set the scene. This will create a very different mood from a bedroom that looks like a tip!
- Use the penis as a kind of vibrator. Hold the shaft and rub the tip of the penis rapidly up and down on the clitoris (this is a great orgasm aid for both partners).
- Use a finger to pull down on the lower part of the vagina during sex.
- Wedge a vibrator between both of your genitals during sex.
- Insert a finger (with short, clean fingernails) just inside your partner's anus during intercourse and press in and out. Alternatively, move your fingertip in circular movements around the rim of the anus.
- A tip for men: hold your partner's labia up around your penis as you thrust inside her.
- A tip for women: close your legs tight in the missionary position to give your partner an extra thrusting area.

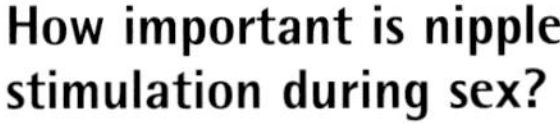

How important is nipple stimulation during sex?
The breasts and nipples are key erogenous zones – a few women can reach orgasm from nipple stimulation alone. Try gently massaging the whole of the breast, tweaking or rolling the nipples between your fingers and licking, sucking and flicking the nipples with your tongue. Men, as well as women, can enjoy nipple stimulation.

Should I wait for my girlfriend to have an orgasm before I ejaculate?
It's not written in stone that you should, but in terms of timing, it tends to make sense. Once you've climaxed you may want to rest, whereas, if your girlfriend is only halfway to orgasm, she will want to carry on – taking a break is likely to create a true anticlimax for her. However, if you're happy to stimulate your girlfriend by hand or mouth after you've ejaculated, then this is fine.

I've always thought that the man should initiate sex. But my partner says that he wants me to be more proactive. Who is right?
The best sex is probably that which happens spontaneously. This means that if you're feeling sexy, it's fine – whatever your gender – to take the initiative. After all, men may feel burdened by sexual responsibility if they always have to take the lead, and women can feel deprived of sexual freedom. Gone are the days when it was perceived as feminine to be the passive recipient of sex. Ideally, there should be no strict roles or rules during sex except, of course, those which are essential for your own health and wellbeing.

Is it OK to have intercourse during my partner's period?
Yes, providing you both feel comfortable with this. You might want to put a towel on the bed first to avoid staining the mattress and, for hygiene purposes, you should wash your penis after lovemaking as sexual fluids and menstrual blood can collect under the foreskin. Beyond this, no other precautions are necessary.

My husband uses a vibrator to make me orgasm. Could this prevent me from climaxing normally?
There is no truth in the suggestion that women can get addicted to vibrators. Rather than limiting sexual opportunities, vibrators have expanded them. They enable greater ease of climax under a wide variety of conditions rather than the other way round – so don't worry!

sextips

The Thai massage

This special Thai massage technique is a great way of giving your partner an unusual and sexy surprise. Prepare both of your bodies by covering them with foaming soapsuds (as the Thais do) or another slippery substance, such as massage oil. The man should lie flat on his stomach on a towel while the woman lies on top of him with her belly to his back. Now the woman uses her entire body as a massage tool by sliding up and down on her partner. She can vary her strokes by wriggling, letting her body slip from side to side and using her arms to propel herself in different directions. She can also impose a definite rhythm to the strokes. The next stage of the massage is to repeat all of the movements on the front of her partner's body.

My wife recently bought a sex manual for us to look at. What does this say about our sex life?
Your wife is probably telling you that she loves the idea of a little novelty and she hopes that you do too. It doesn't mean that she is bored with you – it would be hard to give a sex book to someone you had your doubts about. Take it as a compliment that she wants to explore and expand your sex life. And enjoy your new reading material!

Is it OK to masturbate each other instead of having intercourse? My partner wants to do this occasionally.
Any kind of sexual variation is OK as long as you both agree to it. Mutual masturbation can be an erotic alternative to intercourse – variety is one of the best ways to keep your lovemaking fresh and exciting.
Yet another variation is to stimulate yourself while your partner watches – this can be a good way to break down inhibitions and it teaches your partner how you most like to be touched.

What are the best ways in which to have satisfying non-penetrative sex?
Mutual masturbation, oral sex and genital massage can all be wonderful. So too can whole body massage, touching, rolling and rubbing. You can also experiment with the diverse range of sex toys available (see pages 112–115). If you are having non-penetrative sex for health reasons, read pages 154–155.

Our best sex only ever happens after an argument. Why should this be?
The brain centres for powerful emotional responses, such as anger or even fear, are closely linked to the brain centres that control sexual arousal. To explore this theory in a less destructive manner, try going on a fairground ride, such as the big dipper, with your lover and see how you feel afterwards!

Sometimes, sex after an argument can also provide comfort and reassurance, a way of saying "even though we fight, we still end up back together in the end".

Although having sex after an argument isn't in itself a problem, make sure that you don't start to manufacture arguments as a route to sexual intimacy.

sexual frequency

How often do most couples have sex?

The younger you are, the more sex you are likely to want. People tend to have more sex at the beginning of a relationship but less as time goes on, especially after the two-year mark. Sex surveys have found that the average couple will start off with two to three lovemaking sessions a week, but that this tails off as time passes.

Will it damage our relationship if we don't have sex very often?

Not necessarily, as long as you have settled into a pattern that you are both happy with. Relationships can last a lifetime with no sex involved at all. But lasting over the years depends on how much you care about each other, how many common interests you share, whether you have children and what kind of investment, both emotional and financial, you have in the relationship. Some people don't need much sex to be happy; others compensate for a lack of sex by masturbating a lot. Some people have lovers – they manage to compartmentalize life so that neither partner knows anything about the other. However, it takes a lot of strength to maintain two intimate relationships which are potentially in opposition – and infidelity (see pages 24–27) definitely does have the capacity to damage your relationship.

What does it mean if...

my partner masturbates even though we have a very active sex life?

- Masturbation gives your partner a different type of satisfaction to sex.
- Masturbation is a method of calming anxiety which has nothing to do with sex with a partner.
- Masturbation serves a specific function such as helping your partner go to sleep.
- Your partner has a very high sex drive and masturbation feels like the safest way to fulfil it without being unfaithful.

Sex fact

A 1987 sex survey showed that whereas married couples' sex life declined over time (as measured by the number of sex acts), that of couples who cohabited – rather than married – remained more active, regardless of age.

Is it possible to have too much sex? My partner and I make love at least twice a day.

You can't hurt yourself by having a lot of sex and it can certainly bring you a great deal of pleasure. If you or your body didn't want frequent sex, you'd find yourself making excuses to avoid it. Having said this, the fact that you are questioning the desirability of so many sex sessions might mean that you are getting a) a bit bored or b) worn out. Don't be afraid of saying "I don't feel like it now – let's have a break". This would be perfectly normal.

We used to be in bed all the time when we first met. Now we make love once a fortnight. Does it have to be like this?

How often you have sex depends on so many variables. Hard work, lack of time and energy, stress, illness, having children – these are just some of the things that can deplete your sex life. Even without these, sex studies show that the passage of time causes a natural decline in the rate at which couples make love. But less sex does not mean less love. You need to reassure each other that you still care with loving gestures such as kisses and compliments. Many couples also say that resurgences of passion occur from time to time in their relationship.

My girlfriend doesn't want to have sex very often but then she gets bursts when, over a period of two or three days, she suddenly can't get enough. Why is this?

I would guess that this pattern of desire corresponds with your girlfriend's menstrual cycle (see page 76). The two or three days around the end of the menstrual month tend to be the ones that coincide with high sex drive. Ask your girlfriend if she is aware of the effect her hormones have on her sex drive. If she regularly feels sexy at ovulation (usually mid-way through the menstrual cycle) you can also plan lots of sex around this time or even a weekend away. Don't forget that ovulation is the time when women are most fertile, so, if you don't want to conceive, make sure that you use reliable contraception.

I'm a 42-year-old woman and I'm engaged to a man of 75. How frequent can I expect our lovemaking to be?

Many different sex studies have been carried out on sexual activity in older people and the results are varied. For example, in 1926 bio-statistician,

Raymond Pearl, found that 4 per cent of men aged 70–79 had intercourse every three days and another 9 per cent had it weekly. In 1959, Dr A L Finkle and team questioned 101 men between the ages of 56 and 86 with no illness likely to reduce potency. Some of the results were as follows:

- 65 per cent of the under-69s were sexually active.
- 34 per cent of the over-70s were sexually active.
- Almost 50 per cent of those aged 80 and over managed at least 10 sex sessions per year.

In the group that interests you – the over-70s – the main reason given for sexual inactivity was lack of desire or partner rather than incapacity. So, as long as your husband stays fit and well, you should have lots of sex!

Having seen our sex life dwindle – through my husband's choice, not mine – I'm puzzled by the fact that he's suddenly stepped up our lovemaking. Could he be having an affair?

There are lots of reasons why people step up lovemaking and only one of them is infidelity. If your husband is in his 40s, he could be experiencing the changes of midlife and may suddenly be re-evaluating his relationship with you. This could make him want to re-affirm his sexuality and to relate more sensually to you than he has done in the past. He may indeed be turned on by another person but, instead of having an affair, is directing his feelings at you. And, yes, there is a chance he may be seeing someone else and you are experiencing the spill-over of his heightened sex drive. Think carefully before forcing him to talk. If he is involved with someone else, how would you tackle this?

My boyfriend has never wanted to get married until now. In the past his refusal to make a commitment made me crave lots of sex with him. The problem is, now that he's finally agreed to marry me, I don't seem to want sex so often. What's going on?

Your boyfriend's past attitude towards marriage may have undermined your confidence and, to compensate for your anxiety, you initiated a lot of sex. Now that he is offering commitment, your anxiety is subsiding. As a result, you can get a more realistic picture of how often you wish to make love. And you may be making the surprising discovery that you need a lot less lovemaking than you realized. There is an alternative explanation, however. Now that you feel less worried, you are probably able, for the first time, to feel angry with your boyfriend for all those rejections. This anger may be turning you off sex. If this is true, try taking a wider view of your boyfriend's lack of commitment. Perhaps he was waiting for better financial circumstances or needed time to become more mature – could you find a way to view these things sympathetically? You certainly need to talk frankly about your feelings.

casehistory

"I've been denied sex for years. I'm not going to wait any longer."

Richard, 36

I've been married to Tania for 10 years and during that time there's been very little sex. After about two years together she was always exhausted from her work. It's true that she works very hard, but the gaps between our lovemaking got longer and longer. I woke up the other day and realized that we haven't made love for over six months. I broached the subject with Tania and she turned round and said that she didn't think she wanted to have sex any more. I have a terrible sense of wasted time. I'm nearing 40 and I want to have a family. I've been denied sex for years. I'm not going to wait any longer. As far as I'm concerned my marriage is over.

Anne responds:

"Tania was heartbroken that Richard felt that the marriage was over but still insisted that she couldn't sleep with him any more. She didn't know why, but she just didn't desire him. When Richard suggested that she might go for a medical to see if there was a physical reason for her lack of sex drive, she declined. When faced with the break-up of a long-term relationship, some women are willing to make moves to improve sex. Sometimes the sheer adrenaline provoked by the threat of a break-up can turn people on. Neither of these things happened. Six months later Richard moved out and met a new lover. So, as it happens, did Tania, with the result that her sex drive returned with no difficulty. So hindsight shows that Richard had made the right choice for both partners. By confronting a sensitive problem he was able to start making positive changes. But this kind of choice is invariably tough."

I'd like to have sex more frequently but my girlfriend and I rarely seem to have time because we work so hard. What can we do?

Finding the time to make love can become increasingly hard as work and other pressures build up around you. There are two things you can do. First of all, make the most of "quickie sex". Forget the idea that long sensual lovemaking is the only worthwhile kind of sex. Aim for fast explosive sex that's over in minutes. Do it in the shower, just before you go to sleep at night or as you're getting ready to go out. Secondly, make an appointment to have sex. This may sound clinical but you'll both appreciate having a couple of hours together with no responsibilities other than to have erotic fun. Above all, don't neglect your sex life in the belief that life will soon become less hectic – unless you can seriously reduce your workload, this probably won't happen!

indetail

Negotiating a sex contract

A sex contract is useful when partners disagree about how frequently to have sex, but especially when one partner wants to have sex on a daily basis when the other doesn't. The contract consists of allocating three nights of the week to one partner and three nights to the other. The seventh night is up for grabs. During your allocated days you each have the freedom to choose whether or not to have sex. Whatever decision you make must be respected by your partner. How this tends to work in practise is that the needy partner always says "yes" to sex whereas the not-so-needy partner always says "no". This is beneficial, however, in that the needy partner can still have frequent sex and the not-so-needy partner stops feeling pressured.

My wife wants sex every single day and I'm beginning to feel really stressed by this. How can I change things?

Men and women who want sex every day, year in and year out, usually attribute this to a high sex drive. However, clinical thinking reckons that there are some people who want lots of sex because they use it to dissipate high anxiety levels. Whatever the reason, no-one should be pressurized into having sex when they don't want to. You are perfectly entitled to try to change things – one solution is to create a sex contract (see box above). This takes pressure off you and forces your partner to consider your needs as well as her own.

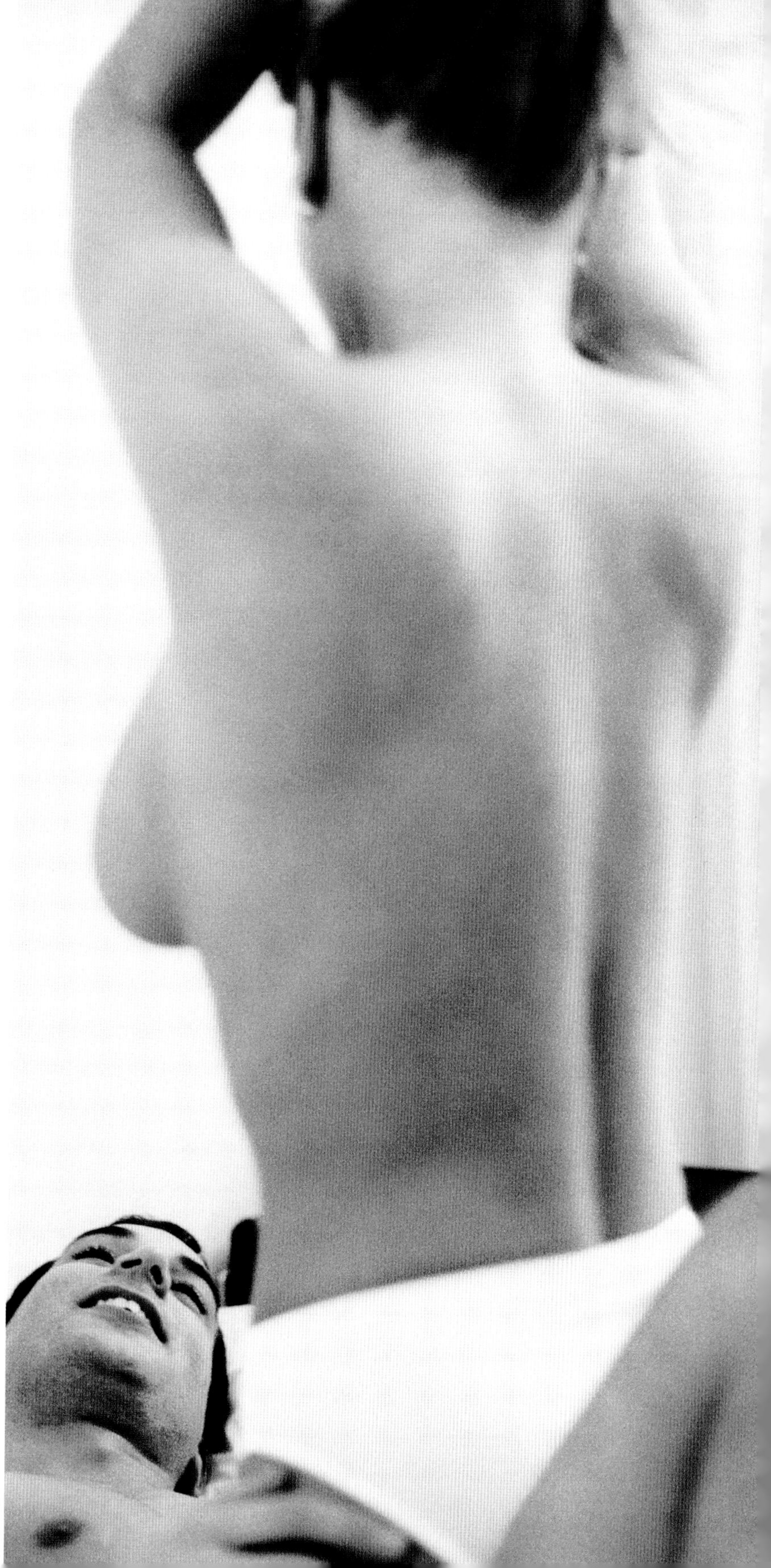

sexual compatibility

I'm feeling smothered by my boyfriend. He always initiates sex and is very dominant in bed. How can I change things?
Rather than criticising your partner's entire sexual approach, it might be better to try to tackle just one aspect of your sex life. This way he won't feel completely undermined. Explain, for example, that you would really enjoy initiating sex sometimes and you'd like him to give you the space to do this. You could try proposing a sex contract (see page 15) in which you both get an exactly equal chance to choose whether or not you have sex, or what kind of sex you have. If your partner is opposed to any kind of sexual change, use the dripping tap technique of negotiation (see box on page 18). If he still won't meet you halfway, it may be worth reassessing your relationship. If your partner bullies you in bed, the chances are he will bully you in other areas of the relationship too.

My partner is incredibly shy in bed and never seems to relax. I love sex and am very open about it. How can I persuade her to be more outgoing?
Spend lots of time reassuring her, stroking her, giving her a relaxing massage and avoiding any sort of sexual pressure. And, if you are at the beginning of your relationship, allow time for you both to get to know one another. If none of these suggestions work, your partner may be one of those people who respond well to a small amount of alcohol before sex (the emphasis here is on small!). Alternatively, in severe cases, where inhibitions are extreme, a prescribed drug called phentolamine, can be helpful. Naturally your partner must want to tackle her shyness. It would be wholly wrong for you to force her.

My lover only wants intercourse. He says he's not interested in foreplay. As a result I never get very turned on or have an orgasm. What can I do?
You could tell him that you know that you can have enjoyable orgasms if you are given the chance to become really aroused. Ask him if he would stimulate your clitoris by hand before you start having intercourse. If he won't agree to this – or to any other kind of adjustment to your sexual routine – there's not a great deal you can do except concede that his lovemaking skills are primitive, and that perhaps he's not the right lover for you.

I really love my girlfriend but she hasn't had much sexual experience. How can I teach her to really turn me on?
Try playing the body map game. It's an excellent way of learning about each other's erogenous zones and helps your partner to learn the best way to stimulate you. You each spend 15 to 20 minutes "mapping" each other's naked bodies. You do this by stroking and caressing small areas of skin using your finger until you have covered the whole body, including the genitals. The recipient rates each touch in terms of how pleasurable it feels (from -3 to +3). When it's your turn to report on the sensations, you can elaborate by telling your partner what type, duration and pressure of touch turns you on most.

indetail

Reducing inhibitions

Sexual problems often arise as a result of hang-ups. There are many different sexual inhibitions but some of the more common ones include worrying about body odours during sex, not wanting to be seen naked, feeling anxious about a particular body part, being nervous about a particular sex act, such as oral sex, or just feeling excessively self-conscious during sex.

Behaviour therapy is a branch of psychology that aims to tackle inhibitions and phobias. It does so by exposing the inhibited person to the source of their inhibition in a series of controlled steps. You can take the principles of behaviour therapy and use them at home. For example, someone who is nervous about having sex with the lights on could start off by making love in a dark room with a single candle burning. If this feels OK, brightness can be increased to several candles, then to a bedside lamp and then to a main light. The idea is that you gain confidence slowly and, if one stage feels uncomfortable, you simply go back to the previous stage until you feel more relaxed. Behaviour therapy also uses relaxation techniques such as deep breathing and muscle relaxation exercises.

emotionaltips

Initiating a difficult conversation

Talking with your partner about sex problems or incompatibilities can be very difficult. It's important to hold your ground while also being sensitive and considerate.

- Choose a time when there will be no interruptions.
- Always speak in the first person. Say "I think..." or "I feel..." rather than starting a sentence with "you". The former feels personal whereas the latter can feel accusatory. This approach helps your partner to listen impartially. And stay calm.
- Don't be put off or deflected. If your partner says: "I'd rather not talk about this", say that you've reached a point of such uncertainty or distress (for example) that you feel you must talk.
- The "dripping tap technique" is useful if your partner is unwilling to give direct answers to your questions. It involves saying the same thing in a number of different ways until you feel you are getting an answer. For example, you could say, "I know that this is hard, but could you explain a bit more", followed by "I need you to go through this with me so that I understand." Keep repeating a version of your original statement until you get somewhere.
- Reassure your partner that you won't criticise/react badly if she/he does reveal his/her feelings.
- Be encouraging. Tell your partner that you rate him/her so highly that you want the relationship to work. This is why you are keen to talk.
- Act as a role model by revealing some of your own uncertainties and vulnerabilities.
- If he/she explodes, stand firm and wait until the anger has subsided. Then acknowledge his/her feelings and encourage him/her to talk more.

Why does my girlfriend seem quite happy to lie there during sex while I do all the work?
Some people are just lazy in bed – they habitually enjoy others making the moves while they reap the benefits. Try allotting "days for you" and "days for me", in which you alternately take responsibility for sex. Another reason for sexual apathy is inhibition. People who don't relax easily during sex need help to build up their sexual confidence. A course in assertion training helps; so does massive encouragement whenever they *are* sexually proactive. A small degree of alcohol or antianxiety medication (if the problem is extreme) can also work wonders. A third reason for your girlfriend's inertia could be a desire to be in control. Being the passive sexual partner – who always receives rather than gives – can make some people feel powerful. If this is the case, help your girlfriend to explore other ways of feeling in control – such as taking charge in bed!

My boyfriend comes too quickly and doesn't have a clue about stimulating me. I'm losing heart. Is there any way in which I can improve things?
I wonder if you have explored the squeeze technique (see page 44) for premature ejaculation. If you haven't,

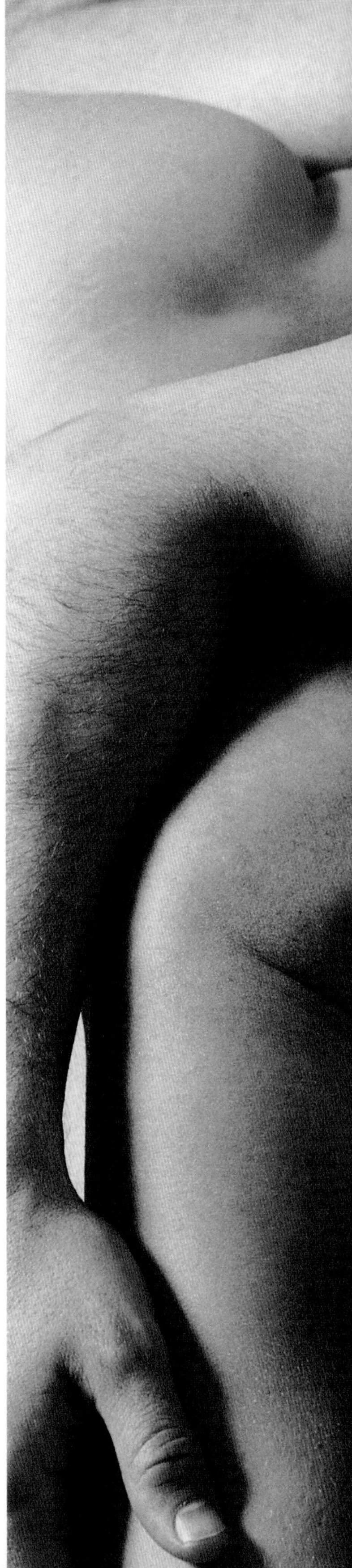

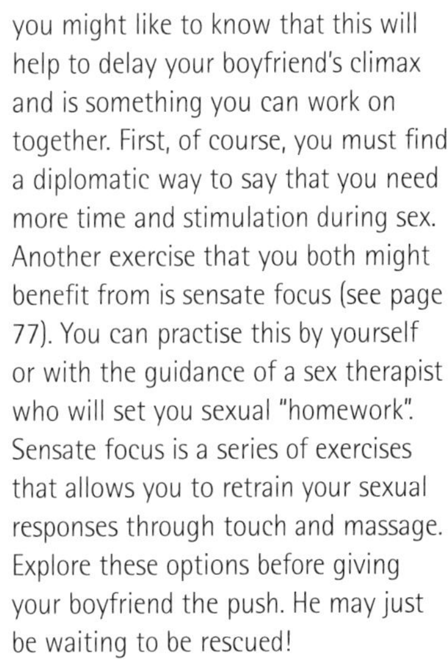

you might like to know that this will help to delay your boyfriend's climax and is something you can work on together. First, of course, you must find a diplomatic way to say that you need more time and stimulation during sex. Another exercise that you both might benefit from is sensate focus (see page 77). You can practise this by yourself or with the guidance of a sex therapist who will set you sexual "homework". Sensate focus is a series of exercises that allows you to retrain your sexual responses through touch and massage. Explore these options before giving your boyfriend the push. He may just be waiting to be rescued!

I'm always too drowsy to have sex first thing in the morning when I wake up. The problem is, my girlfriend loves morning sex. What can we do?

You could give in on the grounds that, although this is not your favourite time for sex, you could manage it occasionally. Or you could have a chat – at some time other than first thing in the morning – when you explain your feelings calmly, without rancour, and see if a good compromise can be worked out. For example, perhaps there are occasions when you are up before your girlfriend (weekends, for example) and could give her a sexual surprise when she awakes.

I don't particularly enjoy S&M games but my partner does. How far should I indulge him?

If by "don't particularly enjoy", you mean you actively dislike playing sadomasochistic games, then you should probably say to your partner "sorry, I'd love to do lots of things in bed with you, but not this". If, on the other hand, you mean you really don't

sextips

Enhancing sexual fit

When a couple don't fit together very well – a large vagina coupled with a small penis or a small vagina with a large penis, for example – you can compensate with specific sex positions.

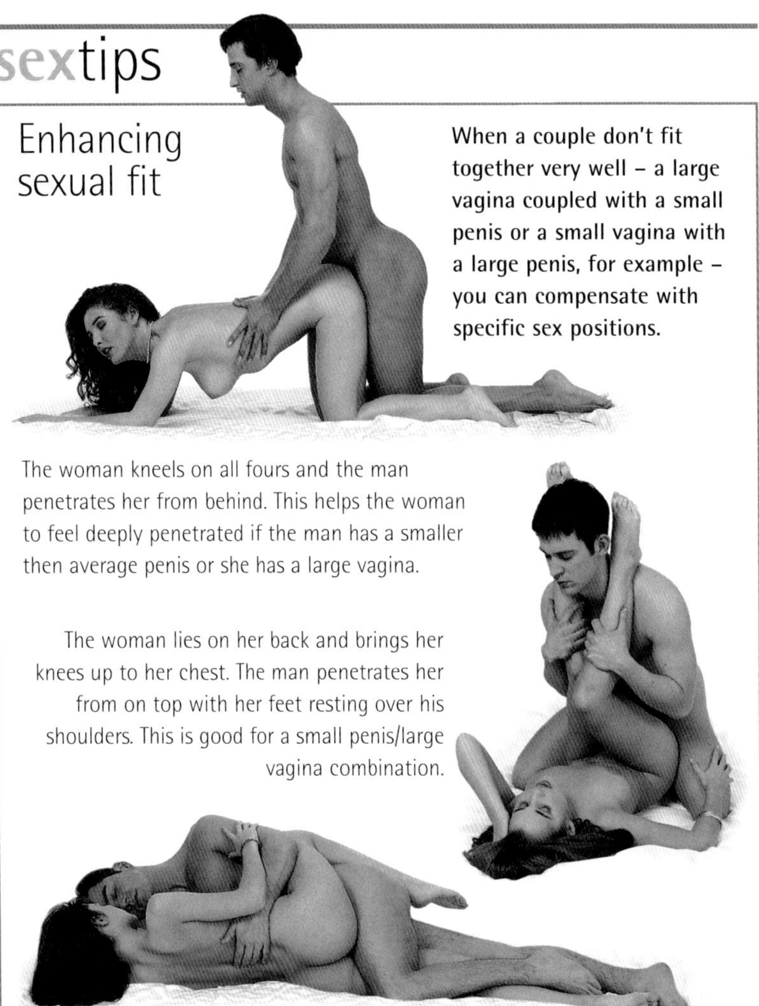

The woman kneels on all fours and the man penetrates her from behind. This helps the woman to feel deeply penetrated if the man has a smaller then average penis or she has a large vagina.

The woman lies on her back and brings her knees up to her chest. The man penetrates her from on top with her feet resting over his shoulders. This is good for a small penis/large vagina combination.

The couple lie on their sides facing each other. She rests her upper leg over his hips and he penetrates her. This is ideal when the woman has a small vagina, the man has a large penis, or both.

The woman lies on her back while the man penetrates her from on top. Then she tightly closes her legs to minimize access to her vagina as he thrusts. This is good for couples who want to cut down on the depth of penetration when the man has a large penis and the woman has a small vagina.

mind much one way or another, then why not go along with your partner occasionally? Perhaps he could indulge you in some of your fantasies in return? Life always involves accepting other people's differences and sex is no exception.

I like to see and feel my partner's naked body during sex, but she always wears her nightie? What can I do?

You could try taking it off in the most sensual way possible. For example, stroke your partner lightly along her legs moving slowly towards her genitals – now sweep her nightie up to her shoulders, stopping to caress her breasts along the way. Now ask her to put up her hands so that you can slip her nightie completely off over her head. If your partner has a problem being naked in front of you, ask her about it. Try to find out what it is that she fears and then offer massive reassurance. People can have all sorts of hang-ups about their bodies and they usually turn out to be very minor – but bear in mind that, for your partner, these hang-ups can assume alarming proportions.

My partner thinks that bodily smells are sexy but I can't have sex unless I've had a shower first. Who is right?

Unless these bodily smells are very strong or unpleasant, I'd say that you probably need to relax a little bit. Smells are indeed a part of sex – they are not just unavoidable, they're also part of the arousal process. As human animals, we are primed to react to chemical triggers, smell being one of them. The smell of male and female genitals and their secretions can be a natural aphrodisiac. It sounds as if you are a bit inhibited about your body – this type of hang-up may have come from parental attitudes or strict rules about hygiene when you were a child. Or perhaps someone has criticised your personal hygiene in the past. Rushing to the shower before sex can impair spontaneity for both you and your partner. If you want to, you can work on overcoming your inhibition by gradually increasing the amount of time that elapses between having a shower and having sex. For example, try having sex an hour after washing, then increase this to two or three hours. Aim to get to the point where you feel comfortable having sex when you've showered either the previous morning or the previous day. If you feel you need help with this, you could consult a behaviour therapist.

I love sex that's wild, dirty and passionate. But I've ended up with a partner who thinks sex ought to be romantic, gentle and adoring. How can we please each other in bed?

This incompatibility means that both of you are going to have to make some changes. This means toning down your desire for wild sex and asking your partner to accept that sex can be adoring without necessarily being gentle. Of course, this approach involves compromise. Try also making a sex contract (see page 15) – you agree that on specified days either you or your partner can choose which type of sex to have and take the lead accordingly. You can combine this with a "give to get" technique in which you do things to your partner that you would like done back to you. If your partner has sexual hang-ups, you could suggest the programme for reducing inhibitions on page 16.

My partner won't let me see him naked. What can I do?

Suggest to your partner that you give him a sensual massage. If he feels uncomfortable taking all his clothes off, let him keep some on. Start with a head massage and move slowly down his body, asking him to undress along the way. The more relaxed he feels, the more likely he is to agree. After a few massage sessions your partner may feel more confident about being naked and, hopefully, will find that clothes get in the way of a whole body experience.

casehistory

"I've always enjoyed talking during sex but my partner wants me to stop."

Connie, 37

In my first love affair, my boyfriend and I talked continually during sex – it became part of how we made love and it was fabulously erotic. As a result, I've always enjoyed talking during sex. I thought my current partner Roy enjoyed it too, but now that we've been together for a few months he's irritated and wants me to stop. I've tried keeping quiet but this makes me feel muffled. I can't get turned on properly and I've got quite angry with Roy for handicapping me like this.

Roy, 43

If I thought Connie was talking to me in bed that would have been fine. But I realized, as time went on, that she was talking *at* me, and that, as long as somebody was there to talk at, it didn't really matter who it was. This made me feel less than important and I told her so. I didn't think she would become completely silent but in fact she has. I don't know which is worse. Sex is now so constrained and I don't know how to put things right.

Anne responds:

"Feelings have been hurt and this needs to be resolved urgently. Since Connie is the "victim", it needs to be Roy who starts the process of change. Roy needs to show Connie love and support and Connie needs to reassure Roy that her sex talk is meant exclusively for him rather than for some generic lover. This exchange should turn into a conversation in which both partners discuss what is and isn't OK in bed. I would also recommend sensate focus exercises (see page 77) to Connie and Roy – these are designed to take couples back to the basics of sexual connection."

stress and boredom

Both my partner and I have incredibly stressful jobs and even when we make time for sex the passion isn't there. What can we do?
If your relationship is sound in other ways, the chances are that stress is spilling over from your work life into your personal life. The body responds to stress by producing bursts of hormones such as adrenaline and cortisol. Provided these bursts are occasional and short-lived we don't suffer any long-term consequences. It's when adrenaline and cortisol levels are perpetually raised that we can start to notice problems such as irritability, mood swings, aggression, fatigue and lack of concentration. And we often try to get rid of these symptoms by using alcohol, cigarettes, coffee and sugary foods – anything that we think will give us a boost or take our mind off things.

Unfortunately, these "quick-fixes" put the body under even more stress. One result of this vicious circle is that sex and relationships get neglected. In your case, when you do get around to having sex, you are too tired or preoccupied to feel passionate. The solution is to tackle the causes rather than the symptoms of stress. Ask whether it is worth persevering with a job that makes life unsatisfactory. Could you downscale and go for something less ambitious? Some people get hooked on stress even though they don't enjoy it. Read the box on page 46.

My 25-year-old boyfriend is always too tired to make love. He's constantly bad-tempered or feeling under the weather. He says he's stressed about work. Should I believe him?
Your boyfriend sounds as though he is suffering from classic burn-out symptoms. If he has been suffering from severe stress for a long time, he may well have reached the point where his physical and emotional health are suffering. Signs of burn-out include depressed mood, lethargy, apathy, irritability, lack of sexual desire and frequent infections such as colds and flu (because natural immunity is impaired). Try to be sympathetic – encourage your boyfriend to look objectively at his stress levels and, if possible, reduce them. If your boyfriend is suffering from depression or erectile difficulties, suggest that he sees his doctor.

My partner spends all her time looking after our two young children and nursing her elderly mother. As a result she's got no time left for sex, romance or intimacy. What can I do to change things?
Your partner is probably under a great deal of stress. The best thing you can do is to find some support for her. This could take the form of more domestic help from you, additional help with childcare or respite care for your partner's mother. It's also important to find a way to nurture your relationship as a couple – even if your sex life is lacking, try to maintain intimacy through small everyday gestures. Allocate time to be alone together – even if this is only

10 minutes a day – and plan in advance for the occasional evening out. Above all, keep talking to your partner, find out how she's feeling and give her your unconditional support.

I'm bored with our sex life. It feels like we have been making love in the same old routine for years. What's gone wrong?
Sex researchers have observed that long-term couples can continue to have sex in the same way for 20 years or more. At first couples usually go through a phase of experimentation in which they try out many different styles of lovemaking. They quickly learn what works well and what doesn't. Having refined their lovemaking skills, people tend to stick with the same routine for the simple reason that it suits them. Problems only start to arise years later when sex starts to become boring. The challenge in long-term relationships is to inject variety into your lovemaking. Try some of the suggestions in Chapter 5.

We have worked at our sex life but the spark seems to have gone. We still love each other but can our marriage survive?
According to psychologist Robert Sternberg there are three building blocks in loving relationships: intimacy, passion and commitment. In the ideal relationship each of these is present in equal amounts. However, relationships don't have to be perfect and many survive with one element lacking or missing. In your case, passion is lacking, but hopefully you have enough intimacy and commitment to compensate. Also, just because the spark isn't there at the moment it doesn't mean that you have to stop making love completely.

infidelity

I suspect that my partner is having an affair. How can I find out for sure?

The only way to know for sure is to elicit a confession from your partner but here are some common clues. Bear in mind that none of these constitute evidence and they may all have alternative explanations:

- A new sense of distance between you and your partner.
- Unusual changes in intimate or sexual behaviour.
- Gifts that are out of character.
- Your partner spends more time out, either on casual drinks with friends or on business (especially if he/she is uncontactable during this time).
- Your partner makes or takes phone calls in a separate room.
- You receive phone calls in which the caller hangs up on hearing your voice (especially when the recall facility reveals that the caller has pressed their privacy button).
- An inordinate amount of time spent e-mailing in private (especially when your partner habitually deletes or hides e-mails).

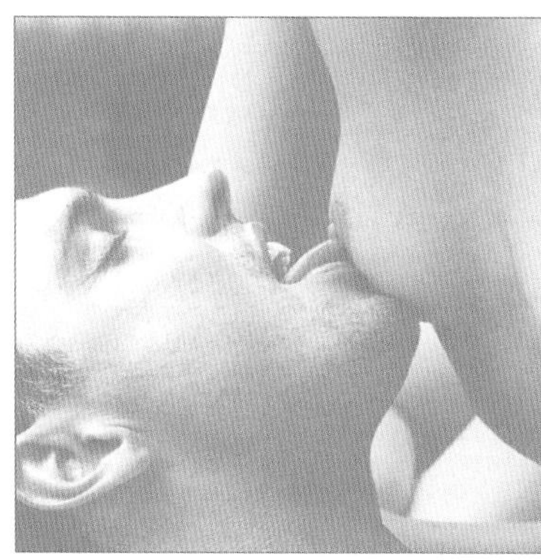

emotionaltips

Weathering the storm of infidelity

If the worst has happened and you have discovered that your partner is having an affair (or vice versa), your emotions are likely to be very raw. Allow time for the dust to settle before you make any irreversible decisions.

- Keep conversation going between the two of you.
- Accept that the weeks and months ahead are going to be painful.
- Rely on friends for support.
- Expect to analyze your relationship in detail if you want to stay together. This could include relationship counselling.
- Try to stay objective even at the most difficult times. Sometimes it can help to see your partner as a friend rather than as a lover.
- When possible, try to stay calm. Do some of your grieving in private.
- Create areas of stability in your life that give you the strength and self-esteem to keep going.
- Avoid having the same conversation over and over again. Try to explore new territory when you talk to your partner.
- Accept the fact that, although one person started the affair, both of you need to work on recovering from it.

My girlfriend is pathologically jealous, moody and aggressive. She thinks I'm flirting or having an affair with every woman I meet. The truth is I'm not. How can I convince her?

This worrying behaviour suggests that your girlfriend is projecting all of her feelings of insecurity and doubt on to you. These insecurities are likely to be considerable, and the chances are – unless you've been unfaithful in the past – that they entirely pre-date your relationship. Personal history has probably taught your girlfriend to regard intimacy with mistrust or to associate it with betrayal. She may have been badly let down in the past by parents, carers or lovers. This means that now, when she becomes intimate, she feels vulnerable and lashes out with aggression and accusations, which is her way of defending herself. It is very important that you avoid "collaborating" in your girlfriend's jealousy. When she accuses you of having an affair, don't attempt a denial as this will only feed her fantasies. Instead, encourage her to talk about herself – about her feelings of unhappiness and insecurity. If possible, suggest that you both talk about the situation in the impartial environment of relationship therapy.

I found a contact magazine in my husband's briefcase with adverts ringed in pencil. Does this mean he's being unfaithful?

It suggests that he's having thoughts or fantasies along these lines. You have obviously questioned his trustworthiness or you wouldn't have searched through his briefcase. If you want to tackle this problem, I suggest you take your entire relationship out for examination, rather than just confronting your husband with this awkwardly-obtained evidence. Start by saying that you feel very cut off from him and ask him whether he feels just as detached from you.

I'm on the verge of having an affair but I don't know whether I'm making a mistake or not. How do I decide?

Affairs can have enormous and sometimes catastrophic consequences so it is good that you are taking the time to reflect upon your choices. Consider the worst possible outcome of an affair and try to envisage how you would cope with it. For example, how would you feel if you lost your primary relationship and all the things that go with it (your home, for instance)? Would this be disastrous or would you consider it a price worth paying? What about if the affair turned out to be misguided and short-lived? Also analyze your reasons for wanting the affair – if they are to do with problems in your primary relationship, could you try to sort out these problems first? And, if you can't, why are you staying in the relationship? Unfortunately, you will only truly know whether an affair is a mistake in hindsight – but by then, of course, it's too late.

Although I am sexually unsatisfied I decided against an affair and took up studying instead. My husband is reacting jealously, as though I am having an affair. What can I do?

This superbly demonstrates that the mechanics of jealousy don't focus on sex alone. Your husband feels neglected, rejected and plotted against because he is excluded from an important part of your life (as he would be if you were having an affair). You, in turn, are sublimating your marital problems rather than addressing them (again, in the same

What does it mean if...

I keep fantasizing about having a passionate affair?

- You are feeling starved of love and affection.
- You are feeling sex-starved.
- You have an active fantasy life and this is one of your staple fantasies (but not something you'd want to enact in reality).
- You are inhibited about expressing passionate feelings in your current relationship.
- You need a focus for your creative energy and an affair is a convenient symbol for this.

way that you would during an affair). You need to decide whether your husband's jealousy is the bad behaviour of a "spoilt child" or whether you are responsible for making him insecure by turning your back on your relationship. This problem might benefit from counselling help.

Sex fact

Research shows that almost 50 per cent of men and women will experience adultery at least once in their lifetime. However, most couples no longer consider a single experience of extra-marital sex to be a reason for divorce.

I had a one-night stand that I regret and that means nothing to me. If I'm sure my partner will never find out, what's wrong with keeping it secret?
There are definitely times when it is appropriate to keep secrets; it is also reasonable for everyone to want some privacy. If you are quite sure that your partner cannot find out about this affair, then perhaps it would be wise to keep it to yourself. But how can you be so sure? An affair means that at least one other person knows about it besides you. Why couldn't this person tell friends who, in turn, tell others? Also, suppose you are affected by feelings of guilt that start to impinge on your relationship? It would be wise to weigh up your options carefully.

I am having an affair and cannot decide which relationship to end and which to continue. Is it possible to love two people at once?
Yes, it most certainly is, and this makes the kind of choice you are contemplating extremely difficult. One way of dealing with it is to wait – your feelings may crystallize over time. But if each of your lovers knows about the other, this approach will create a great deal of pain for them. This has never seemed to me to be a very loving thing to do. Plus, your lovers may take the choice away from you by making their own decisions. If you are choosing between a long-term relationship, in which you still love your partner, and a new sexually-charged romance, I would remind you that romance and passion tend to dwindle after around the first six months. For this reason, it's worth examining your new relationship in terms of its long-term prospects. Try to imagine where and with whom you would like to be in five years time.

I always said I would leave my husband if he had an affair. Now he has, I don't know what to do. He says he doesn't want me to go but I am so angry and upset. What can I do?
You are probably shaky and uncertain because you don't know what will happen next. Your anger indicates the strength of your attachment to your husband. You would be wise to think very hard before leaving. Sometimes couples can learn from extra-marital affairs and move on to improve their relationship. Of course this is painful but you can't usually have change without pain. Don't feel you have to stick to your principles – it can be

more mature to change your mind because you have learned something new. Try taking the problem to a counsellor who would give you a safe space in which to shout and scream. You may need to do a lot of this before your relationship can improve.

My girlfriend has been sleeping with someone else and I feel destroyed. How can I ever let her near me again?

You are registering the "appropriate" feelings of someone who has been let down very badly. You are shocked, upset and angry – and so you should be. But at the moment you can only see things in one way. Intimacy with your girlfriend is unthinkable at the moment, but you may not feel this way forever. If you could tell your girlfriend exactly how you feel and if she could show you that she understands, it's possible that your relationship still stands a chance. You might not want to get close to her in a hurry, but if you let the relationship have a future in your mind, your heart may eventually catch up.

How can I learn to trust my partner? He has been unfaithful to me in the past.

If your partner has told you that he is now prepared to work towards a committed future with you, you need to work on building up trust slowly over a period of time. First of all, you need to understand why your partner was unfaithful, and you need to know that things are different now. You also need to keep talking very honestly and openly with your partner. If you are able to voice your anxieties and he can offer you genuine reassurance, then your relationship stands a good chance of surviving. If you feel that your lack of trust is eroding your relationship, consider going to counselling with your partner.

Why has my sex life with my girlfriend improved now that I've started having an affair?

Your affair provides excitement, eroticism, increased physical arousal and a sense of danger – as a result some of your surplus sexual energy is spilling into your relationship with your girlfriend.

An alternative explanation is that you are consciously putting more effort into sex with your girlfriend because you feel so guilty about having an affair.

casehistory

"I carried on seeing both men."

Janet, 42

Laurence and I married very young. I was only 17 and so it wasn't really surprising that I should fall in love with someone else when I was 27. My sex life with Laurence had never worked very well for me, but with Robert it was great. Having said this, I never wanted to leave Laurence. He was part of me. It would have been like losing a limb. Besides, we had three children we loved deeply. So I carried on seeing both men and each of them knew about the other. After about seven years Robert finished with me. He finally realized that I was never going to live with him. By now, Laurence was spending most of his time in our country home. The important thing is that we stayed married and I continued loving him.

Laurence, 48

Surviving Janet's affair with Robert was painful and I wouldn't wish it on my worst enemy. I sublimated a lot of my feelings into competitive sports and I even had one affair myself (it ended when it became clear that I wasn't going to leave Janet). Now that we're older, Janet and I are much more settled with each other. We commute between our two homes, spend a lot of time apart, but are loving friends. We still have sex, if only occasionally. Even though we argue, we're comfortable together. Janet is committed to me for our old age and that counts for a lot.

Anne responds:

"This wouldn't be most people's ideal marriage but Janet's and Laurence's relationship was strong enough to stand up to a great deal of buffeting – and it has emerged even stronger. Ultimately, a relationship lasts because one or both partners carry a very strong personal belief that it continues to be valuable and worth hanging on to. In this case, Laurence's deep sense of commitment to the idea of companionship helped to preserve the relationship."

sexual dilemmas

I have lied about my sexual history to my partner. I've actually had more partners and a far more colourful sex life than I admitted to. I now want to be open about this but I'm afraid of the consequences. What should I do?

Whether or not you decide to tell your partner partly depends on how seriously you take your relationship. If, for example, you plan to spend the rest of your life with this person, then it might be advisable to come clean so that you don't have to face a lifetime of feeling guilty (only you can assess how much guilt you will feel). Your decision may also be based on how likely your partner is to find out about your sexual history. Are you still friendly with any of your ex-lovers, for example? Total honesty will allow you to relax in the knowledge that your partner loves and accepts you, whatever your past. Another issue to consider: if your partner judges you critically, do you want to be with someone who holds a different set of sexual standards to you?

If you do opt for honesty, bear in mind that people rarely respond well to revelations of past lies. Explain why you wanted to cover up your past and be prepared for anger or upset.

I've been having virtual sex with someone in an Internet chatroom. I've kept this secret from my girlfriend. The problem is that the girl I've met online wants to meet me in the flesh. What should I do?

The normal etiquette that operates between strangers is absent in Internet chatrooms and people feel few, if any, inhibitions. This can create intense online relationships which can quickly become sexual and which can feel as emotionally engaging as "real" relationships. If you agree to meet your online friend, you should be clear about your motives, which – if you are completely honest – are probably to have fully-fledged sex. This would be fine if it wasn't for the fact that you already have a girlfriend. You need to take an objective look at your current relationship and decide how important it is to you. Don't deceive yourself that this meeting is innocuous. You have already been sexually intimate – albeit remotely – with this girl and you would effectively be going on a first date with her.

My wife spends hours in Internet chatrooms every evening and I believe she's having an Internet affair. She says she's having fun and that nothing will come of it. Am I wrong to feel upset?
No, you're not. Internet relationships can and do become sexual (sex in this context consists of an exchange of explicit messages accompanied by masturbation). Many people who meet online and have virtual sex feel that their relationship is as real and intense as a conventional relationship and, because of this, they may feel compelled to meet. Some couples have separated or divorced as a result. On the other hand, many virtual sex relationships are casual and last the length of one exchange or, at most, a few days or weeks. Your wife needs to understand that by cutting herself off from you she is stifling the emotional growth and communication that a good relationship requires. She also needs to understand that virtual sex and flirtation can seriously damage your relationship. For your part, try to accommodate your wife's need for excitement – arrange for the two of you to go out in the evenings, for example. If her interest in chatrooms is the sign of a deeper malaise in your relationship, you might benefit from going to see a relationship counsellor.

emotionaltips

Resolving a dilemma

- A dilemma involves making a difficult choice, so start by being clear about exactly what your alternatives are. Is there a third (or fourth) way that you haven't yet considered?
- Be clear about the consequences of each course of action.
- Talk things over with an impartial third party, such as a trusted friend or a counsellor.
- Once you have decided on a course of action, commit to it wholeheartedly; don't backtrack or be hesitant.

We stopped having sex a long time ago and recently my partner suggested that we go for sex therapy. The problem is, I think I just want to leave the relationship. Should I try sex therapy as a last resort or should I just leave?
If you tried going to sex therapy, you would at least feel that you had made the effort. If you still want out once you have begun the therapy, you could use the sessions to discuss your decision to leave. Your partner will need to talk about such a dramatic action – even though you have made up your mind, she clearly hasn't. She is likely to be shocked and upset and it's not unreasonable to give her some help in this painful event. There is also a tiny chance that you might gain something from sex therapy and change your mind. It's worth giving therapy a try, even as a last resort.

My husband and I don't make love or talk properly any more. I want to go for some sort of marriage guidance, but I know he would never agree. Do I go on my own behind his back or do I try to broach it with him? He's very bad at talking about emotional issues.
It's very common for a woman to want to have therapy while her partner flatly refuses. What is also common is that when the woman attends sessions on her own, the man becomes curious. If, after a couple of sessions you tell your husband that the therapist would like to hear his side of the story - you may be surprised by his consent. So, to begin with – if your husband won't see a therapist with you – go by and for yourself. By discussing your options with a therapist, you may learn how to improve your marriage.

My boyfriend is a fantastic lover but a lousy partner. If it wasn't for our sex life I'd leave him. But I'm terrified I will never have such good sex again. What should I do?
Sex is only one part of a long-term relationship – a part that is extremely important in the early years, but one

that shakes into place as time goes on. I think yours is doing the "shaking" right now. If your boyfriend doesn't value you or is in any way abusive, you probably need to leave him in order to rebuild your self-respect. There is an excellent novel called *Falling* by Elizabeth Jane Howard that illustrates the kind of exploitation that can happen in the name of good sex. Your relationship is probably not as scary or as dramatic as the one in the book, but read about it anyway. It might help you to see that making an absolute break could be the best thing to do. If you are worried about craving sex, be comforted by the fact that, after a while, many women experience "sleeping beauty syndrome" and don't actually miss sex as much as they anticipate.

My wife brought home a lesbian magazine which we both found very erotic. Now I know how turned on she is by women I'm worried about her sexuality. Should I bring it up with her?

Many of us fantasize about things we don't actually want to happen. Clearly, your wife enjoyed "imagining" lesbian sex scenes, or at least she did on that one occasion. This doesn't prove anything. Talk to her if you like, but first accept that there is usually a clear line between fantasy desires and real desires. Some homosexuals are capable of being excited by imagining straight people in bed, but they still wouldn't want one for Christmas!

I discovered a pile of porn magazines hidden in my husband's workshop. I feel very upset, mostly because we don't have a regular sex life. Should I let this go or should I confront my husband?

For some men, looking at porn is a kind of sexual hobby that has no deep meaning. But when a preoccupation with porn is combined with a poor sexual relationship, something else is happening. Porn can provide sexual pleasure that is free from the demands and responsibilities of "real" sex. In other words, it's much easier to feel in control if a woman is on a magazine centrefold rather than next to you in bed. Talk to your husband about the magazines you found. Encourage him to commit to jointly improving your sex life. If you can't get over this problem on your own, seek sex counselling with an expert.

I need sexual humiliation to feel turned on. I don't know whether to broach this with my girlfriend. I don't want to scare her off. Can a committed love life include S&M?

Sometimes sexual relationships form on an S&M basis and sometimes S&M partners turn into wives (and husbands). Since S&M has not yet featured in your relationship, you need to tread carefully. How well do you

know your girlfriend? How sexually adventurous is she in other ways? Could she cope with your requests? When people want something badly, they often convince themselves their partner can cope with their revelations. And they can turn out to be spectacularly wrong. It's also worth considering the fact that humiliation from a long-term partner may lack the edge of excitement that you're looking for. Try playing some sex games that involve mild restraints and spanking and see how your girlfriend responds.

My boyfriend wants me to be his sex slave. I'm a bit nervous about this. What should I do?
You need to ask your boyfriend exactly what he means. On the simplest level he may mean that he wants to lie back while you indulge him in his favourite erotic acts. For most people, being a sex slave is about sexual role-playing and is not to be confused with abuse, pain or mutilation. The point of role-play is to explore domination and submission on a voluntary basis. Some people find feelings of power or vulnerability during sex very erotic. For a celebrated fictional portrait of a sex slave, read Pauline Reage's *Story of O*. If you like the idea, you might agree to play, provided there are built in safety guarantees (see page 122). If not, don't have the slightest doubt about saying that this is not for you.

I'm a 42-year-old woman and I'm thinking about having a sexual relationship with a 22-year-old man. But the age gap bothers me and I'm afraid of what my friends will think. Does age really matter?
If it doesn't matter to the two of you, then a sexual relationship doesn't have to pose problems. You may learn a lot from each other sexually and have an exhilarating time in the process. Having said this, there are some built-in difficulties to a relationship between people of unequal ages. If your relationship becomes serious and long term, how will you negotiate different life stages? The lifestyle that you want in your forties may be quite different from what your partner wants in his early twenties. How willing and able would both of you be to compromise? And what about in five years time? It's worth considering these issues before you become too emotionally entangled. Don't worry about your friends – if they get critical it's more likely to be due to jealousy rather than disapproval.

are you compatible lovers

You meet, you fall in love and you settle into a relationship – but how compatible are you in bed? Do you like doing the same things at the same time or are there major differences in your sexual styles?

Would you say that your and your lover's sex drives are:

☐ **A** Just about equal?

☐ **B** There's a slight imbalance, but it's not a problem?

☐ **C** There's an imbalance that might cause problems?

Your partner is keen to try anal sex. Do you:

☐ **A** Think its a great idea – you're keen to try anything?

☐ **B** Feel unsure but willing to experiment?

☐ **C** Tell him/her that you're not up for it?

Your partner suggests dressing up and doing a bit of role playing to add a twist to your lovemaking. Do you:

☐ **A** Get into costume and discuss some sexy scenarios?

☐ **B** Agree to some play acting, but refuse to dress up?

☐ **C** Think it's a terrible idea – you'd rather just be yourself?

Your partner starts talking dirty while you're making love. Do you:

☐ **A** Love it and return the favour?

☐ **B** Find it mildly amusing?

☐ **C** Find it embarrassing?

Is your favourite sexual position:

☐ **A** The same as your partner's?

☐ **B** Different to your partner's but he/she likes it too?

☐ **C** Different to your partner's and he/she tries to avoid it?

When it comes to oral sex, does your partner:

☐ **A** Readily give you as much as you need?

☐ **B** Oblige you from time to time, but you'd love more?

☐ **C** Need lots of encouragement?

Is the amount of foreplay your partner enjoys:

- [ ] **A** Exactly in line with your needs – you're always ready for sex by the time you get there?
- [ ] **B** Slightly at odds with your needs but the difference is manageable?
- [ ] **C** Completely at odds with your needs. One of you is always ahead of the other?

When your partner is masturbating you, do you:

- [ ] **A** Lie back and enjoy the blissful sensation?
- [ ] **B** Enjoy it but guide your partner's hand from time to time for greatest effect?
- [ ] **C** Keep your hand over your partner's to make sure he/she does it right?

When it comes to controlling the action in bed:

- [ ] **A** Do you both have input, depending on how you feel?
- [ ] **B** Are things a bit one-sided but that's OK?
- [ ] **C** Are things so one-sided that it makes sex less enjoyable?

Are the orgasms you have with your partner:

- [ ] **A** Fantastic and reliable?
- [ ] **B** Usually pretty good?
- [ ] **C** Good when they happen?

You want to try sex standing up, does your partner:

- [ ] **A** Excitedly pin you to the wall?
- [ ] **B** Say he/she will give it a go?
- [ ] **C** Suggest another position of his/her own liking?

Do you like to have sex:

- [ ] **A** Anytime?
- [ ] **B** Not always at the same time as your partner?
- [ ] **C** At different times from your partner?

Are the positions you and your partner enjoy:

- [ ] **A** Many and varied?
- [ ] **B** Predictable but OK?
- [ ] **C** Predictable and boring?

When it comes to discussing your sex life do you:

- [ ] **A** Find it easy to talk to your partner?
- [ ] **B** Talk about things only when a problem arises?
- [ ] **C** Find it difficult to talk to your partner?

ANSWERS

Mostly As A perfect match! You and your partner work well together and are happy to discuss sex and try out new things. This is a balanced relationship with a lot of sexual variety and a willingness to listen to each other's sexual needs. You are both confident and can communicate honestly. You know your way around each other's bodies and can rely on each other to keep sex fulfilling.

Mostly Bs You two are good together and enjoy a satisfying sex life although you could work a little at spicing things up from time to time. You're up for new challenges and care about each other's needs. However, talking about sexual desires and spending more quality time together will enhance what happens in bed. It may be that initiating sex is a little one-sided. If it is, try taking it in turns and whoever is a little nervous (be it you or your partner) will soon gain confidence.

Mostly Cs This relationship has potential, but you need to talk about sex and sort out what each of you is looking for from lovemaking. If the relationship is in it's early stages, there is no reason why you can't work together to develop a mutually satisfying sex life. It may be that inhibitions get in the way. Set some time aside to talk through your needs and anxieties. Building a sexual relationship can take a while before you discover what really works for both of you.

questions men ask

Men are expected to be confident, knowledgeable and experienced when it comes to sex, despite the fact that they aren't always encouraged to ask questions. These Q&As cover all aspects of male sexuality throughout life.

sexual self-esteem

I don't have the right physique to attract women. One partner even told me that she found me a turn-off. How can I increase my sex appeal?
Sex appeal is one of the hardest things to pin down and, since it's such an individual and subjective judgement, it's not something you can easily manipulate. Just because one woman doesn't find you sexually attractive doesn't mean that others will feel the same. Instead of focusing on the things that you can't change, focus on the things you can. Bathe or shower regularly so that you always smell fresh, wear clothes that make you feel confident, and look after your body by eating healthily and exercising. Perhaps most importantly, cultivate a sense of humour about yourself. The ability to laugh is something that women rate very highly.

I'm overweight and I can't believe that any woman would fancy me. Should I just give up the idea of a sex life?
The amazing thing about the world is that if you have enough confidence, all sorts of people will find you attractive, regardless of physical appearance. For a start, reassure yourself with the fact that a potential lover will be equally worried about the impact she makes on you. If your weight continues to be an insurmountable issue, you could get a doctor to assist you in a medically controlled diet, but, believe me, your appearance is unlikely to be a major problem in forming relationships. Some women adore overweight men. Many women marry overweight men. The only real difficulty is in your mind.

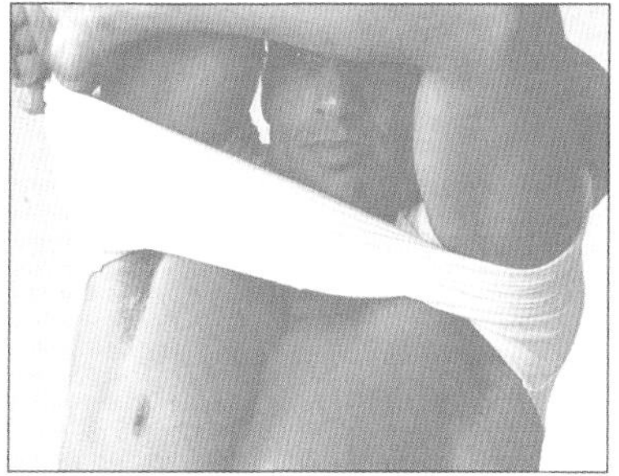

I'm in my late 20s and am rapidly going bald. I can't see a woman ever fancying me again. Is there anything I can do?
Women don't date heads of hair – they date human beings. No evidence suggests that women are deterred from going out with bald men. Your hair loss proves you to be a normal, virile male with the right levels of sex hormone in circulation (testosterone triggers baldness following a genetic blueprint). Perhaps you are feeling insecure for other reasons. Have you been dependent on your looks in the past? Has this meant that you haven't needed to feel confident about talking to women? If this is the case, try to build communication skills instead of focusing on your hair.

the penis and foreskin

I am worried that my penis is too small. What is the average length of the erect penis?
Out of 1,200 penis measurements, taken from men aged 16 to 77, and recorded by sexologist Kenneth S. Green, the mean average was 15.6 cm (6.14 in). The shortest measured penis – that of a 27-year-old Native American – was 5 cm (2 in) erect but 7.6 cm (3 in) in diameter. Alfred Kinsey reported 16 cm (6.3 in) as the mean length from a sample of 4,000 men. Many men get hung up on penis size, believing that bigger is better. Bear in mind that the most sensitive part of a woman's vagina is the lower third – an area that even the smallest penis is able to penetrate.

How big can an erection be?
Various studies have found that the largest erect penis can go up to 26–35 cm (10.2–14 in) in length. It's also possible to find posters of men with penises so long that they look as though they could have knots tied in them! Nationality affects penis size – American men, for example, have been found to have bigger penises than Thai men. But beware of becoming too phallocentric – remember that skill with your hands, mouth and whole body counts for more than the length of your penis.

What do women really think about penises and penis size?
A series of questionnaires carried out in the mid-1970s found that men believed that women would rate the penis as the sexiest part of the male body. In fact, women rated the buttocks as the sexiest part, with the penis coming very low down on the list. Although men tend to link penis size with sexual prowess and potency, women's attitudes are far less predictable. Some women find large penises appealing, others worry that a large penis won't fit comfortably inside them and others are indifferent to penis size, focusing instead on feelings such as emotional attraction to a partner.

My erect penis has a slight bend in it. Is this normal or should I see a doctor?
If the bend is truly slight, and provided it remains at the same angle over a period of time, this is perfectly normal. Erections often bend to the right or to the left. However, if your bend has been slowly increasing, you may be suffering from Peyronie's disease and you should consult a doctor. Peyronie's disease is a result of fibrosis. It happens when the normal spongy tissue of the penis gets replaced with scar tissue on one side. This distorts the erection, causing it to take on a banana shape. As the condition worsens, simply getting an erection can become extremely painful. Rubbing the area with vitamin E cream is recommended to maintain skin elasticity but, unless Peyronie's disease resolves by itself, treatment, including surgery, may be necessary.

Does the fact that I am circumcised mean that my penis is less sensitive?

Objectively, it may do, since the scar tissue left after circumcision must, in theory, render the area less sensitive. However, since no-one else can be inside your body or indeed that of any other man, we don't really know. Some men who were circumcised as babies may feel cheated of what they consider to be an integral part of their genital anatomy. But this is unusual – most circumcised men say they lead happy and fulfilling sex lives and don't consider circumcision a disadvantage.

It hurts to pull back my foreskin during an erection. Should I be circumcised before I lose my virginity?

It would be worth trying to massage your penis regularly with vitamin E cream to try to ease it back naturally. The medical name for a tight foreskin is phimosis – although it isn't a dangerous condition it can cause the glans to become inflamed, which can be uncomfortable and, in the long term, can lead to scarring. If self-help measures, such as vitamin E cream, don't help, your doctor may be able to carry out a simple operation to help you draw back your foreskin. If not, circumcision may be the answer.

Is it more hygienic to be circumcised?

Not as long as uncircumcised men pay careful attention to cleanliness. The inner skin of the foreskin contains glands that secrete an oily substance. When this mixes with dead skin cells it forms a substance called smegma that becomes white and foul-smelling if it is not regularly washed away. Poor genital hygiene in uncircumcised men can sometimes lead to an infection of the glans called balanitis. Although this can be treated relatively easily it causes symptoms such as soreness, itchiness and inflammation.

indetail

Penis enlargement – is it possible?

It is, although only in a very few countries. Fat can be sucked from the abdominal wall and introduced just under the penile skin by injection. This procedure aims to increase the general width of the penis and is known as CAPE (circumferential autologous penile engorgement). If the operation is successful, the fat cells remain viable and attach themselves naturally to the penile shaft. But if the fat cells die, the fat deposits harden and the man may find, to his dismay, that his treasured organ has become lumpy.

In China there is an another type of operation that extends the penis by up to 50 per cent. Surgery lasts one hour, is performed under general anaesthetic and involves cutting the suspensory ligament attaching the penis to the front of the pubic bone. This allows the root of the penis (40 per cent of which is hidden in the pubic mound) to be pulled forward and re-attached with stitches. The operation carries with it a couple of slight side effects but sexual activity can usually be resumed after a three-week recovery period.

masturbation

How do most men masturbate?

There are so many different styles of masturbation that it would be impossible to list them all. Every man works out his own particular pattern and hones it over the years. Many men simply enclose the shaft of the penis in their fist and rub up and down until they ejaculate. Others rub against a tactile object or surface such as a towel, pillow or mattress. Some men like to use sex toys to thrust into. Men may masturbate in the shower, on a bed, standing up, kneeling or sitting down. Some men prolong the event; others keep it short. Some use saliva to lubricate the penis, while others may use lubricating gel or masturbate "dry". Some men are incredibly rough with their genitals, others caress themselves gently.

What does it mean if...

I fantasize about an ex-lover when I masturbate?

The best thing about masturbation is that you're free to fantasize about anything you like. It doesn't have to be something that you'd want to happen in real life – in fact, fantasizing about something taboo, illicit or forbidden can add extra excitement to masturbation. Fantasizing about ex-lovers is very common – it doesn't constitute a betrayal of your current partner (if you have one) and it doesn't necessarily mean that you crave a sexual reunion with your old lover. Women are just as likely as men to fantasize about old sexual encounters. The diversity of masturbation fantasies is endless.

Is it possible to masturbate too much? I do it at least every day.

Many men do masturbate daily. How frequently you masturbate depends on a huge range of factors including your age, your libido, your lifestyle and even your mood from day to day. Whereas young men may masturbate up to several times a day, a middle-aged man may masturbate once a week or less. It all depends on the individual. Unfortunately, it's still common to feel guilty about how often you masturbate. Rest assured that the only type of masturbation that is not normal is compulsive masturbation. This is when you do little else except masturbate. If this applies to you, then you should seek your doctor's help. But, as long as masturbation doesn't interfere with your everyday life, there is no reason to worry.

Why do I feel guilty when I masturbate?

Historically, masturbation was frowned upon and boys were strongly discouraged or even punished for handling their genitals for pleasure. In the past, parents may even have told their sons that masturbation would cause them to go blind. Unfortunately, these negative messages still hang over modern society. Perhaps you were brought up in a family where sexual expression was not permitted. Or were you told off for touching yourself as a baby or child? Whatever the origin of your guilt, you should know that the modern view is that masturbation is a normal part of everyone's sexuality.

I enjoy masturbating with sex aids. My problem is that now masturbation is more exciting than sex with my partner. What can I do?

Perhaps you should introduce a few of your favourite sex aids into mutual lovemaking. Your partner might turn out to enjoy them as much as you do. You never know, you might find that you extend your sex life by getting your partner to do all the things that you have, up till now, been doing to yourself. If your sexual

relationship is going to thrive you will need it to stay fresh, varied and exciting.

My girlfriend says that I shouldn't need to masturbate now that we live together but this doesn't change the fact that I want to. Is there anything wrong with this?

No, many people in relationships masturbate by themselves in addition to having intercourse – masturbation is a natural form of sexual self-expression that can complement your relationship with your girlfriend rather than detract from it. The problem might be that your girlfriend interprets your masturbation as a rejection of her. You need to reassure her that masturbation is not a substitute for sex and that you love having sex with her.

How can I show my girlfriend how to masturbate me?

You can play the body mapping game (see page 16) while focusing on the genitals or you can try the following technique. Ask your girlfriend to lean against a pile of pillows or cushions at the head of the bed. Now sit between her legs and lean back against her. If she's too small to support you, lie down on your back and ask her to sit by your side. Ask her to put her hand around your penis, then place your hand over hers. Now guide her hand in the way that you like to be touched. This is a great way for her to learn about the speed and pressure that you need to feel stimulated.

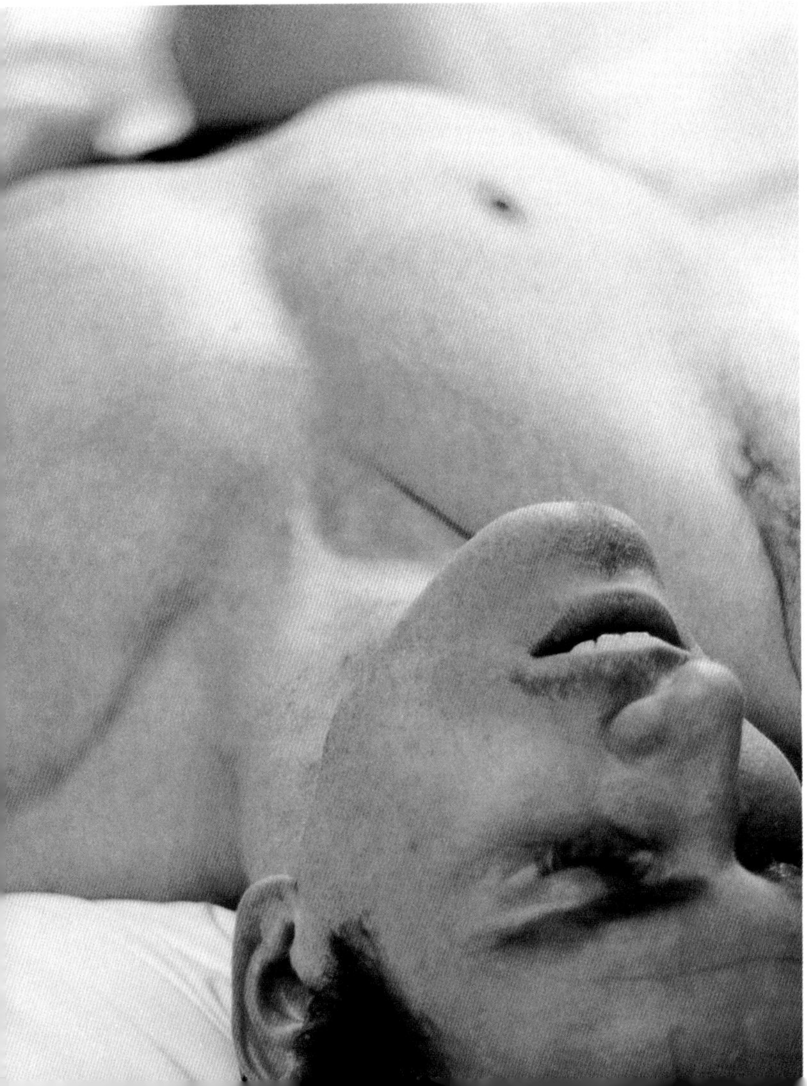

I masturbate to orgasm in private before I have sex with my girlfriend. It helps me to last longer. Is there anything wrong with this?

In theory, no. But in practice you may be forming a habit that becomes very hard to break in the future. How will you feel if you find yourself in a situation where it is difficult to masturbate before sex? Would you feel anxious that you wouldn't be able to perform? And bear in mind that the best sex is often spontaneous. It's also worth thinking about how your girlfriend would react if she found out and how you would cope with her reaction. Occasional masturbation to help you last longer is OK but if it's becoming a habit, consider other techniques to stop yourself ejaculating too soon. Try the squeeze technique (see page 44), for example, or the self-help programme on page 40. And, if possible, enlist your girlfriend's support.

Sex fact

Sex therapists recommend special masturbation exercises as a way of gaining control over the timing of ejaculation. See the exercise on page 40 to prevent premature ejaculation.

erections and orgasms

How long should I be able to keep an erection for?
Some people would say for as long as it takes to satisfy your partner. The truth is that you don't strictly need an erection to do this as you can give your partner an orgasm with your hands or your mouth (and she may prefer this). If you are one of those people who adores spending a long time on sex, keeping a continuous erection isn't really necessary as you can allow your erection to wax and wane before you finally ejaculate. For example, if you stop full body contact in order to concentrate on giving your partner oral sex, you are likely to lose your erection until the sexual focus returns to you. You just need to trust that your erection can be revived – and it can. If you are concerned that you ejaculate too quickly during sex, try the squeeze technique on page 44 or follow the advice for lasting longer in bed in the box below. And remember that sustaining intercourse for long periods isn't always desirable – both you and your partner may find that sensation becomes blunted and your genitals can feel as though they've been anaesthetized.

How can I make my erection last longer during intercourse?
You could try the self-training programme specially created for men who want to last longer in bed (see box below). But just in case you are one of those exceptional men who only have to look at an attractive partner in order to come, it may be helpful for you to know that drug therapy can now help to slow down ejaculation. Consult your doctor about this or ask to be referred to your nearest sex therapy clinic.

indetail

Teaching yourself to last longer in bed

This programme uses tried and tested techniques to help you learn greater ejaculatory control and increase your sexual staying power. Take it slowly and you should start to see results in several weeks. If you need extra help delaying ejaculation during these exercises, try the squeeze technique (see page 44).

1. Masturbate with a dry hand until you can last 15 minutes before ejaculating.
2. Masturbate with a lubricated hand until you can last 15 minutes before ejaculating. You may find that these two steps alone help you to sustain your erection for longer during sex. Alternatively, you can go on to do the following exercises with your partner.
3. Let your partner masturbate you with a dry hand until you can last for 15 minutes before ejaculating.
4. Let your partner masturbate you with a lubricated hand until you can last for 15 minutes before ejaculating.
5. Lie on your back with your partner astride you and your penis inside her vagina. Both of you should keep your movements to a minimum. Keep practising this until you can last 15 minutes before ejaculating.
6. Repeat step 5 with your partner thrusting gently. Practise until you can last for 15 minutes.
7. Repeat step 5 with you thrusting gently. Practise until you can last for 15 minutes.
8. Repeat step 5 with both of you moving freely until you can last for 15 minutes.

I'm 17 and I get extremely embarrassed when I get an erection in public. How can I stop this happening?
Spontaneous erections are very common when you're a teenager and become less frequent as you get older. There's not a great deal you can do about them except to wear baggy clothes and try your best to remain unflustered. This type of erection doesn't last too long, usually because you are so busy feeling embarrassed rather than aroused.

I can get an erection but I don't think my penis rises as much as it should. It doesn't even get up as far as 90 degrees to my body. Is there something wrong?
If your penis becomes hard, it's very unlikely that you have a problem (if it doesn't get hard, consult your doctor). The angle the erect penis makes with the body varys from man to man and also depends on your age and how big your penis is. The older the man, the lower the angle of erection (the penis may become hard but continues to point downwards). The longer and heavier the penis, the more difficult it is for the genital muscles to pull it into an upward-pointing position.

I'm healthy and I play a lot of football yet I can't always get an erection. Could it be because I drink too much? I don't have more than the other guys on the team.

And the guys on the team probably drink too much too! What's more, every individual has their limit of alcohol. Some people may be drunk after one glass and others completely sober after six. The effects of alcohol on sex drive and performance are complex. The first few drinks can make you feel merry and uninhibited – at this stage you are still able to have sex. A few more drinks down the line, however, and the story is different. High doses of alcohol have a sedative effect and cause your thinking, memory, speech and movement to become impaired. You may have extremes of mood, such as becoming maudlin or violent. It will be difficult for you to achieve or maintain an erection or you may simply lack the co-ordination to have sex. Long-term heavy drinking can damage testosterone levels, libido and sexual function. Impotence is a common symptom of alcohol abuse. Consider the fact that your problems may be related to your drinking habits. Cut down on your alcohol consumption and see if your sex life improves.

Why can't I keep my erection during sex?

Losing your erection is an upsetting problem particularly when it happens frequently. If you suffer from persistent erection problems, see your doctor. Whereas young men often lose their erection for psychological reasons, older men are more likely to suffer from physical problems. The following are all possible reasons for erectile dysfunction:

- You are very nervous or suffering from performance anxiety.
- You are stressed or depressed.
- You have lost your erection on previous occasions and this is making you nervous.
- You are not sufficiently aroused.
- You have a physical problem such as diabetes or cardiovascular disease.
- You are taking medication that influences erection.
- You suffer from long-term alcohol abuse.
- You have low levels of the male sex hormone testosterone.

I always seem to lose my erection when I put a condom on to have intercourse. What can I do?

Try putting on a condom when you are on your own. If you don't lose your erection in these circumstances, then you are almost certainly suffering from performance anxiety. The best way to overcome this is to stop focusing so hard on the condom and make putting it on part of the entire act of sex. And don't worry about losing your erection – it's normal for erections to come and go during sex – you can always get an erection back again. One solution is to ask your partner to put the condom on you while you lie back and enjoy the sensation of her touching your penis. She could do this while she's masturbating you or, if she wants to be really clever, she could even slip it over the head of your penis as she gives you oral sex. The key is to make the experience sexy. If your penis does go limp when you've got the condom on, hold the base of the condom in position with one hand and stimulate yourself back to erection with the other hand.

How many orgasms is it possible to have in a row?

Most young men can enjoy between one and three orgasms within an hour or so – this is true of a few older men as well. However, with age, the refractory period (the time between ejaculating and being able to get another erection) does become longer. In compensation, mature men may be less prone to premature ejaculation, meaning that they can keep going for longer, giving and getting greater sexual satisfaction from a single lovemaking session.

How can I have more powerful orgasms? I'm not feeling satisfied by sex with my girlfriend but I don't want to start sleeping with other women.

Perhaps you don't get enough physical and mental stimulation before orgasm. Extending foreplay and spending ages teasing and tantalizing every possible part of each other's body might make sex more satisfying. Research by sex therapists Masters and Johnson has shown that the longer you spend on stirring up arousal, the more powerful experience you will ultimately enjoy. Would you like your girlfriend to give you new types of stimulation or try new sex positions? If you want oral sex, for example, you might start by offering it to her, then suggesting that she honours you with the same – it's called the "give to get" principle. Plan on spending much longer in the bedroom, but don't rely only on the physical aspects of sex. Really great eroticism includes a mental exchange between lovers. Talk to her and seduce her into talking back!

I've heard that some men can have multiple orgasms. All I can say is that this doesn't happen to me. Is there any way in which I can learn?

Although US sexologists William Hartman and Marilyn Fithian maintain that it's possible to train yourself to experience multiple orgasm, there appear to be few men who have actually done so. The trick seems to be learning to stop yourself ejaculating. This may make it possible to have a number of orgasmic sensations in a row (these may be peaks of sexual excitement rather than true orgasms, but who's quibbling!). To attempt this you need strong muscles in your penis and around your testicles. You'll need to practise flexing your penile muscles and contracting and relaxing your testicles (if your testicles hurt when you do this, stop and carry on the next day). When you think you have developed enough muscular control, try to squeeze your penile muscles tight when approaching ejaculation during sex or masturbation. (Another tip for blocking ejaculation is to pull down on the testicles from the rear.) With some luck you may experience orgasmic sensations without actually ejaculating and then you'll be able to go on to reach further orgasmic heights.

Would it be disastrous if I faked orgasm occasionally? Sometimes I find myself straining to reach a climax during sex.

Of course you can fake orgasm if you want to, but it won't solve the underlying problem of why you are straining to climax in the first place. It's worth spending some time thinking about the reason for this. Are you having sex when you don't really want to? Do you feel insufficiently aroused when you have sex? Are there difficulties in your relationship with your partner? Could your difficulty with climaxing be your method of backing off from your partner? It may be that you need to postpone sex on the occasions when you are too tired or distracted to become properly aroused. Alternatively, if you feel the problems lie at the core of your relationship, you need to talk them through with your partner and possibly seek therapy depending on how anxious or depressed you are feeling.

indetail

The path to orgasm

Male arousal can start with sexy thoughts, an erotic fantasy or seeing or touching your partner's body. Or sometimes you just feel sexy for no obvious reason. The brain sends a message along nerve pathways to the penis instructing it to become erect. The intricate network of vessels within the sponge-like penile tissues fill up with blood and the penis becomes long and firm. The testes pull up towards the body and the wall of the scrotum thickens and tightens. If your penis is stimulated at this point, you will feel more and more aroused. The tip of the penis deepens in colour and a few droplets of fluid may appear. Your blood pressure, heart rate and skin temperature increase; your pupils dilate and your nipples may become erect. There is an increase in muscle tension all over your body.

As you approach orgasm your breathing gets faster and some men experience a skin flush. Men usually know when orgasm is imminent because they recognize the "point of no return" – a sense that ejaculation is inevitable. Semen is pumped out through the urethra in a series of short muscular contractions. This is accompanied by a feeling of intense sexual pleasure.

After orgasm the penis loses its firmness and the body reverts to its normal state within around 10 minutes. There is a period after ejaculation when you can't get another erection. In young men this is usually a matter of minutes.

I've worked hard at achieving a simultaneous orgasm with my girlfriend but it's elusive. She says it doesn't matter but I'd still like to do it. Any tips?
She's right – simultaneous orgasm doesn't matter. It's a hangover from the 1940s and 50s when, for some reason, the myth abounded that the only "right" way to climax was simultaneously. We now know, mainly through common sense, that many people have better orgasms when they experience them separately. That's because they don't have to struggle to synchronize their responses with their partner's and they can concentrate on their own orgasm without distraction.

If you still want to try, simultaneous orgasm depends on one or both of you holding back your orgasm. This means bringing your girlfriend close to orgasm and then holding back on the clitoral stimulation and, in your case, using the squeeze technique (see box below) or pulling down on your testicles. Have fun trying, but don't be heartbroken if you don't manage it.

I come so quickly that sexual intercourse is impossible. Squeeze techniques don't work and just the idea of sex is enough to make me ejaculate. Is there any way I can get over this problem?
You are one of a tiny minority of men whose sexual responses work on a hair trigger basis. Ejaculating before you have even penetrated your partner can be extremely frustrating for both of you. Your best bet would be to seek pharmacological help from your doctor. Thioridazine and monoamine oxidase inhibitors have been used for this problem, but the drug most widely used is clomipramine, a tricyclic antidepressant. The effect of the drug on your ejaculatory control will last only for as long as you continue to take the drug.

I'm in my first relationship and I can't ejaculate during intercourse. I can go on and on for hours but I just wear my girlfriend out. I can climax OK when I masturbate. What's gone wrong?
Either you're not getting enough friction from intercourse or, more likely, you are feeling inhibited and this is preventing you from "letting go". Because this is your first sexual relationship, your reticence may be caused by nervousness or a lack of confidence in your sexual ability. Take heart from the fact that these feelings are very common in first-time lovers. Spend more time talking intimately with your girlfriend so that you can learn to trust her. If possible, try masturbating together so that she can understand what you like and what stimulates you. Then try a combination of masturbation and intercourse. The more open you are with your girlfriend, the more accepted you will feel and the easier it will be for you to ejaculate. If you still need a little more help, have a small drink before you make love. This might release your inhibitions. But beware of drinking too much – that can put you off your stroke altogether.

sextips

The squeeze technique

Premature ejaculation is a common problem among men but there are several reliable ways of treating it. The squeeze technique is one of the most straightforward. It involves grasping the tip of the penis (just below the glans) between your thumb and fingers. Simply apply firm pressure when you feel that you are close to ejaculating. Don't worry if this causes your erection to "wilt" slightly – it will come back again. You can also apply this squeeze technique to the base of your penis. This can be useful during intercourse when you don't want to withdraw from your partner. Another way to overcome premature ejaculation is the self-help programme on page 40. If none of these techniques work, try consulting a doctor or sex therapist.

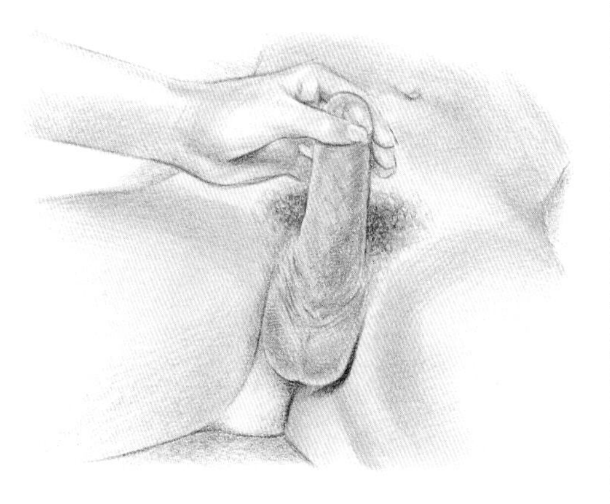

sex drive

When does a man's sex drive peak?

Sex drive can experience peaks and troughs throughout life depending on the nature of the relationship you are in and your state of mind. In terms of age, a man's sex drive tends to be highest in his late teens and early 20s. However, there is a great deal of variation from one man to the next.

Sometimes I don't feel like having sex but I make the effort for my partner. My mates seem to have sex all the time. What's wrong with me?

There's a myth abounding that men crave sex all the time. This is nonsense. Men are not machines to be driven automatically any time of day and night. Sexual desire is a finely tuned emotion and what is right for one person will be entirely unsuitable for the next. It's perfectly normal to have times when you don't feel sexy. Don't worry about how you shape up in relation to your male friends – and ask yourself how much of their sex stories are male exaggeration? It's great that you care enough for your partner to make an effort with lovemaking. Just don't be so hard on yourself.

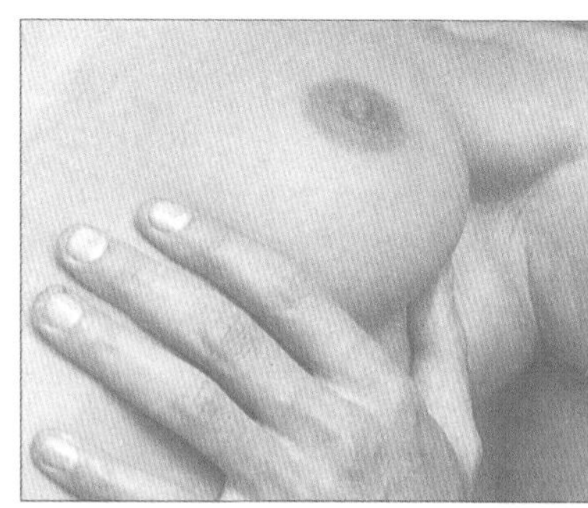

I'm 22 and under-sexed. I've only recently felt any real urge to get a girlfriend and I hardly ever have spontaneous erections. But I don't want to go through life without having a family. What can I do?

It sounds as though you fall on the low libido end of the sexuality scale. Clinicians are finding that many men like you have low testosterone levels and that regular hormone therapy can completely alter your sexual responses. Men who have never had an erection until past the age of 20, can, with treatment, go on to have happy and successful sexual relationships. Ask your doctor to refer you to a hormone specialist.

Can stress affect my sex drive?

Yes, it can. Stress can burn you out so that you become too exhausted to do little more than survive from day to day. Sex is often one of the first activities to be deprioritized during stressful times. Although a little stress may be good for you in that it sets

What does it mean if...

a man constantly wants sex?

Men in a state of sexual high-alert may fall into one of these categories:

- Being at the beginning of an intense new relationship when sexual feelings are running high.
- Being in an erotically charged atmosphere or environment.
- Feeling highly anxious – anxiety can confer a state of high arousal.
- Being driven by hormones.
- Feeling pressurized by cultural stereotypes to appear super-sexual.
- Being frustrated at not being able to find a suitable sexual outlet.
- Needing sex because it makes you feel attractive, desirable or loved.

emotionaltips

Relieving stress

Your sex life can be an accurate barometer of your stress levels. If sex gets shelved in favour of work, then it may be a good time to figure out which situations and people put you under pressure. Then you can tailor your lifestyle accordingly.

- Set yourself realistic targets – don't try to over-achieve.
- If struggling to make money causes you stress, actively change your lifestyle so that you can make do on less. Don't be afraid to downsize.
- Work at your own pace and resist pressure to speed up.
- Say no to extra work.
- Stressful situations can be addictive. Force yourself to take breaks for at least a week at a time and leave the computer and mobile phone behind.
- Expect to make mistakes – it's normal.
- Make time for sex. It can be an excellent way to relax, unwind and remind yourself of what your priorities should be.

adrenaline going and gives you a buzz, too much stress depletes testosterone levels and dampens sex drive. Stressed people are also likely to drink and smoke too much, both of which can cause problems with sexual function in the long term.

I have no interest in sex at the moment. My doctor says that I am suffering from depression. Are the two things linked?
Almost certainly. One of the hallmarks of depression is a loss of interest in previously enjoyable activities – sex being a classic example. As soon as your depression is treated with drug therapy or psychotherapy you should find that your libido starts to return.

I've always been highly sexed and I need a range of outlets for my sex drive. Because my girlfriend is always willing to have sex she can't understand it when I say I need other partners. And to be truthful, neither do I. What's going on?
Many people have a natural and compelling curiosity about sex and a strong desire to explore that curiosity. Sociobiologists might say that you are driven to sleep with a range of partners in order to spread your genes as widely as possible. Alternatively, sex with multiple partners may be a way of affirming your masculinity – "proving" to yourself that you are attractive – or alleviating underlying sexual insecurities. Whatever the reason, there is bound to be an emotional price to pay for sleeping with other people without a partner's acceptance. Weigh up how much your girlfriend means to you and how much you want her to stay with you. And then tailor your behaviour to fit.

stimulating a woman

How can I make sure my partner is really turned on before we have sex?

The key to this is to offer her a great deal of touch at the beginning of your lovemaking. Spend 15 minutes on stroking, caressing or "finger-tipping" each other. Explore the art of kissing. Just roll around having fun together. Laugh, giggle, talk, tell sexy stories, tell her she's gorgeous, attractive, sexy and beautiful. Eventually, touch her boldly on the area around the clitoris. Most women have far more sensation focused on the clitoris than they do on any other part of the body, including the breasts. Make sure that you draw out the proceedings in the earlier part of lovemaking rather than the later part. Once you get to clitoral stimulation and intercourse you need to be consistent – a languorous or stop-start approach can be frustrating at this stage. But you don't need to be hurried. Above all, arouse every part of her skin so that genital feelings are part of overall eroticism.

I'm not very sexually experienced. What's the best way to touch the clitoris?

Most women prefer stimulation on the area around the clitoris, rather than directly on the clitoris which is a highly sensitive place packed with nerve endings. Try massaging around the clitoris using a light circular or backward and forward movement with your fingertip. If she is very sensitive, try stroking her through thin fabric. But if she needs a lot of stimulation, then circling directly on the clitoris itself may be the best idea. If you are in doubt, ask your partner to guide your hand to where she wants to be touched or, even better, let her show you how she masturbates.

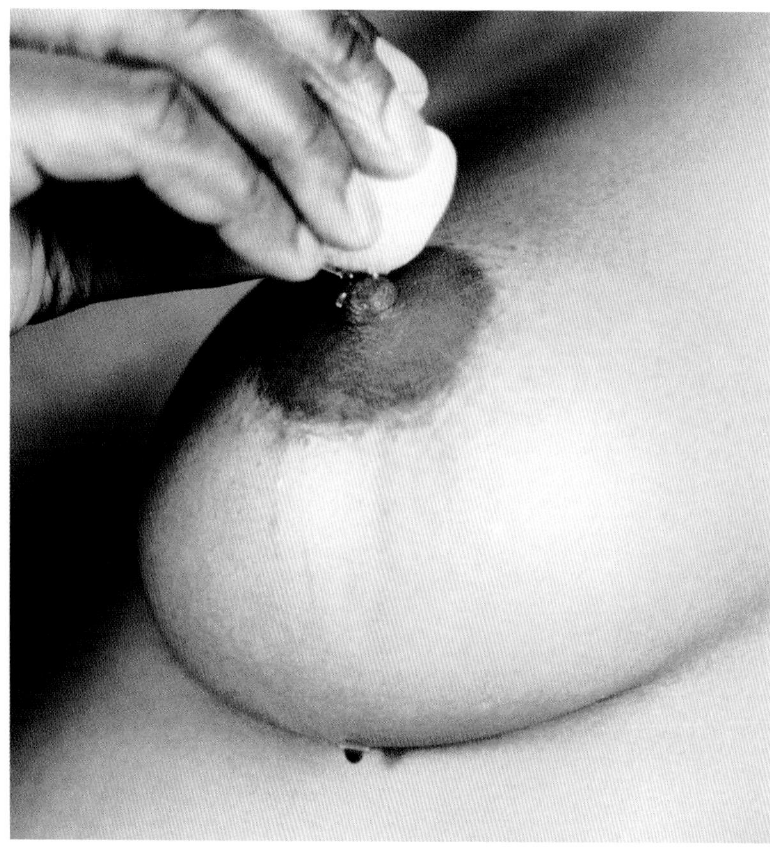

I'd like to become a true expert at stimulating my partner's genitals. Do you have any tips?

There are some special genital massage techniques that feel wonderful. Ideally these should all be done after giving your partner a whole body massage.

- The first technique is called the duck's bill: make your fingers and thumb into the shape of a duck's bill and hold your hand above her clitoris. Drizzle warm massage oil over your fingers so that it slowly drips onto her clitoris and seeps through her genitals.
- The second technique is gentle hair torture: using both hands softly tug tufts of her pubic hair – work your way from the top of her pubic triangle down each side of her vulva.
- The third technique is wibbling, named after the sound it makes. It involves gently pulling and releasing the labia in a rhythmic manner (much like you'd pull your bottom lip out!). Try wibbling both outer labia and then move on to the inner labia.
- The final technique involves the clitoris. Using a well-lubricated finger begin by circling the head of the clitoris at a steady pace, then stop and circle in the opposite direction. Keep

sextips

Oral sex strokes

Most women really enjoy receiving oral sex and some women say it's the easiest way to reach orgasm. Here are four imaginative ways to use your tongue and give your partner the maximum amount of pleasure.

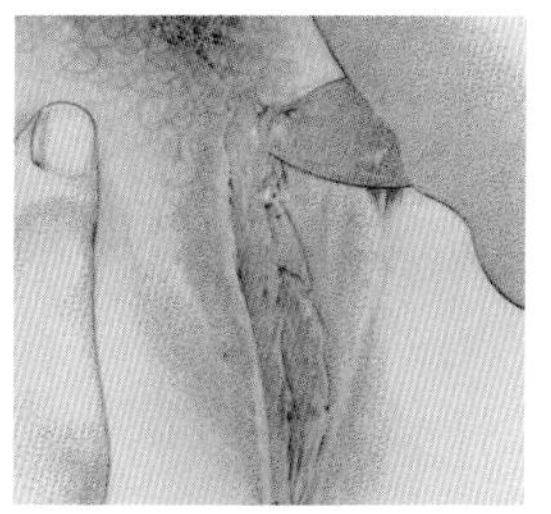

The tongue twirler – twirl your tongue in featherlight movements on top of the clitoris itself.

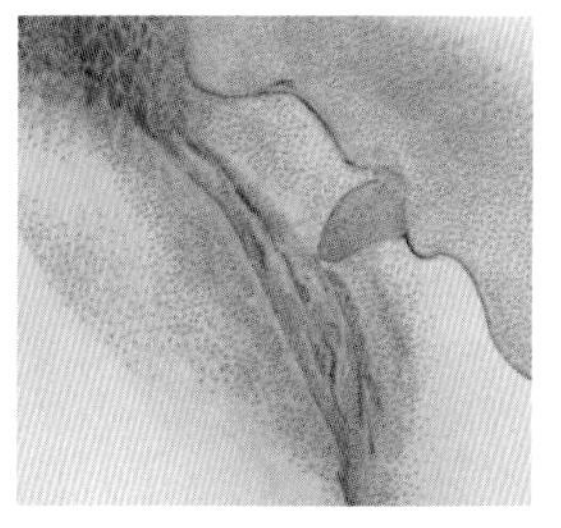

Firm circles – make your tongue firm and move it in circles around the head of the clitoris.

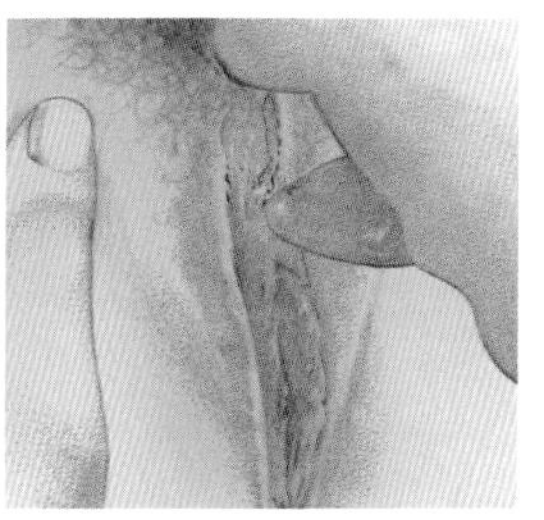

Butterfly flick – flick your tongue from side to side immediately underneath the clitoris.

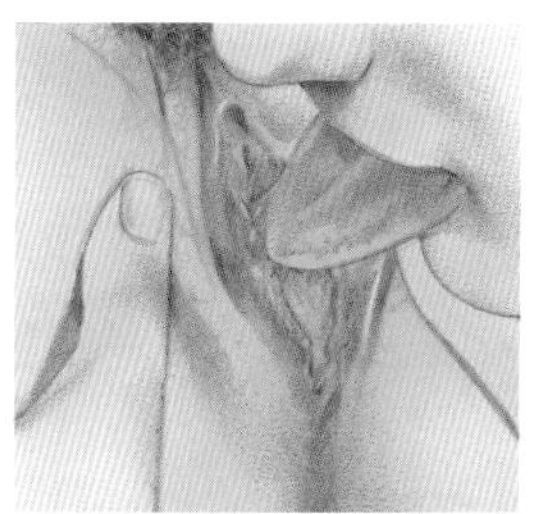

French lapping – use the broad blade of your tongue in a swirling movement between clitoris and vagina.

the pace even and regular. After 20 or so circles each way, rub the tip of your finger lightly up and down on either side of the clitoris. Do this 20 times. Finish with 20 light strokes from the clitoris down to the opening of the vagina and back again.

How do I give oral sex?

The form of oral sex done by a man to a woman is called cunnilingus. It consists of manipulation of the clitoris and vulva by the tongue. For really sensational cunnilingus your head needs to be right between your partner's thighs and preferably slightly below them so that you can stroke your tongue upwards against her clitoral shaft. She could lie on the edge of a bed with you kneeling between her legs or she could kneel on all fours with you underneath her. From here you can experiment with different strokes – use the tip and then the blade of your tongue and try occasionally pushing your tongue into her vagina. Stimulate one side of the clitoris and then the other, always from underneath. Try using your fingers for extra clitoral stimulation or to penetrate her vagina. Ask her for feedback so that you learn what she likes best. Some people enjoy sucking the clitoris, but a word of warning: don't do it too hard – this can make her numb rather than aroused.

How do I stimulate my partner's G-spot?

Try reaching inside her vagina with your longest finger. The G-spot is thought to be located 5 cm (2 in) up on the front wall of the vagina. If you stimulate this area you may be able to feel it as a kind of elevated bump. Many women say that it takes a steady pressure to stimulate the G-spot – not the backwards and forwards motion of masturbation or intercourse. Ask your partner for feedback and bear in mind that not all women are sensitive in this area. Also, when you first stimulate the G-spot, it can make your partner feel as if she needs to urinate!

How can I keep my partner on the edge of orgasm for as long as possible?

The more you stop and start clitoral stimulation, the more drawn out the sexual experience will be. Be warned though – many women will get irritated by a "give it then take it away" approach. Or they may even give up hope of reaching orgasm and slump into a sort of sexual despair. A better bet might be to stimulate every inch of her body, including her clitoris, extremely slowly. This will create a build-up of sexual tension that leads to a fabulous orgasmic experience. It's also worth knowing that sometimes sex can be amazing because it's rapid and explosive.

sextips

Ten tips for erotic sex

A simple way to improve sex is to make sure that your partner is really aroused before you have intercourse. The best way to do this is to spend lots of time on long, languorous and sexy foreplay.

- Caress her through her clothes and then slowly undress her.
- Wash each other in the bath.
- Kiss passionately.
- Tell her how aroused you feel.
- Pay attention to her breasts and nipples – stroke the area to the side of the breasts and under the armpits.
- Kiss and nuzzle her neck and ears.
- Kiss and lick her genitals with your mouth and tongue.
- Roll around so that every area of your body makes sensual contact with hers.
- Ask her what she would most like you to do to her.
- Don't force the pace - let arousal grow between you.

What does it mean if... *my partner always wants sex in the woman-on-top position?*

Sometimes people just slip into habits when it comes to sex but it's likely that your partner has a specific reason for favouring a particular position. Woman-on-top positions allow her freedom of movement and this can help her to reach orgasm. Your partner's preference may mean any of the following:

- She finds it difficult to climax in any other position.
- She likes being in charge.
- This has been her sex pattern in a past relationship and she is assuming it will be the same in the present.
- She enjoys the sensations that she gets in this position.
- She is afraid of being dominated and this is her pre-emptive strike to prevent such a situation.

My girlfriend gets close to climaxing but doesn't quite make it. Is there a sex position that can help women to reach orgasm?

Yes, one particularly good one is to remain pressed against her pubis once you have penetrated her in the missionary position. Instead of thrusting in and out, move back and forth in a grinding motion so that her clitoris is constantly being stimulated. This steady friction can help her to have an orgasm, especially if she is quite close to climaxing already. You could also let her go on top during sex so that she can move in a way that directly stimulates her clitoris. Alternatively, try stimulating her by hand during intercourse – having sex from the rear allows you to reach around her with one hand and stroke her clitoris.

How can I tell if my partner has had an orgasm? She says that she has, but she doesn't make much noise.

It can be difficult to tell. Some women keep absolutely still and barely make a sound during orgasm. However, if you are in the habit of stimulating her by hand or of giving her oral sex, you might be able to actually see or feel the contractions that take place during orgasm. This is especially true if you have one or more fingers inside her vagina.

I can't bring my girlfriend to orgasm. Am I a failure for being incapable of such a simple thing?

Making love takes two people so you can start by shifting 50 per cent of the anxiety off your shoulders. Next you should ask your girlfriend whether she has ever had an orgasm. And if she has, how? If she has never experienced orgasm during sex or masturbation, the cause is probably little to do with your lovemaking skills and everything to do with her unique sexual background, experiences, attitudes and responses. Modern thinking has it that we each need to be responsible for our own orgasm and not for those of others. So your best bet is to help your girlfriend achieve an orgasm by herself, perhaps through masturbation or by experimenting with a vibrator. Once she can bring herself to orgasm she should teach you how to stimulate her. Don't forget that most women don't climax from intercourse alone – most need extra clitoral stimulation.

My girlfriend – whom I haven't slept with yet – tells me that she has multiple climaxes, as many as 15 in one go. What if I don't have this kind of effect on her?

If she's that orgasmic, you may find it almost impossible to sabotage her response, so try to relax and take things in your stride. Just be yourself and make love as you would normally. Multiple orgasms come in many different shapes and sizes. Some women go in and out of gentle waves of climax, others have steep, sharp climaxes with as much as five minutes in between each. Try not to go into lovemaking with too many preconceived ideas.

I love my partner giving me oral sex and I know I ought to return the favour, but the truth is I hate the idea. Why am I so irrational?

Perhaps you regard the female genitals as unclean? Perhaps you have a horror of natural secretions, or somehow associate the genitals with toilet training? In some men, this dislike almost amounts to a phobia. The way to overcome phobias is by desensitization. This usually consists of a step-by-step approach to slowly getting closer to the object of your fear. With your partner's co-operation, you could try doing this at home. Alternatively, you could seek the advice of a sex therapist. People suffering from extreme phobias can also be helped by prescribed antianxiety medications. You are the only person who can tell if your dislike of the female genitalia is sufficiently intense to merit these measures.

sex in midlife

What is a normal sex drive for a man in his 50s?

The 1994 National Survey of Sexual Attitudes and Lifestyles found that men aged between 55 and 59 years made love around twice a month (compared with five times a month for men aged between 25 and 34). However, sex drive is highly individual and can increase or decrease at any age depending on your physical and emotional health, your lifestyle and the relationship you have with your partner.

Do men have a menopause?

Although men do not experience the dramatic physical changes that affect women at menopause, they do undergo a gradual decline in the level of the male sex hormone testosterone. Testosterone is manufactured by the testes, and to a lesser extent by the adrenal glands (located just above the kidneys). It is responsible for energy levels, sex drive and, above all, for the hardness of erections. It also acts in a variety of other ways on the male body and, due to its complexity, is difficult to measure and quantify. However, it's thought that testosterone decline can have various physical and psychological effects, for example, weakening the bones, making osteoporosis more likely, decreasing sex drive and making men more prone to mood changes and irritability. These effects and others are known as the "andropause".

Why do erections get less powerful with age?

This is usually a direct result of declining testosterone levels. A man of 50 may need significantly more penile touching and friction to stay erect and achieve orgasm than, say, a man of 30. Sensation may be less and so may ejaculatory power. This is normal. However, habituation may also be part of the problem – if you have been making love in the same way to the same person for many years, sheer familiarity may make it harder to become aroused. Fortunately, it is never too late to inject variety into your sex life (see Chapter 5).

I'm 41 and having erection problems. Could this be the start of impotence?

Yes and no. You may have erection problems because you are taking certain medications, because there are problems in your relationship, because you are stressed or depressed, or because you are drinking too much, too often. These are just a few possible explanations. Forty-one is young to develop impotence. If self-help measures, such as reducing stress or resolving relationship problems, don't help, consult your doctor who will check for underlying physical problems.

At 50 I'm always too tired for sex. I'm not impotent - just exhausted. My wife has started nagging me for sex but I can't seem to get it together. What can I do?

There may be good reasons for your fatigue, such as over-work or stress, and if there are, your extreme tiredness should force you to change your pace. There may also be physical reasons, including certain illnesses, and you should seek your doctor's advice about this. Another possibility is that you are suffering from depression. Fatigue is a classic sign of depression. And depression, in turn, decreases sexual desire. If you suspect that this is the case, ask your doctor about taking antidepressants and having counselling. The drugs will lift the depression and the counselling will help you to work out the origin of the problem and, hopefully, how to avoid it in the future.

I'm suffering from middle-age spread and I don't feel happy undressing in front of my wife any more. Is my sex life coming to an end?

It certainly doesn't have to. How does your wife feel about your body? The chances are that she still loves and desires you as much as ever and that you just need some reassurance. On the other hand, if you have gained a substantial amount of weight that is putting your health at risk (obesity in midlife is linked to a range of problems including heart disease and diabetes), it would be a good idea to recruit your wife's help in devising a programme of diet and exercise. The most important thing is to share your feelings and anxieties with your wife so that you can resolve this together.

sextips

Sex with a partial erection

If your erections are less firm than they used to be, it's still possible to have intercourse with a partial erection (consult a doctor about chronic erectile problems, however).

- Hold your penis with a finger along the side – as if the finger were a splint – to aid insertion.
- Ensure that your partner is very lubricated so that your penis can slip in easily.
- Ask your partner to slide on and off your penis as you hold it in place. Your erection should become firmer as stimulation increases.

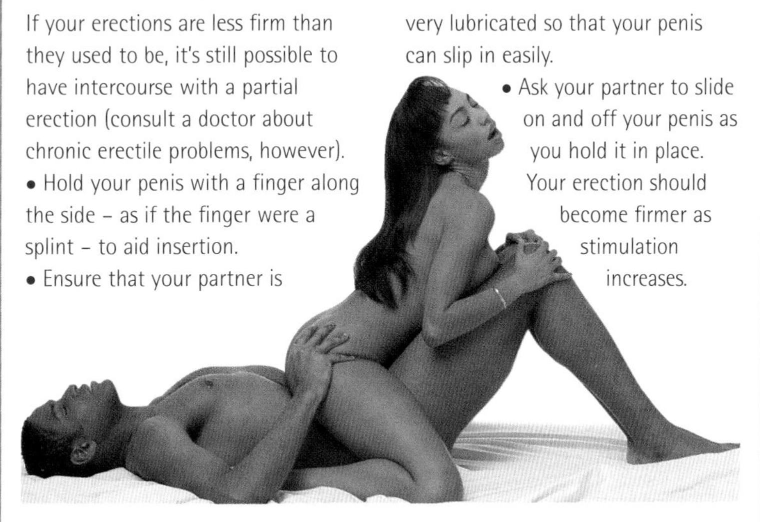

My sex drive remains as high as ever but my 49-year-old wife's appears to be flagging. What can we do?

Your wife is probably going through the menopause and is likely to need your love, patience and support. Sex drive can decline at the menopause and this is partly a side effect of physical and emotional symptoms, such as hot flushes, night sweats, irritability and mood swings. Female sex drive often returns post-menopausally, with the added advantage that you no longer have to worry about contraception. Reassure your wife that you still find her attractive. Talk to her about your mutual sexual needs at this time. Some specialists believe in putting women on hormone replacement therapy (HRT) early on in the menopause and your wife may choose to seek professional advice about this. HRT may alleviate her menopausal symptoms and this could have a spin-off effect on her sex drive. A natural alternative to HRT is nutritional supplements (see page 87).

Since having a hysterectomy my wife feels anxious that I will no longer want to make love to her. Why should she feel this way?

A possible male equivalent to a hysterectomy might be having your testicles removed. It's worth imagining how you would feel in this situation. The chances are that, rather than feeling sexy and positive, you would feel similar to your wife – worried about your sexual attractiveness and identity. Try to give your wife as much patient understanding as you can and encourage your family and friends to do the same. On a medical note, if your wife's ovaries were taken out along with her uterus, she might need to consider starting HRT.

HRT for men

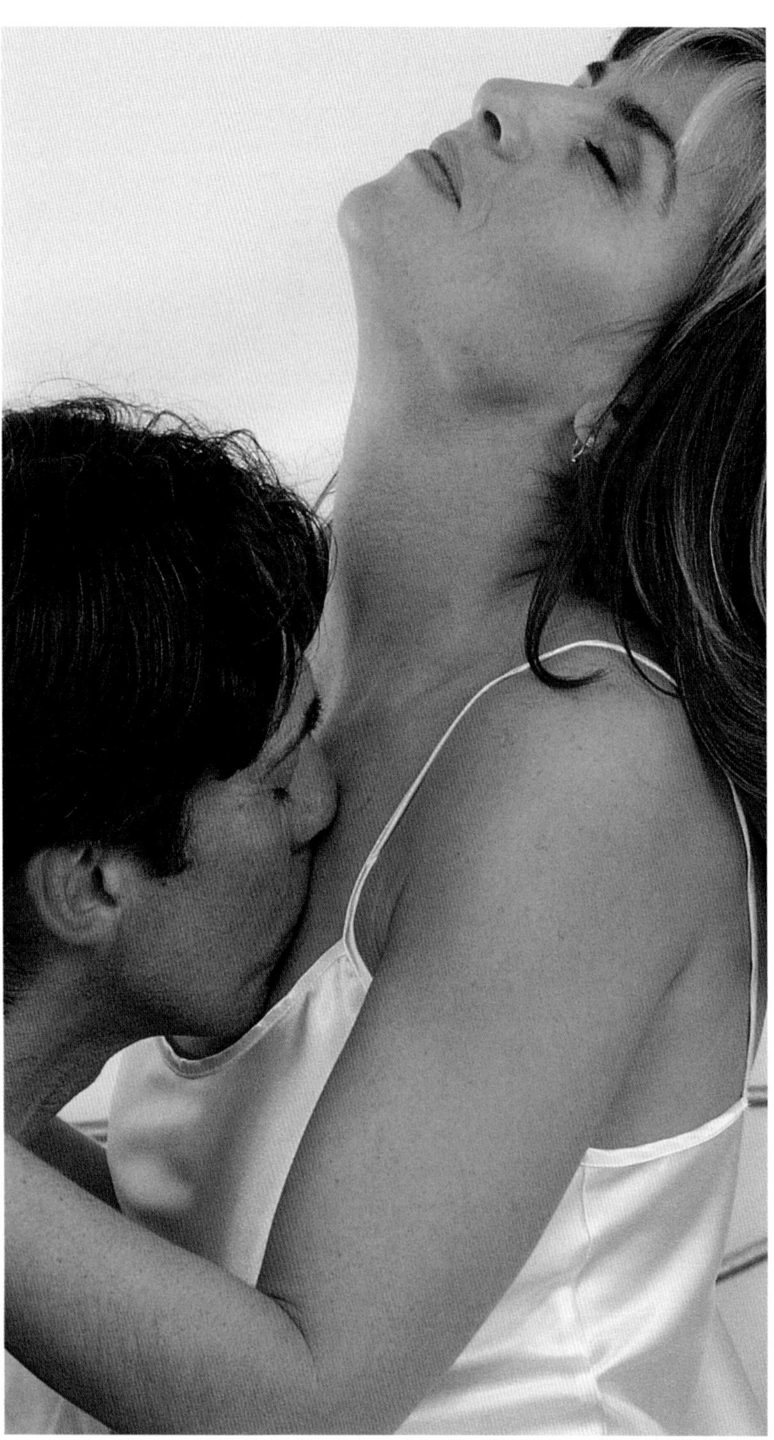

What is hormone replacement therapy (HRT) for men?

HRT for men consists of testosterone. It can help to restore libido and sexual sensitivity and is prescribed in patch or gel form. Doctors are divided about the wisdom of prescribing testosterone regularly for men since some experts believe that it may increase rates of prostate cancer. However, Dr John Moran, a UK hormone specialist, says that the latest findings show that men who have no signs of prostate cancer are at little risk from taking HRT. As a safeguard, all men considering HRT are first given tests that can detect prostate cancer even in its very early stages.

What are the benefits of HRT?

Testosterone not only restores sexual function, it can also help to alleviate symptoms of the andropause (see page 55) and prevent cardiovascular disease and osteoporosis. Although osteoporosis is a disease that is most common in postmenopausal women, men start losing bone mass roughly five years after women and also become vulnerable to bone fractures resulting from weak, brittle bones.

How do I know whether HRT is right for me?

Although some men undoubtedly benefit from HRT, this is not the case for all men. There will always be a percentage of men whose natural free-ranging testosterone levels remain high enough to make HRT unnecessary. In addition, there are some men who just don't appear to benefit from additional testosterone. In their case the hormone DHEA may be preferable (consult a hormone specialist about this). One way of deciding whether or not HRT is for you is to answer the question below. Men who answer "yes" to items 1 and 7 and/or any other four items on the list may be suffering from testosterone decline and could benefit from HRT. (However, please note that these symptoms can also be caused by other conditions – it is important to be screened for both thyroid disorder and depression.) Do you suffer from any of the following?

1. Decreased sex drive.
2. Lack of energy.
3. Decreased strength and endurance.
4. Loss of height.
5. Decreased enjoyment of life.
6. Sadness and/or grumpiness.
7. Erections that are less strong.
8. Deterioration in sporting ability.
9. Fatigue.
10. Deterioration in work performance.

I am wary of taking hormones. Are there any natural alternatives that will keep me sexually energetic?

There are a variety of natural supplements that help to maintain the health of the reproductive tract and prevent some of the signs of aging. For example, phytoestrogens (derived from soya and seaweed products) have a proven protective effect against enlargement of the prostate gland (a common problem in middle and old age). Gingko biloba protects against memory loss and (hopefully) encourages the imagination to continue working well.
Co-enzyme Q10 is an antioxidant supplement that promotes good general body maintenance. Calcium, preferably in the form of skimmed milk, helps prevent bone loss which can indirectly become a sex killer.

casehistory

"He became so irritable I nearly asked him for a divorce."

Sandra, 58

We had a great marriage until a few years ago when Lester started to become bad tempered and moody. We started to have a lot of arguments and our sex life ground to a halt. He became so irritable I nearly asked him for a divorce. In a last ditch attempt to save our marriage we went to counselling together. This didn't seem to change Lester's mood. The counsellor suggested that Lester got his health checked out to see if there was a physical reason for his lack of interest in sex. We saw a doctor and then a specialist who prescribed a hormone gel that Lester rubs into his arm. This has really improved things. We've started having sex again for the first time in years.

Lester, 63

I didn't realize how bad things had got until Sandra suggested counselling. In hindsight things were bad: I was constantly irritable or angry about something, tired all the time and sex seemed irrelevant to me – I barely even masturbated. The doctor prescribed a hormone gel because he said I had low testosterone levels. Using the gel has helped me enormously. I feel much more energetic and enthusiastic than I used to. But I must admit that, although I've got my sex drive back, I do feel a bit rusty. I think it's because I've neglected my sex life for so long.

Anne responds:

"Lester was suffering from some of the classic symptoms of andropause – fatigue, irritability and low sex drive. The counselling sessions revealed that there was nothing fundamentally wrong with Lester's marriage and no specific event that had triggered his foul moods. Neither the counsellor nor the doctor felt that Lester was suffering from depression. After a comprehensive health check, including a hormone analysis, Lester was found to have low levels of free-ranging testosterone and was prescribed HRT in gel form by a hormone specialist. His testosterone level rose, his grumpiness disappeared, his wife started to feel happier and his sex drive returned. Although Lester's sexual confidence has been dented over the past few years, a couple of sessions of sex therapy could help him and Sandra to rediscover the intimacy and sensuality that they have shared in the past."

sex and aging

Do all men become impotent eventually?

Not necessarily. Research conducted in 1984 found that in the over-70 age group 59 per cent of men were still having sex with their partners. A further 22 per cent reported sexual activity which was assumed to consist of masturbation. Men over 80 are more likely to be impotent – 75 per cent in Alfred Kinsey's study. Kinsey noted that there is a natural and gradual decline in sexual activity over the years. Later research has confirmed this but has found that people who have a lot of sex when young are likely to continue having sex in old age.

What is the oldest age at which men may become parents?

Theoretically, men may sire children throughout life – Picasso was a notable example, begetting his last child when he was well into his 80s. However, older men are prone to impotence which can make conception through normal sexual intercourse difficult or impossible. Fortunately, men who suffer from impotence may have a normal level of fertility, and modern reproductive technology can help impotent men become fathers through assisted conception techniques.

A couple of years back I began to have problems getting an erection and the doctor diagnosed diabetes. Although my diabetes is now under control, my erections haven't returned. What's happened?

Adult-onset diabetes is an illness that is increasingly common in middle and old age. It can damage sexual function in two ways. Firstly, it can cause deterioration of the nerves that supply the penis and, secondly, it can damage the arteries so that there is insufficient blood flow to the penis. Both of these can make it difficult to get an erection. Unfortunately, bringing diabetes under control does not necessarily restore a man's ability to have an erection. Ask your doctor about available treatments, such as a penis pump.

I've been told by my doctor that I must have a operation for an enlarged prostate gland. I've heard that this can result in loss of sexual ability. Is this true?

Many men find that their prostate gland gets larger with age and the pressure that this creates on the urethral tube can interfere with normal urination and ejaculation. Some men receive hormone treatment for this problem, a side effect of which may be reduced sex drive. Other men have surgery. There are at least three surgical methods (transurethral, suprapubic and retropubic) that should not interfere with sexual function at all. However, in these three cases, orgasm will be "dry" because semen is ejaculated backwards into the bladder rather than forwards out of the penis.
The least commonly performed type of operation (perineal surgery) damages nerves supplying the penis, and this frequently results in impotence. Talk to your doctor or surgeon about your concerns and ask about the most probable outcome of your surgery.

If I wake up in the morning with an erect penis, does this mean that I should be able to manage intercourse?

In general, the answer is yes. A total lack of spontaneous erections whether during sleep, on waking or during the day can suggest that there is an underlying physical problem that is preventing you from having an erection. On the other hand, if you have regular spontaneous erections but experience problems when you come to make love with a partner then the cause may be anxiety-related. Men suffering from erection problems should consult a doctor for a professional diagnosis.

indetail

How the penis pump works

The penis pump works on a vacuum principle. A cylindrical container is fitted over the penis and the air is then gently pumped out, creating a vacuum around the penis. This causes blood to rush into the penis, creating an erection. A specially designed penis ring is then slipped onto the base of the penis to sustain the erection, and the cylindrical container is removed. Now the man has sex as normal and removes the penis ring afterwards (the ring should not be left on for more than 30 minutes). An alternative to the pump is a penis sheath which functions in a similar way. The sheath looks like a condom, and is wrapped around the penis.

What are the best ways to overcome impotence?

There are several methods and you should discuss them with your doctor. It is worth bearing in mind that impotence always has a psychological component even if the underlying cause is physical. When sex goes wrong you often feel bad about yourself – your impotence treatment should take this into account.

These are the options that you should discuss:

• Sildenafil (Viagra) is a prescribed medicine in pill form and works by increasing blood flow to the penis.

• Caverject is a hormone that can be injected directly into the shaft of the penis using a special device at home. (Injection methods have been largely but not entirely superseded by sildenafil.)

• The penis pump is a device that induces erection by mechanical methods (see box opposite). It is used in conjunction with a penis ring – a specially designed rubber band that is placed around the base of the penis to sustain the erection. This is an inexpensive and reliable way of inducing erection that many men prefer to drug treatments.

• Various different types of implants are available which are surgically inserted into the penis.

• Sex therapy or other types of counselling. During sex therapy a couple will be asked to attend for counselling, given homework to carry out and asked not to attempt intercourse. Instead, in domestic privacy, they practise massage and relaxation exercises culminating in the rebuilding of a joint approach to sex and its performance. Sensate focus (see page 77) is a commonly prescribed sex therapy exercise.

I'm suffering from intermittent impotence. Is there anything I can do to improve my sex life?
Different causes require different treatments and so you need to find out the reason for your impotence. You should start by having a thorough medical to rule out health problems such as diabetes or atherosclerosis (blocked and narrowed arteries). One of the commonest causes of impotence is venous leakage – this means that although blood flows into the penis, making it stiffen and stand up, it also drains away again because the natural "locking" system that keeps blood in the erection is faulty. One way to establish whether you are suffering from venous leakage is to take sildenafil (Viagra) under your doctor's guidance. If you still have erection problems when you take sildenafil, the chances are you are suffering from venous leakage. Although microsurgery can be used to repair the penis' locking mechanism, it is difficult, expensive and may not work. These days, doctors fall back on something simpler and cheaper – the penis ring. This is a surgically designed band that is put around the base of the erect penis. It works by constricting the blood vessels at the base of the penis and can be used in conjunction with a penis pump. Intermittent impotence may also have a psychological origin, in which case your best option is to seek sex therapy.

Can sildenafil (Viagra) cure some cases of impotence?
No, sildenafil only ever treats impotence. You take a pill about an hour before you plan to have sex and this helps you to get an erection by increasing blood flow to the penis. Sildenafil doesn't automatically give you an erection – you need to feel sexually aroused and stimulated first. If you're not aroused, the pill won't have any effect on you.

Is sildenafil (Viagra) suitable for everyone?
Sildenafil isn't right – or doesn't work – for all men with erection problems. You may not be able to take it if you have cardiovascular, liver or kidney

problems, stomach ulcers or blood problems, such as leukaemia or sickle cell anaemia. Sildenafil can also react badly with other drugs. For example, it should never be taken with nitrate drugs (nitrates are commonly found in prescription drugs for angina, and recreational drugs, such as amyl nitrate, known as "poppers"). This can cause a dangerous, even fatal, drop in blood pressure.

Does sildenafil (Viagra) have any side effects?
Side effects may include headache, facial flushing and an upset stomach. These are usually mild or moderate and tend to pass within a few hours. If you have severe side effects, cardiovascular problems or an erection that lasts for many hours, seek medical help immediately.

My wife still turns me on after 40 years of marriage but I'm finding it more and more difficult to climax. What's wrong with me?
This is almost certainly age-related. You can help yourself by increasing stimulation both physically – using friction – and emotionally – using fantasy. The fantasies I'll leave to you (although legal erotica and sex games are worth contemplating). For increased friction, place a pillow under your wife's buttocks in the missionary position. Alternatively, ask her to clamp her legs together during sex so that thigh pressure maximizes your stimulation.

I find that at the age of 60 I can't have intercourse as much as I'd like. Last year I married a woman 10 years younger than me who expects a fully active sexual relationship. What can I do?
She can have an active sexual relationship provided she doesn't expect you to behave like a teenager with the reflexes of a leopard and the stamina of a stallion. You can take her to bed morning, noon and night, for hand, mouth and cuddling bliss. In the absence of two disabilities – actual disease and the belief that older people should be asexual – sex can continue for as long as you want it to. If you are suffering from erection problems or low sex drive, consult your doctor about the treatments that are currently available.

emotionaltips

Overcoming negative attitudes

Negative attitudes about sex and age can have a damaging effect not just on how you express yourself sexually, but on your overall self-esteem. You can help to overcome negative sexual stereotypes with the following ideas.

- Stay fit and healthy through a combination of diet and regular exercise.
- Pay attention to and take pride in your appearance.
- Develop a wide range of interests. Self-identity affects your approach to sex.
- Flirt with the opposite sex. Use assertion techniques to boost your confidence.
- Learn to look for the individual beauty that lies beneath an aging face or body.
- Campaign vigorously to combat ageism.

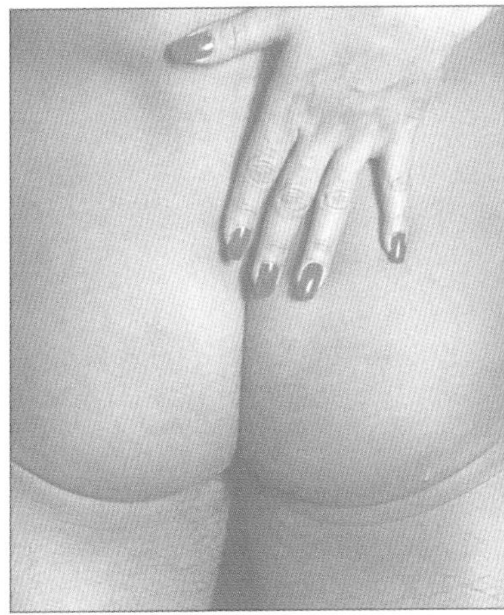

My 72-year-old partner says she is convinced that our sex life kept her young in the past. Can this be true?
Sexual activity in old age can indeed help to keep the sex organs healthy and functioning (hence the old adage: "use it or lose it"). There is also a belief that the hormones and nutrients in ejaculate keep the vagina moist and youthful – a kind of intra-vaginal HRT. On an emotional level, continuing to enjoy sexual intimacy as you grow older can help to give you a sense of youth and vitality.

My wife died a year ago and I mourn her a lot. She could never be replaced and I will never remarry. Lately, however, I've been experiencing some violently erotic dreams. Why?
Although mourning needs to take place, sometimes for months or years, physical life goes on, including that to do with sexual desire. Moreover, the complexities of grief may cause you to feel anger that she has "left" you as well as "relief" that you are free. These could feed into your fantasy dream life. Try to accept your erotic dreams and don't feel guilty about them.

are you a confident lover?

Many men believe that sexual confidence comes from sleeping with lots of different women. In fact, all you really need is a sense of openness and curiosity about sex.

You wake up next to your lover and you're dying to have sex. Do you:

- ☐ **A** Kiss her passionately and make her an offer she can't refuse?
- ☐ **B** Snuggle up and tentatively stroke her body until she becomes aroused?
- ☐ **C** Give her a peck on the cheek and hope she wakes?

When it comes to foreplay, do you begin by:

- ☐ **A** Kissing, caressing, stroking and fondling the areas where you know she is most sensitive?
- ☐ **B** Fondling her nipples and genital area?
- ☐ **C** Rubbing your body against hers until you think she's ready?

When you are giving your lover oral sex are you:

- ☐ **A** A tongue-twirling genius? You always bring your partner to a delicious orgasm.
- ☐ **B** A hit-and-miss man? You try it, but rarely have the technique or patience to let your lover reach orgasm.
- ☐ **C** An occasional visitor? You don't do it much because you're not completely sure that your lover enjoys what you're doing.

When you are stimulating your lover's clitoris with your hand, do you:

- ☐ **A** Go straight for the right spot and slowly and tantalizingly bring your lover to orgasm?
- ☐ **B** Aim in roughly the right direction and hope that your lover will give you a guiding hand?
- ☐ **C** Try to avoid it unless your lover requests it?

Your partner is trying to masturbate you, but she's not doing it the way you like and you are rapidly losing interest. Do you:

- ☐ **A** Give her an erotic explanation of how you'd really like her to touch you?
- ☐ **B** Give her a helping hand?
- ☐ **C** Allow her to continue – it might get better?

You're having sex and your lover says she is about to climax. Do you think:

- [ ] **A** How can I make her orgasm as intense as possible?
- [ ] **B** Great, now you can have your orgasm or lie back and relax?
- [ ] **C** What a relief, you were worried she wasn't going to?

Do you and your lover have sex:

- [ ] **A** In a wide variety of positions, depending on the mood and location?
- [ ] **B** In three or four different positions?
- [ ] **C** In one or two different positions?

Your lover seems to have difficulty reaching orgasm when you have sex. Do you:

- [ ] **A** Talk about it with her and try a few positions and techniques that may help?
- [ ] **B** Grind harder when you're having sex?
- [ ] **C** Hope things will get better in the future?

On the subject of your lover's G-spot, do you think:

- [ ] **A** The two of you can have fun finding it together?
- [ ] **B** If you discover it along the way, great, but you won't seek it out?
- [ ] **C** You're not sure how to go about locating it?

When it comes to making the first move for sex, do you:

- [ ] **A** Take the initiative, but love it just as much when your partner does?
- [ ] **B** Prefer that one or other of you habitually takes the lead?
- [ ] **C** Have a set pattern for initiating sex and dislike variation?

If you're having intercourse and your lover wants to stop before you've climaxed, do you:

- [ ] **A** Ask her to stimulate you manually or orally until you come?
- [ ] **B** Finish yourself off?
- [ ] **C** Stop - you can always try again later?

ANSWERS

Mostly As You seem to know what you're doing when it comes to keeping your partner happy in bed and making sure that your sex life is mutually satisfying and varied. You understand how to stimulate your partner and have the patience to learn about what she needs – and you take many of your cues from her. You also have the confidence to allow your partner to take the initiative when it comes to lovemaking. Don't fall into the trap of growing complacent though – it's always possible to keep learning.

Mostly Bs Although you enjoy sex and want your partner to be satisfied, you're not always entirely sure what she wants and needs. You're willing to try new things but sometimes lack the confidence and patience to see them through. Although your sex life is quite satisfying for you most of the time, it may not always be so for your partner. Try to accept some guidance from her. It would also help to improve your knowledge of your body and your partner's and to see your sex life as a true partnership.

Mostly Cs You would benefit from letting go a bit more when it comes to sex. You are a sensitive individual and tend to avoid areas where you lack confidence. By experimenting physically and talking to your partner about what she wants, you will quickly find that you know far more about your lover's body than you think.

questions women ask

Women's sexual responses change throughout life and even from one relationship to the next. Understanding your sexuality can help you to enjoy your body and have a satisfying sex life whether you are in your 20s or your 80s.

sexual self-esteem

I've been dumped by my boyfriend for someone much more glamorous. I feel unattractive and dull. How will I ever meet anyone else?
I firmly believe that appearance isn't solely responsible for attracting men – what really does the trick is a kind of inner spark. However, it doesn't hurt to feel that you look good, and if you're happy about your appearance, your inner spark gets a bigger and better chance to emerge! Eat a healthy diet, take exercise and invest in some new clothes and make-up. And be objective – my work in women's sex therapy groups has taught me that some women place undue emphasis on the negative aspects of their appearance, imagining, for example, that they have a terrible complexion when in fact they have one spot!

My partner often loses his erection during sex and I'm worried that it's because

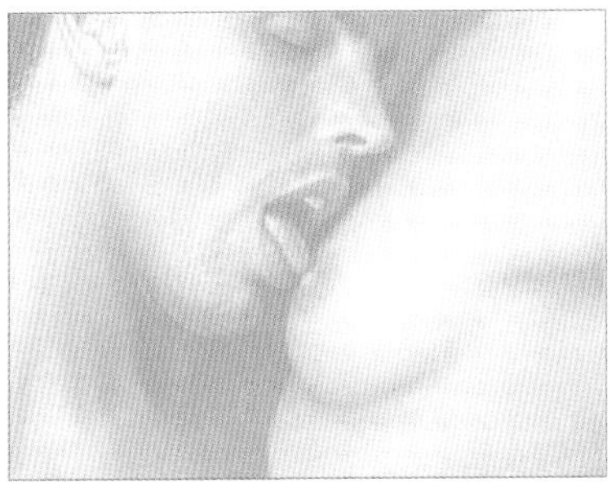

I'm not sexy enough for him. What can I do?
It's perfectly normal for erections to come and go during sex – it happens to most men. Talk to your partner and find out what his feelings are about the situation. If he's not worried, try to concentrate on building up your own sexual confidence.

I'm too shy to ask for what I want in bed. How can I find the right words?
You need to practise some assertion exercises. Make a list of 10 things that you would like to change in your life and rate them in order of difficulty. Then, starting with the easiest thing, work your way up the list. The more accustomed you get to doing difficult things the easier it gets. When you get to sex, preface your requests with some praise. An example might be: "I think the way that you touch my breasts is wonderful. I'd love you to stroke my clitoris in the same way."

I always get nervous and inhibited in bed which means that most guys give up on me fairly quickly. What can I do?
You could explain to new lovers that you feel scared about letting go, and need their support. Or you could insist on a getting-to-know-each-other period before you have sex. Above all, you could work on your own confidence. If you could be more outspoken about what you would like in bed (even if what you want is very simple), you would feel much stronger. Try the "yes/no" exercise (see page 98).

the breasts and genitals

indetail

Pain during sex

The medical name for pain during sexual intercourse is dyspareunia. If you suffer from dyspareunia, you should seek help from your doctor or from the genito-urinary clinic at your nearest hospital. Some of the common reasons for painful sex are as follows:

- Your vagina is not sufficiently lubricated and the penis is causing painful friction against the vaginal wall. Make sure that you feel "ready" before you attempt penetration.
- Deep penetration during sex can "bump" one of the ovaries and cause pain. Try changing sexual position.
- Your vaginal muscles tense up or go into painful spasm when you attempt intercourse. See your doctor.
- You have had a recent episiotomy (a surgical cut made to the vaginal entrance during childbirth). Wait until the vaginal area has healed before you attempt intercourse.
- The glands on either side of your vagina are sore, inflamed and painful. This is a sign of bartholinitis and should be treated by a doctor.
- You are suffering from a gynaecological problem or a sexually transmitted infection (STI). Consult your doctor.
- You have had frequent sex and your vagina and vulva are feeling sore or irritated. Wait until you feel better before you have sex again.
- Your hymen is still intact. If it doesn't break naturally, seek advice from your doctor.

One of my breasts is larger than the other. Is this normal?
It's very common for one breast or nipple to be a different shape or size from the other one. Breasts come in all shapes and sizes – it's normal to have inconsistencies.

I'm very large-breasted and I'm worried that men are only interested in me for this reason. What can I do?
Many large-breasted women suffer from unwanted sexual attention or feel that they attract interest for no other reason than their breast size. You could try dressing in colours and styles that de-emphasize your breasts and cleavage or, if this is too much of a compromise, you can be outspoken with men about your anxieties and invite them to be outspoken back. Alternatively, you could adopt a "wait and see" approach – it may be easy to guess what someone's motivation is. Only as a last resort should you think about cosmetic surgery.

I'm ashamed of my breasts because they sag. Is there anything I can do?
As a woman grows older her breast tissue becomes less dense and the breast ligaments lose their elasticity. These changes encourage the breasts to sag. You can help to support the breasts by wearing a good quality, professionally fitted bra, but it's important to be aware that there is no such thing as the "perfect" breast. The media frequently present us with idealized images of young, pert breasts, but the majority of women have breasts that sag or point in different directions, or nipples that are uneven or irregularly shaped. The breasts also change in appearance at different times of the menstrual cycle, often becoming more full or swollen in the days before menstruation.

I'm virtually flat-chested. I don't even need a bra. Will men find this unattractive?
Because society and the media pay so much attention to breasts, more and more women are feeling insecure that their breasts don't match up to the stereotypical ideal. Fortunately, men have a great variety of predilections when it comes to breasts. Don't worry about being flat-chested – breast size rarely dictates the quality of sexual relationships. Consider cosmetic surgery only as a last resort.

My boyfriend says that I get a bright red flush on my breasts and chest when I'm nearing orgasm. Sometimes it extends up to my neck and face and I can feel myself getting hot. Is this normal?
Yes, it's perfectly normal and it's often referred to as a "sex flush" (see the box on page 74 about the path to orgasm). Take pride in the fact that your sexual responses work so well. Take a look at your boyfriend during sex – some men get a sex flush too.

My pubic hair grows on my inner thighs and up to my navel. What can I do about it?
Rejoice in the fact that this probably means that you have a high sex drive. Women who have a lot of body hair, a tendency towards acne and sometimes a slightly greasy skin are usually women who possess a lot of natural

testosterone. This not only gives you a high sex drive, it should also make it easy for you to become aroused and reach orgasm. If you decide to remove your body hair, choose a long-lasting method such as waxing. If hair is fine and sparse, consider plucking or bleaching. Severe cases of hirsutism can be tackled with laser treatment.

My lover says that my vagina is too big. I'm really upset. Is there anything I can do?

If you have never had a baby, it is extremely unlikely that your vagina is particularly big. The reverse is usually true, especially for women who have only recently started having sex. Try putting a finger inside your vagina and then "grasping" it by contracting your vaginal muscles (imagine that you are trying to stop urinating in mid-flow). Even if the movement you can feel with your finger is only slight, that's fine – you don't need to worry about having a large vagina (after all, compare the girth of your finger with the girth of a penis). If you want to improve the strength of your vaginal and pelvic floor muscles, there are special exercises known as Kegel exercises (see page 67) that you can practise. You should also be aware that men who are finding it hard to get or to sustain an erection may complain about vaginal size. I wouldn't mind betting that if you help your lover to a stronger erection by giving him some sensual genital massage he'll stop complaining.

I'm worried that my genitals are ugly, especially my vaginal lips which seem really long and floppy. What can I do?

Don't worry, it's absolutely normal to have vaginal lips that extend outside the outer lips of the vulva. And there are as many genital appearances or "styles" as there are facial features – none is more beautiful or ugly than another.

I want to find out if I have a G-spot. What exactly is it and is it true that you can ejaculate from it?
"G" stands for Grafenburg. Ernst Grafenburg was the German gynaecologist who located and identified a sensitive erogenous area around two-thirds of the way up the front wall of the vagina. If pressed in a certain way, the G-spot can yield rapid orgasm in some women and this may also cause women to "ejaculate" a thin arc of pale fluid. There is much controversy over this fluid – some experts say that it is just urine while others say that it is similar to prostatic fluid (a component of seminal fluid secreted by the prostate gland in men). The G-spot is thought to derive from the same structure as the prostate gland during fetal development. It can be quite difficult to feel your own G-spot because it is often situated a long way inside the vagina. Many women find it's easier for their partner to locate it because a man's fingers tend to be longer and it's easier for a man to angle his hand into position (see page 49).

My ex-partner used to say that my genitals smelled bad even though I washed meticulously. I can't smell anything myself but it's made me so nervous that I'm scared of getting close to new men. Is it possible that I've caught a sexual disease?
It's possible, but it's unlikely. To rule this out, visit your doctor or a local STI (sexually transmitted infection) clinic for a professional diagnosis. If you don't have an STI and you regularly wash your vulva and perineum with water and unscented soap, then your ex-partner may have had an aversion to natural bodily smells. You should consider this his hang-up rather than letting it become yours. Fortunately, the majority of men are turned on by a woman's "cassolette" - literally, her perfume-box.

My vagina makes fart sounds during sex. I find it really embarrassing. How can I prevent it?
Many other women experience exactly the same thing. It's caused by air entering your vagina during intercourse and then being noisily released. You may find that air gets pushed into you more easily during some sexual positions than others, so try to note which positions are the

worst offenders. However, by far the best approach is to make it into a shared joke with your partner and simply laugh it off as one of those natural quirks of sex.

My boyfriend has a huge penis. I haven't had intercourse with him yet and I'm worried in case he hurts me. Are there any special positions that we should use?
It might be sensible to avoid positions that allow deep thrusting and this includes the missionary position and the doggy position. One method of creating more room for him is to lie on your back with your legs out straight and clamped together quite tightly – this means that he is thrusting between your thighs as well as into your vagina. A side-by-side facing position would also allow extra room. Alternatively, if you go on top of your boyfriend, you will be in control of the depth of penetration.

When I try to have sex, my vagina just tenses up so much that my boyfriend can't enter me. I really love him so it's not that I don't want to have sex with him. What's my problem?
You are suffering from vaginismus. This involves involuntary spasms of the vagina which experts believe are triggered by the unconscious mind as a result of some physically or emotionally traumatic event that happened in the past. For example, some women may have experienced an unpleasant gynaecological examination when they were younger; others may have had a frightening sexual encounter – both can instil a profound fear of penetration. A therapist can help you to overcome

this problem by teaching you how to insert "safe" cylindrical objects (known as vaginal trainers) into your vagina. You start with small-sized trainers and gradually move on to bigger ones, so that you and your vagina slowly but surely get used to degrees of penetration. It sometimes (but not always) helps to talk about your anxieties about sex and penetration.

My boyfriend and I have been trying to have sex for the first time for nearly a month now but he can't manage to penetrate me. How will I ever lose my virginity?
Take a close look at your genitals. Use a small mirror so that you can see whether the entrance to your vagina is open or obscured by a thin membrane. If you can see a membrane, this is your hymen and it needs to be broken to make intercourse possible. When the hymen proves too tough to break during normal intercourse (as in your case) medical help is needed. Ask your doctor for advice. If, on the other hand, your hymen has been broken, then you may be suffering from vaginismus (see previous question).

sextips

Kegel exercises

Pelvic floor or Kegel exercises (named after their inventor, Dr Arnold Kegel) are exercises that are often recommended to women before and after childbirth in order to improve the muscle tone of the pelvic floor and vagina. However, any woman can practise Kegel exercises to improve vaginal muscle tone at any time of life. In fact, Kegel exercises may improve your sex life by enhancing sensation during intercourse. It may take around six weeks of practise to start feeling the benefits.

1. Locate the pubococcygeal (PC) muscle. Do this by trying to stop and start the flow of urine when you go to the lavatory. The muscle that you are using is the PC muscle.

2. Squeeze the PC muscle for three seconds, then relax it for three seconds. Repeat. Do this 10 times on three separate occasions every day.

3. Refine the exercise by imagining that your vagina is an elevator and that the PC muscle is a method of halting the lift at each floor. Take the lift up for three floors halting at each floor and then come down in the lift halting at each floor again. Practise this three times a day.

Sex fact

The clitoris resembles the penis in structure. It has a glans and a shaft and, although it is only visible as a tiny pink tip, the clitoris actually goes back several inches into the body.

masturbation

Is it normal for women to masturbate?

Women of all ages and backgrounds, whether they are married, cohabiting, single or involved in casual sexual relationships, enjoy masturbation. Female masturbation is not only accepted as a healthy and enjoyable way of expressing sexual feelings, it is also a good way to learn about your body and its responses so that you can pass on this knowledge to present and future sexual partners.

How do women masturbate?

Women masturbate in many different ways. Shere Hite was the first person to ask large numbers of women about their favourite masturbation techniques (as well as about many other aspects of female sexuality). The results of her surveys are published in *The Hite Report* (1976). She found that although most women masturbate by rubbing the clitoris with their fingers, there were various refinements to this method. For example, a woman may insert a finger or dildo into the vagina while rubbing her clitoris or she may also caress other areas of the body, such as her breasts or anus. Some women stimulate the clitoris with a vibrator or a jet of water from a shower head. A few women masturbate by crossing their legs and squeezing their thighs together rhythmically or by thrusting against a soft object such as a pillow.

casehistory

"One of my friends bought me a vibrator as a joke."

Jenny, 25

I've had two serious boyfriends and I'm single at the moment. I never found it very easy to reach orgasm during sex and I only managed it very occasionally with both of my ex-boyfriends – and then only in certain sex positions. I enjoyed sex but it always seemed a bit anti-climactic – literally! I've tried masturbation in the past but I always felt quite inhibited and I usually gave up before I had an orgasm. Then, for my last birthday, one of my friends bought me a vibrator as a joke. After letting it sit in the drawer for a few weeks I finally got around to using it. It was really good – it made me aroused very quickly and I even had an orgasm. It's changed my attitude to masturbation and I feel really pleased that I've found a way to get sexual satisfaction when I don't have a boyfriend.

Anne responds:

"*According to* The Hite Report *it's common for women to feel uneasy, inhibited or even guilty about masturbating despite the fact that they enjoy the feelings and sexual release that masturbation can offer. It's great that Jenny has found a way to overcome her reticence. Masturbation has not only brought her sexual confidence and independence – it also means that in her next relationship Jenny can show her partner how she stimulates herself so that she will no longer have to rely on the occasional orgasm during intercourse.*"

I've never masturbated before but I'd like to try. Where do I start?

First make sure you have the time to relax in absolute privacy. Start by taking a luxurious bath. As you soap yourself run your hands all over your body savouring the sensations as they glide over your skin. After your bath give yourself a sensual massage using oils. Don't touch your genitals yet – concentrate on touching and caressing erogenous zones such as the belly, buttocks, lips and breasts. If you like, you can start to fantasize. Now move your hands to your genitals. Simply massage them as you have done the rest of your body. Note any really good feelings you experience and begin to build on that, focusing on the spots that feel special. If you have an orgasm that's fine, but it doesn't have to be the goal of the exercise.

Next time you stimulate yourself, follow the same formula but spend less time on the whole body and more time concentrating on your genitals. Continue to build on the stimulation you give to the really sensitive areas. If the feelings of pleasure become intense, keep going until you reach orgasm. If you don't reach orgasm after practising this self-massage several times, try repeating the technique using a vibrator.

Why do I have more powerful orgasms during masturbation than I do during intercourse?
This is normal – the penis doesn't stimulate the clitoris very efficiently during intercourse. In fact, the majority of women can't reach orgasm from intercourse alone. In contrast, the fingers are ideally designed to stimulate the clitoris.

How can I show a man how to masturbate me?
Famous US sex researchers Masters and Johnson suggest that couples sit propped up against some cushions with the woman between the man's legs and leaning back against him. She begins to stimulate her genitals with her hand and then she substitutes her partner's hand for her own. She places her hand on top of his so that she can direct the movement, speed and depth of pressure of his fingers (this is known as hand-riding). This way he gets to see and feel what type of stimulation she enjoys most.

I've always used masturbation as an aid to sleep. Now that I live with my boyfriend I find it difficult to sleep on the nights we don't have sex. Unfortunately my partner caught me masturbating the other night and went mad, saying that he ought to be enough for me. I love him and want to make him understand. How do I do this?
Try explaining your sleep patterns to him. Say that you've always used masturbation as a sleeping aid and that it does not reflect on his skills as a lover or mean that you are unhappy with your sex life together. Reassure your boyfriend of your love for him and say that you don't want to put pressure on him to have sex all the time. However, invite him to help you reach orgasm every night – this doesn't have to mean intercourse, it could also mean your boyfriend stimulating you with his hand or a vibrator. This way, you are putting the ball very firmly in his court.

reaching orgasm

What do orgasms feel like?

Some women describe intense feelings of erotic bliss centred around the clitoris, others describe waves of sensual pleasure that flow over the whole body. Orgasm can be both an emotional and a physical experience. It is described as a build up and release of sexual pressure, tightness or tension in the clitoris and/or vagina; or simply as the relief that comes from scratching an intense itch. Some, but not all women, can feel the muscular contractions that take place in the vagina during orgasm.

How long should an orgasm last?

Sex researchers who have studied the physiology of female orgasm say that most women experience orgasms that last 15 seconds or less. During this time the vagina contracts rhythmically at 0.8 second intervals. There are usually between three and 15 of these contractions – the spaces between the contractions grow longer at the tail-end of the orgasm.

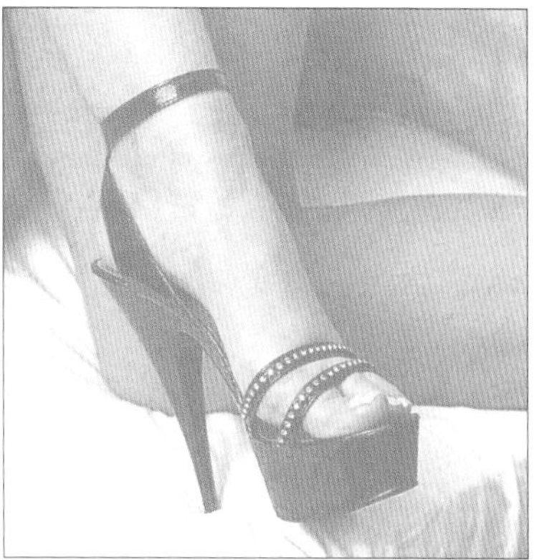

However, this is an extremely clinical description of orgasm and many women would say that the feelings of intense arousal beforehand and the glow afterwards make orgasms hard to quantify in terms of time.

How do most women reach orgasm?

Most women need direct and ongoing stimulation of the area around the clitoris to reach orgasm. Stimulation can come from a vibrator, your own hand or your lover's hand or tongue. There are also many other sex toys and masturbation tools (both improvised and specially designed). To climax during intercourse most women need lots of clitoral friction from rubbing against the penis or the man's body.

How can I have more intense orgasms?

By making sure that you are fully aroused in the build up to orgasm. You may find that fantasizing during sex gives you a more powerful orgasm. Immersing yourself in fantasy also helps you to forget any inhibitions you may have, and this in itself can enhance orgasm. Other tips include making a noise during sex or doing anything that heightens eroticism, such as making love in front of a mirror or dressing up in sexy clothes (see Chapter 5).

My friend says she can have multiple orgasms. I'd like to do this too. How could I manage it?

First of all, not everyone can experience multiple orgasms. So, if you find you can't, don't feel bad – value what you are capable of rather than dwelling on what you miss. The secret to having multiple orgasms is to continue with sexual stimulation after your climax. Practise with your fingers or with a vibrator and try to relax into the extreme sensations of orgasm and see if these turn into more climaxes.

I can masturbate several times in a row with gaps in between. I climax each time. Is this the same as multiple orgasm?

If you take a break between orgasms, let your body relax and then restimulate yourself, this is not the

indetail

Vaginal versus clitoral orgasm

Old-fashioned psychological theory says that a vaginal orgasm (one where the focus of pleasure is within the vagina) is a better and more mature sort of orgasm than a clitoral one, which is seen as being shallow, immature and only locally experienced. Over the past 30 years sex therapists have made it quite clear that any sort of orgasm is great and that there are indeed many different varieties. Orgasm can be felt practically anywhere – the clitoris is thought to receive and transmit sensations to all over the rest of the body. Also, many women feel orgasmic sensation in both the clitoris and the vagina making it inappropriate to divide vaginal and clitoral orgasms into separate experiences.

same as a multiple orgasm. In *The Hite Report* this type of orgasm is known as a sequential orgasm. Many women are able to have sequential orgasms, providing that they or their lovers have the energy and desire to keep going.

How many orgasms is it possible to have in a row?
It's possible to go on indefinitely but you might find that you get tired or that your clitoris becomes uncomfortable or loses its sensitivity – it depends on you as an individual. Some women enjoy two or three or even 10 orgasms in a row. In theory, the sky's the limit!

I can't bear my clitoris to be touched after I've had an orgasm. Is that normal?
Yes. It's normal for the clitoris to be hypersensitive after you've climaxed. This feeling takes a varying amount of

What does it mean if...
I could reach orgasm during intercourse with my previous partner but not my current one?

- Your present partner is a less skilful lover than your previous one and does not yet make the moves that fully stimulate you.
- You have got used to a certain pattern of lovemaking and need time in which to adjust.
- You do not yet fully trust your new partner and cannot "let go" during sex – you need to practise talking things through and establishing trust.
- You are still grieving for your former boyfriend and perhaps need a period of mourning before your next sexual relationship.

time to disappear. If you hope to have a further orgasm, go back to some gentle foreplay until your genitals have become less aroused. But please be aware that not all women can carry on once they have climaxed.

Can I suffer physically if I get aroused but don't reach orgasm?
No. You may feel a sense of uncomfortable tension, fullness or congestion in your pelvis and genitals (or throughout your body). This is because when you are aroused, blood flow increases to the genitals and pelvic organs. If you don't have an orgasm, this feeling of fullness can take a while to fade, but it is not physically damaging. Emotional reactions may be as noticeable as physical ones. For example, if stimulation is withdrawn just as you are about to reach orgasm, you may end up feeling cheated, frustrated or resentful.

It takes me ages to climax - at least 40 minutes. My partner gets exhausted. How can I speed things up?
Learning about timing would be a good idea. I suggest that the two of you consciously prolong foreplay and begin intercourse only when you sense you are close to the "point of no return". This will shorten the duration of intercourse and take some of the physical demand away from your lover. You could also use a vibrator if this kind of stimulation works for you. Experiment by jamming it in between the two of you so that it hits the important areas during intercourse. Your lover might enjoy this too!

I find it really hard to let go when I'm making love with my boyfriend. I get excited but I just can't climax. So why is it that I can reach orgasm on my own?
You are probably feeling inhibited with your boyfriend. Perhaps you are

What does it mean if...

I climax very quickly?

Some women reach orgasm extremely quickly either during masturbation or intercourse, or both. This should not pose a problem because sex can continue after a woman has climaxed and she may be able to have more orgasms if she wants to. Men, in contrast, need a period of time before they can have an erection if they have just ejaculated. Reaching orgasm quickly can happen occasionally or habitually, and it can mean any of the following:

- You receive enough of the right kind of clitoral stimulation.
- You receive enough of the right kind of lovemaking approach – this could mean loving with words, cuddles, kisses and caresses – not just genital stimulation.
- Your environment or situation is extremely exciting or erotic.
- Hormones, natural or artificial, predispose you to climax quickly.

worried about how you look or sound when you are in the throes of climax. Perhaps you are afraid of losing control in front of your boyfriend. You may find a sex therapy exercise known as sensate focus (see page 77) useful. This is used for a great diversity of sexual difficulties. It involves touching and massaging each other and exchanging information about what feels good and what doesn't – most importantly you are under no pressure to have an orgasm. Quite often, removing performance pressure from sex is enough to solve the problem.

I've heard that you should relax in order to experience orgasm. But when I relax I stop feeling aroused. What am I doing wrong?
There are two types of relaxation: mental and physical. You certainly need to relax mentally so that you feel safe with your partner and trusting enough to let go and experience orgasm. But, in contrast, there needs to be a certain amount of muscle tension in your body for orgasm to happen. The legs, abdomen or whole body may become tense or rigid as sexual arousal intensifies. Don't fight this tension – it can help you to reach orgasm.

I cannot feel my orgasms but my boyfriend assures me I have them. He says he can see my vagina contracting. Could this be true?
Yes, it could. You may be one of those rare women who experience a kind of anaesthetized orgasm. No-one knows why this is. One guess is that orgasm feels scary and the sensations are blocked. I suspect there is a physical cause which is, as yet, unknown.

I can't climax during sex even when my partner uses his hand. What's wrong with me?
There could be several reasons for your difficulties in reaching orgasm. Are you able to masturbate to orgasm by yourself? If you are not, have you tried using a vibrator? It may be that you need faster stimulation than hands can provide. If a vibrator works, try using one during sex with your partner. A small percentage of women find it extremely difficult to climax either due to extreme inhibition or because they naturally possess low levels of testosterone. In the case of extreme inhibition, small amounts of alcohol can aid relaxation, as can a drug called phentolamine. In the case of low testosterone levels, a prescribed hormone gel (see page 74) can help you to reach orgasm.

I've never climaxed and I'd really like to. Where do I start?
Start by teaching yourself to masturbate using your hand or a vibrator (see page 68). Then, if you have a partner, you can teach him how to bring you to orgasm when you make love together.

indetail

Why it's hard to reach orgasm during intercourse

Most women don't reach orgasm from the thrusting movements of intercourse because of the way that the clitoris is positioned in relation to the vagina. Whereas the clitoris is positioned on the upper part (or front) of the female genitals, the vagina is situated at the lower part (or back). This means that the movement of the penis during intercourse only indirectly stimulates the clitoris. As few as 30 per cent of women experience orgasm regularly through penile thrusting. The other 70 per cent need a little extra help – around 55 per cent of those use fingers or a vibrator. A vibrator has the advantage of not only being able to target accurately the area on or around the clitoris, but it also runs at a high speed of oscillation which, research has shown, helps many women to tip over into climax.

indetail

The path to orgasm

The sexual response cycle is very similar for men and for women. It consists of three stages: desire, arousal and orgasm. Desire focuses on the preliminary feelings of attraction and interest. Arousal is all about sexual excitement – the vagina lubricates, lengthens, distends and becomes engorged with blood in the same way that the penis does during erection. This makes the labia swell and turn deep red in colour and the clitoral shaft become erect. Many of the body's muscles become tense, and areas of the body, such as the breasts and nipples, enlarge as sexual tension increases. At the height of arousal, 75 per cent of women develop a "sex flush" – a measles-like rash that spreads rapidly over the rib cage and breasts. Also during the later stages of arousal, the outer (bottom) third of the vagina closes a little due to engorgement. This helps the vagina to grip the penis during intercourse. The clitoris can nearly disappear as it withdraws into the folds of engorged flesh.

During orgasm, a woman's breathing is at least three times faster than normal. Her heart drums at more than twice its usual rate and blood pressure increases by a third. Most of the body's muscles are tense. Orgasm begins with contractions in the outer third of the vagina – these can spread up to the uterus. After orgasm the body rapidly returns to its pre-aroused state.

My partner gets upset if I don't have an orgasm when we make love. I really feel as if I've failed in some way. Is it excusable to fake it sometimes?

If you fake an orgasm, you are effectively teaching your partner the wrong way to make love to you. If he believes you are satisfied, he will think he is "doing" sex the right way and will have no incentive to change. If, on the other hand, he knows you need a different kind of stimulation, then hopefully he will make adjustments. However, your partner also needs to understand that perhaps you don't always need to reach orgasm to enjoy yourself. He should learn to accept this fact and not burden you with guilt. If you suspect that he feels inadequate when you don't have an orgasm, explain to him that there are times in your menstrual cycle when you naturally feel sexy (see page 76) but also times when you don't. Tell him that your lack of orgasm has nothing to do with him and everything to do with your hormonal chemistry. But avoid faking orgasm – this can lead to other problems.

I've got into the habit of faking orgasm. I know it's stupid but I can't seem to stop myself. How can I break this instinctive habit?

You probably fear that your lover will reject you if you cannot respond orgasmically. (Please examine this fear carefully – if your partner would reject you, then he is not the right guy for you.) Improving your relationship will inevitably mean taking a risk. Try experimenting on yourself with your fingers. If you can climax on your own, ask your partner to incorporate some finger skills into lovemaking. If he wants to know why, tell him that you know you will have a more enjoyable experience as a result. Alternatively, you could try using your own fingers during intercourse. Tell your partner that recently your response has felt muted and you want to heighten it. Incidentally, a small proportion of women find it extremely difficult to climax and the use of testosterone gel can help to improve their sexual response.

If you go on to a new relationship in the future, do your best to be honest about your sexual needs and responses from the outset.

indetail

Testosterone gel

Current sexological thinking has it that testosterone is the hormone responsible for sexual response, desire, arousal and sensitivity in both men and women. For purely accidental reasons some women are born with masses of the stuff (and are highly sexed as a result); the great majority of us possess an average amount; and a few of us are short-changed and don't respond sexually as we would like to. The last group of women can be helped by taking testosterone. It is now available in a gel form, which is rubbed into the skin – this is a safe route of administration since the hormone bypasses the liver and goes straight into the bloodstream. The effects of testosterone include having more energy and more erotic sensation, especially in the genitals.

sex drive

I've noticed that there are times when my sex drive is much higher than others. How can I feel this sexy all of the time?
You can't! Your sex drive is partly determined by the rise and fall of the hormones that govern the menstrual cycle. Although everyone is different, many women report peaks in their sex drive around the time of ovulation. (If you have a 28-day cycle, you usually ovulate around the 14th day.) The few days leading up to your period and/or during your period can also be a time of heightened sex drive.

How can I work out which are my most sexy days?
Start keeping a diary of your menstrual cycle and make a note of the days on which you feel particularly sexy:
• Count the first day of your period as day one of your menstrual month. Start charting your moods and sex life from now.
• Make a note in your sex diary whenever you masturbate, initiate sex with your partner, fantasize or dream about sex, have a particularly erotic sex session or powerful orgasm, or even just when you feel attractive and sexy.
• Keep the diary for three months and then compare each of the three months. Work out the times when you regularly feel sexy and the times when you would much rather read a good book!
• Act on this information by setting aside special time for sex or even by planning a night or weekend away with your partner.

Is it normal to want sex every day?
Everyone's sex drive is different. Some women desire sex several times a day and others are content with sex once a month or even no sex at all. The important thing is to settle into a sexual pattern that meets your needs – don't worry about comparing yourself with other people. Sex drive is determined by many things. Hormones play a major role in libido but so also do thoughts and feelings. For example, if you are at the beginning of an intense new relationship, you may feel sexually charged most of the time. If you are having relationship problems on the other hand, this is likely to dampen your sex drive.

I've stopped being interested in sex and I don't know why. I like sex and I like it when my boyfriend climaxes but I don't have orgasms myself. Is it normal to have such a low sex drive?
I suspect that you have got near to climax yet been disappointed so many times that your sexuality has gone on strike and that you have effectively locked away your sexual feelings. If you consult a sex therapist, you may well be given a series of exercises known as sensate focus to practise at home (see box right). The idea behind sensate focus is that couples relearn their sensual and sexual responses through touching exercises in which they are not allowed to reach orgasm until the final stage. This takes the performance pressure off both partners so that they can enjoy the basic sensual and tactile experience of sex. If, however, you are happy with your sex life as it is, then don't worry.

indetail

Sensate focus

These sex therapy exercises can be applied to any sex problem, but they're very useful for low sex drive:

- Start by agreeing that you won't have intercourse. Undress and take it in turns to touch and massage each other (exclude the sexual parts of the body). Ask your partner to give you detailed feedback about what feels good. When it's your turn to receive a massage, lie back and concentrate on the sensations that different types of touch provoke. Tell your partner if there is a sensitive part of your body where you enjoy being touched or if you find anything distracting or unpleasant. Repeat this exercise until you both feel confident about touching each other in a truly sensual way.
- After two weeks you can start including each other's genitals in your massage but still avoid orgasm and intercourse. Keep giving each other detailed feedback. Gradually alter the balance of the massage so that you focus on the genitals. This should build up feelings of arousal without pressure to have intercourse.
- The final stage of sensate focus is intercourse. Try to integrate your knowledge of sensual genital touch with intercourse. Don't feel under any pressure to have an orgasm – just focus on the sensual experience of sex from one moment to the next. Finally, work towards having an orgasm by experimenting with different sexual positions and genital massage.

stimulating a man

What is the best way to masturbate my partner? I want to give him a great sexual experience.

First, discover how he most likes to be touched. You can do this in the following way: start by sitting behind him so that he is between your legs and leaning back against you (if he's too big for this, sit or lie side by side in bed). Now put your hand around his penis and ask him to place his hand over the top of yours. Tell him that you are a sex student and that you want him to teach you the perfect stimulation skills. By turning this into a game, you will enjoy learning first hand (literally!) what kind of touch he prefers, how firm and how fast it should be, and exactly where he likes it. And he will have the pleasure of showing you. When you feel this lesson has taught you all you need to know, you can try adding your own special touches such as fondling his testicles with your spare hand, using slippery lubricant or stimulating him with sex toys.

My new partner is circumcised and I don't know how to go about touching his penis. What should I do?

Whether your partner is circumcised or uncircumcised, the rule is the same: find out how your partner likes to masturbate (try the game in the previous question) and adopt this as your basic template for touching him. Because your partner doesn't have a foreskin that slides back and forwards over the tip of his penis you might find it easier to cover your hands in lubricant before you masturbate him – this will create a smoother sensation.

I've been trying out oral sex on my boyfriend but don't feel I've worked out an effective technique. Can you give me any tips?

You don't need to wait until your boyfriend has an erection before you start. Take him into your mouth while he's still soft and partially suck and partially swallow. This sucking/swallowing motion creates a distinct pressure around his penis and if performed rhythmically, it will encourage his erection to take shape. When his penis is erect, treat it like an ice-cream cone by holding it at the base with one hand and licking it all over, running your tongue up and down the shaft. Then, when it is covered in your saliva, take his penis between your lips and slide your mouth gradually down as far you can and back again. If you've got a small mouth and he's got a large girth, cover your teeth with your lips to avoid giving him a nasty nip. Now continue rhythmically moving your mouth up and down his shaft or try stimulating him by hand at the same time as fellating the head of his penis (see box opposite).

Should I keep my partner's penis in my mouth when he comes during oral sex? I'm not sure I like the idea.

I suspect that until you've tried it once you aren't going to know how you feel. You can ask your partner to tell you when he's about to ejaculate so that you can pull away beforehand. Or you can let him ejaculate into your

sextips

Oral sex techniques

The secret of enjoyable oral sex consists of varying your strokes so that you give your partner a series of erotic surprises. Practise these four techniques on your lover or try inventing your own.

Tongue shaping – hold his penis with one hand and lightly run your pointed tongue up one side, across the tip and then down the far side. Now use your tongue more firmly like a sculpting tool, so that you are literally licking him into shape.

Running around in circles – move your mouth up and down his shaft. Keep doing this in a rhythm, then circle your tongue around the head of his penis. Alternate these movements so that his penis is subjected to two separate strokes and counter-rhythms.

Lips and fingers – put the head of his penis in your mouth and your wet hand around his shaft. Now move your mouth and hand up and down. For extra sensation vary the pressure of your lips and hand – don't be afraid of squeezing quite hard.

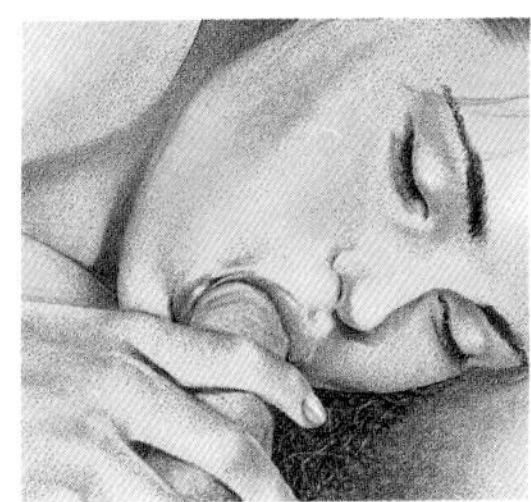

Swallowing up – move your lips as far down his shaft as you can manage so that a large part of his penis is inside your mouth. Don't move your head but simply concentrate on sucking with your mouth. This creates a sensation of being swallowed.

mouth but let the semen run back out again (or spit into a tissue). Or you can let him ejaculate into your mouth and swallow his semen. Needless to say, swallowing is purely optional – whatever you choose to do is fine.

Do men have a G-spot?

The male equivalent of the G-spot is the prostate gland. It is the size and shape of a large walnut and it surrounds the urethra. Its function is to supply the prostatic fluid that sperm is bathed in. The prostate gland is located at the end of the anal passage and can be accessed via the rectum. It is extremely sensitive to touch and massaging it can result in a rapid and easy orgasm.

I'd like to initiate sex with my partner for a change. How should I begin?

Work out some routines for yourself in advance. For example, you could tell your partner that you are going to give him a sex massage. Then you could rub and stroke his whole body with sweet-smelling oil. Tantalize him by touching him around his genitals during your massage and "accidentally" brushing his penis. If your massage hasn't already turned into sex, try climbing on top of him and having sex in a woman-on-top position. Alternatively, you might snuggle into your partner's body one evening, spoons-fashion, with your back against his front so that you are pressing against his genitals. You can help to give him an erection by putting your hand behind you and stroking his penis. This could develop into rear-entry sex. Another, more blatant approach is to climb on top of your partner and slide down his body until your head is level with his genitals. Now give him oral sex. This is a useful trio of "start routines".

How can I keep my partner on the edge of orgasm for as long as possible?

Try giving him a sensational, drawn-out massage before you make love. You could turn on every part of his body with your tantalizing touch and only when he is begging for sex, give

in and climb on top. You could try repeatedly arousing him with oral sex or genital massage but withdrawing stimulation when you think he's getting too close to orgasm. There are also plenty of sex games that you can play with your partner that will keep him hovering on the edge of orgasm (see pages 116–127).

How can I give my partner a wonderful sensual massage?
Massaging your partner can be a blissful prelude to sex. It's very easy to feel swamped with massage instructions so take it slowly and stick to one or two basic strokes and you will find that your hand movements come naturally. Virtually anything you do will feel fantastic.

• Choose a sensual-smelling massage oil and warm it up by putting the bottle on a radiator before you start (or just rub the oil into your palms). Make sure you wash away the oil before you use a condom though (oil-based products can damage latex).

• Start with some simple circling strokes: place both hands, palms down on your partner and move them in opposing circles. Work out and away from the spine, first down and then up his body. Always move your hands very slowly and don't be afraid of repeating strokes and patterns.

• Apply flexible pressure: this is the secret of turning a routine massage into a sensual experience. Whereas a strong massage feels thorough and "medical", a lighter one feels pleasurable and sensual, and a fingertip massage feels arousing and erotic (a fingernail massage can send your man right out of his mind!). Whatever style you choose, you can use a basic circling stroke throughout the massage.

Sex fact

Men are more likely to develop fetishes than women. Common objects that are fetishized are stockings and high-heeled shoes, so try incorporating these into foreplay.

I think my partner ejaculates too quickly. How can I help him to last longer?
You could say, "I adore the way we make love. I get incredibly turned on by you but I need a bit more time to enjoy a climax". This allows you to explore ways of prolonging sex together. At some stage you may want to talk to him about the self-training programme for men who want to prolong their ability to thrust (see page 40). Make sure that you take a positive and loving approach rather than a critical one. You could also try the squeeze technique (see page 44) on your partner. When he feels close to orgasm use your forefinger and thumb to grasp his penis at the ridge at the tip or at the base of his penis. Squeeze hard. This blocks the exit route for ejaculation and although your partner may partially lose his erection he will be able to get it back through further stimulation.

sextips

Maximizing sensation during sex

These sex positions can enhance the sensations you and your partner experience during intercourse. They're easy to do and they're straightforward variations of the missionary position. Try drawing one or both of your knees up toward your chest, wrapping your legs loosely or tightly around your partner's waist or putting one or both legs over his shoulders. These variations in leg position alter the tilt of your pelvis and so change the angle at which your partner enters you. Your partner can also penetrate you more deeply in these positions.

sex in midlife

Will the menopause change my sex life?

The combined physical and emotional symptoms of the menopause may have an impact on sex. Some menopausal changes have a direct effect on your pelvic and sexual organs and can make intercourse uncomfortable. These include vaginal atrophy and dryness, and bladder disturbances, such as frequent, urgent urination and a burning sensation on passing urine. Other menopausal symptoms, such as mood swings, anxiety, irritability and depression, are psychological and can mean that you aren't in the mood for sex. General physical symptoms, such as hot flushes, night sweats and insomnia, can also dampen sex drive. All of these changes can be alleviated by hormone replacement therapy (HRT).

sextips

Changing your sexual routine

If you find you are bored and dissatisfied with sex in midlife, these suggestions can help you to break away from old sexual routines. But the golden rule is: don't try the same suggestions repeatedly as you'll simply be setting up a new routine. Always aim to keep sex varied.

- Lie on the other side of the bed from the one you habitually occupy.
- Go to bed earlier than usual with an invitation for your partner to join you (without even mentioning sex).
- If you normally wear a nightdress, wear nothing at all.
- If you normally wear nothing, buy yourself a seductive nightgown.
- If he wears boring pyjamas, buy him a silken nightshirt.
- If he normally makes the first move, just start innocently caressing him instead.
- If he invariably offers routine foreplay, play much harder to get or initiate a complete quickie.
- Make love in a different room of the house.
- If he never goes down on you, go down on him.
- Whatever happens by routine, imagine and implement the opposite.

I've heard that some women stop having sex at the menopause. Is this true?

Those who do are mainly influenced by a prejudice that sex is restricted to the young and fertile. Some women find that lowered levels of sex hormones – testosterone in particular – do make them lose desire, but many women are more affected by a loss of confidence than a loss of hormones. The best action is to maintain a regular sex life through intercourse or masturbation. If you have a partner, make sure that you devote time to nurturing your relationship. A strong and mutually supportive relationship can be invaluable during the menopause and beyond. Women may also find that HRT – possibly including testosterone – can help to restore their sex life.

Will my vagina get smaller after the menopause?

The vagina may get smaller and dryer but this takes some years since your adrenal glands continue to produce sex hormones even after your ovaries stop. Also, if you have regular intercourse, your vaginal size is unlikely to change significantly. HRT can prevent the vaginal tissues from shrinking and drying; you can also apply oestrogen cream directly to the vagina with the same result.

Will the menopause affect my ability to have orgasms?

No, you will still be able to have orgasms, but you may find that they take longer to happen and that the sensation is not as strong as previously. You can compensate for this with longer foreplay and extra mental and genital stimulation. If you do suffer from orgasm difficulties, HRT and testosterone therapy can work wonders.

I'm 50 years old and I've never had an orgasm. Is it too late?
Absolutely not – many women of your age climax for the first time when they teach themselves self-pleasuring techniques (see page 68). A vibrator can be especially useful.

Is it true that a woman's sex life can improve after the menopause?
Sex can indeed become more erotic because you don't have to worry about pregnancy (provided you've gone two years without a period). Many older women have shed inhibitions they had when they were younger and know exactly what sort of stimulation they need to feel aroused. Plus, you may have more time, freedom and privacy (especially if your children have left home) and fewer financial constraints. These lifestyle changes can all have a great knock-on effect on your sex life.

At the age of 45 I'm bored by my husband's routine in bed. How can I change it?
You can start by changing yourself and your own approach to sex – this may well have the effect of transforming your husband too. Give him advance warning of your intentions and be as friendly and light-hearted as possible. For instance, if he's in business, you could say you're going to "do an audit on yourself" or that "you feel the need for a product overhaul" to improve your sexual performance. Try some of the suggestions in the box opposite.

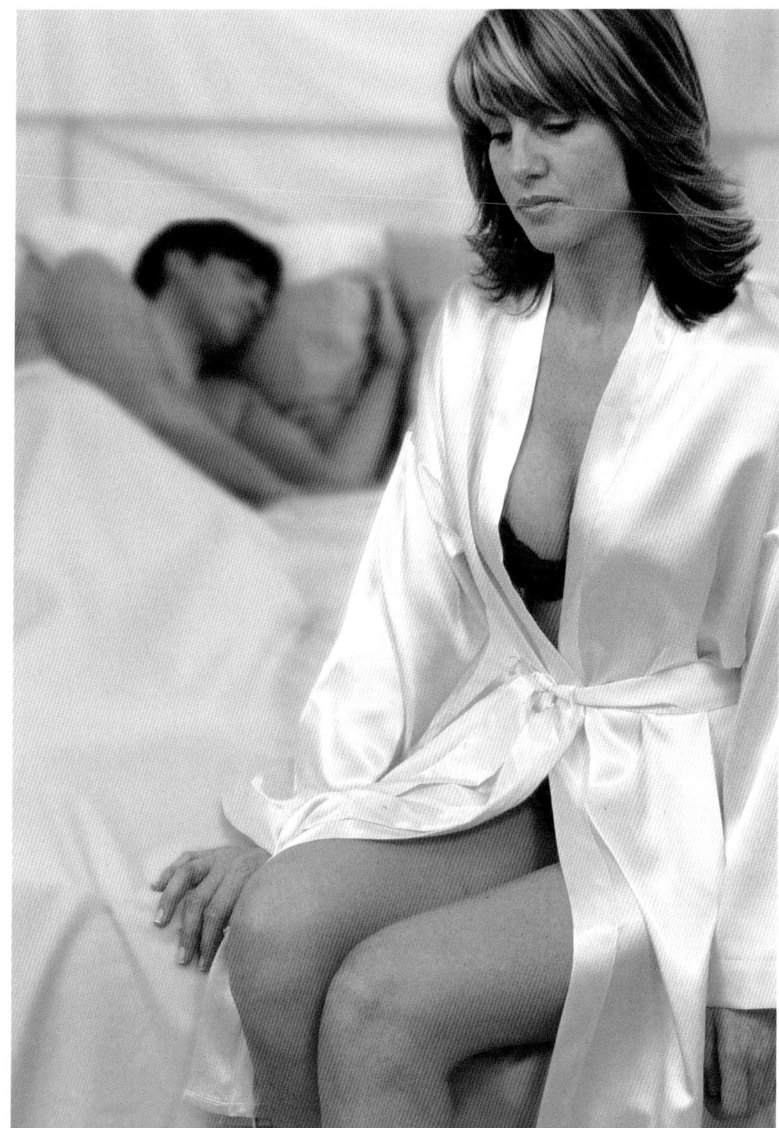

How can I make sure that I stay fit and sexually attractive through the menopause?
By looking after your mind, body and spirit. Try some of the following suggestions. Take some exercise every day: walk, swim or work in the garden. Eat plenty of fruit and vegetables, especially leafy greens and skimmed milk products which are both rich in calcium. Drink alcohol in moderation (a couple of glasses of wine a day is healthy – more isn't) and if you smoke, give up. Exercise your mind by continuing to work, even if it is to a lesser extent. Take spiritual or mindful exercise such as yoga or Pilates, or go to philosophy classes. Make sure that you don't neglect sex – try to make love in the form of sensual massage, oral sex, penetrative sex or passionate kissing once a week.

I have turned from being a sunny-natured, affectionate human being into a snappy, snarly monster thanks to the menopause. My husband is finding me hard to take and I'm worried that I'm driving him away. He doesn't approach me so often for sex any more. How can I control my moods?
It would be helpful to tell your husband what is happening inside your body. Explain that, just as adolescents are hit by huge hormonal storms of feeling, so too are menopausal women. Ask him to try, during the times you are being completely impossible, to think of you as a teenager battered to and fro by internal tempests. This might encourage him to sympathize with you rather than write you off.

You can also help yourself: do your best to get enough sleep, take nutritional supplements (see page 87) and consult your doctor about taking HRT. Counselling or therapy is also a very good idea at this stage of your life because it can help you to get a new perspective on old situations. Above all, try not to lose touch (literally) with your husband. Offer to scrub him in the bath, soap him in the shower and caress him all over in bed. If you haven't made love for more than a week, try to initiate sex even if you're feeling exhausted. It's important to maintain intimacy now because later on your energy will return and you will want to be sensual with your husband once again.

indetail

Your changing body

When you reach your mid-40s your ovaries stop manufacturing so much oestrogen and progesterone with the result that you go through a variety of physical and emotional changes in the build-up to the menopause. This period is known as the perimenopause and it may be characterized by hot flushes, night sweats, irritability, nervousness and insomnia. In addition, the density of your bones starts to diminish. It is a good idea to have a bone scan at around the age of 45 so your doctor can compare your bone mass later at the age of 50 or 55 and assess your risk of osteoporosis. Most women have lost up to 5 per cent of their bone density by the time their periods actually stop.

At some point in your late 40s or early 50s you will experience the menopause - your last menstrual period (you can only identify this retrospectively). This marks the end of your fertility. Some hormones, such as testosterone, the hormone that controls sex drive, continue to be manufactured by the adrenal glands in midlife but this also declines quite rapidly with the result that sex drive, desire and response can start to fade. The good news is that all of the changes associated with the menopause can be prevented by the judicious use of HRT (this can also include the hormone testosterone to preserve your sex drive).

My partner and I have been together for over 20 years but I'm worried that we're drifting apart. I've noticed that he's started flirting with younger women. Is our relationship coming to an end?

Flirting with younger women probably means that your partner is feeling his age and looking for confirmation that he is still attractive (reassurance from you may not be sufficient). Rest assured that this behaviour is common in middle age. Midlife is undoubtedly a time of wobbly self-esteem and making changes is one way in which you can boost your ego. So take this opportunity to reassess the quality of your life and relationship. Are you happy with your routine or would you benefit from moving house, job or neighbourhood? What would you like to achieve that you haven't yet managed? Persuade your partner to make changes with you – it may sound corny but try to take up a new mutual project. It could help to revive your relationship.

Do women in their 40s make suitable partners for younger men?

Biologically, yes. Women reach their maximum capacity to have orgasms and multiple orgasms in their middle to late 30s and early 40s. They also tend to feel more comfortable with their sexuality by this stage. Men, in contrast, reach their sexual peak between the ages of 18 and 22 and are able to have several orgasms a day with small intervening time gaps. They often make vigorous, athletic lovers. The drawbacks to relationships between older women and younger men are usually emotional – one partner tends to possess an unhealthy concentration of power, making the other feel over-vulnerable. Apart from this, age is no bar to any loving relationship.

At 49 I'm newly single and miss having a man in my life. I still look quite young and attractive, but I'm very aware that men of my age go for younger women. Realistically, what are the chances of meeting a new lover?

Realistically, about the same as they always were (given that the number of potential partners we're exposed to at any time of life is relatively small). Observation has shown me that many older women of all shapes, sizes and backgrounds meet new lovers. Provided you have energy, are fun and possess a real interest in sex, the chances of finding a new partner are high. One older woman reported that bright red lipstick combined with the ability to flirt and be versatile in bed meant that she was never short of lovers. However, until you do meet someone who has partner potential, concentrate on making friends with a wide range of people. Friends can be invaluable, especially at times of change.

HRT for women

What is hormone replacement therapy?

Hormone replacement therapy (HRT) usually consists of replacing the hormones oestrogen and progesterone, which the ovaries stop producing when women go through the menopause. Oestrogen helps to prevent a host of menopausal symptoms – most notably hot flushes, depression, tiredness and a lack of wellbeing. There are several different types of oestrogen that act in different ways on the body – one type may suit a woman much better than another. Furthermore, optimum dosages may vary from one woman to another. A good doctor will encourage women to experiment with types and dosages of oestrogen until the right combination is found. Progesterone is included in HRT because it safeguards against cancer of the uterus.

Sex fact

As well as alleviating menopausal symptoms, HRT can preserve a premenopausal body shape. The waist and hips keep their curvy shape instead of filling out.

At what point in life should women start taking HRT?

Opinions differ on this. Many women start taking HRT when they are already menopausal because the additional hormones help to make the passage of change easier. However, we now know that by the time women's periods cease women will already have lost 5 per cent of their bone density (as a consequence of oestrogen decline). As a result, some experts believe that women should start taking HRT around three to four years before the menopause. Although it is impossible to predict when periods are going to end, women may benefit from starting HRT around the age of 46 (the average age of menopause is around 50).

Should all women use HRT?

It is estimated that 85 per cent of women experience one or more menopausal symptoms and many of these women benefit from the symptom relief that HRT provides. The remaining 15 per cent of women who don't suffer from menopausal symptoms can benefit from the long-term effects of HRT, such as protection against osteoporosis, a degenerative disease that causes a decline in bone mass. A low dosage of HRT is thought to be sufficient to prevent bone loss. However, some health problems, such as breast cancer, may mean that you will not be able to take HRT.

What effect does HRT have on sex?

Oestrogen confers a sense of health, energy and wellbeing, and prevents the vagina from becoming smaller and dryer. However, oestrogen isn't responsible for sex drive and won't restore a flagging libido – the hormone therapy that you need for this is low-dosage testosterone.

What effect does testosterone have on sex?

It not only restores sex drive but also increases genital sensitivity and sensation during orgasm. It also appears to enhance sexual imagination and makes you physically stronger. Testosterone can be prescribed in addition to oestrogen

indetail

New hormone treatments

Two comparatively new hormone treatments that may be useful in midlife are dehydroepiandrosterone (DHEA) and melatonin supplements.

DHEA is described as a "mother" hormone and it is produced naturally by the adrenal glands (situated on top of the kidneys). As hormone specialist Dr Michael Perring explains, DHEA is the precursor of testosterone in men and progesterone and oestrogen in women; without DHEA, the other hormones don't function properly. In clinical trials, individuals with a DHEA deficiency (most people over 30) who were given supplements experienced increased energy, wellbeing, memory and immunity to infection.

Melatonin is a hormone that is secreted by the pineal gland in the brain and is responsible for good sleep. Since sleep promotes health, energy and healing, it is thought that melatonin supplements may enhance these effects. However, there are still doubts about the safety of taking melatonin regularly over long periods of time and research into this supplement is continuing.

and progesterone. It comes in the form of a gel that is rubbed into the skin. It is also available as an implant.

I'm not sure that I want to take HRT. Are there any natural treatments that I can use instead?

You can prevent many age-related changes by simply cutting down on alcohol and quitting smoking (women who smoke have an earlier menopause by one or two years compared to non-smokers). Regular weight-bearing exercise, such as walking or low-impact aerobics, together with a diet that is rich in phyto-oestrogens appears to promote or maintain hormone production in the body and prevent weight gain. Phyto-oestrogens are contained in foods such as tofu, miso, pulses, alfalfa, fennel and celery. It is also important that you get enough calcium-rich foods, such as skimmed milk products, leafy, green vegetables and dried peas and beans – these will maximize bone health. Dietary supplements that may be useful include antioxidants, evening primrose oil, boron and magnesium. Consult a dietary therapist or naturopath for advice.

Are there any other times apart from the menopause when women should get hormone treatment?

Women with postnatal depression or severe premenstrual syndrome (PMS) may be prescribed hormones. Premenopausal women who have had their ovaries surgically removed should seek advice about HRT (removal of the ovaries causes premature menopause). Finally, some women may benefit from testosterone to boost libido at times other than the menopause.

sex and aging

Is it true that sex and masturbation will keep my sex organs young as I get older?
Sex with a male partner who regularly ejaculates inside you does appear to allow the vagina to retain its youthful shape and moistness. This is thought to be a result of the testosterone contained in ejaculate. Women who do not have regular intercourse may find that the vagina shrinks and becomes dry. Masturbation is also thought to help to maintain the youthful state of the vagina.

How can I be sexually adventurous in later life?
In much the same way as when you were younger. Socialize in places where you will meet men who would be sexually interested in you. Be as open and frank as possible and use the confidence of age to ask for what you really want. Try surfing some of the sex sites on the Internet. This can also be a way to meet people, but bear in mind the potential drawbacks of Internet relationships (see pages 28–29). If something experimental, such as swinging, is what you long for, check out the various groups that abound. You can usually find these in magazines or on the Internet – many are for older rather than younger individuals. As always, be aware of the potential risks of having sex with people you don't know.

At 68 I masturbate regularly yet my doctor expressed surprise that I should still want sex. Am I abnormal?
Of course not. What you are discovering is that doctors don't receive much sex tuition as part of

their training and that they are as capable of being prejudiced about age as the next person. Take heart from this example of a female advertiser in a magazine column who is at pains to announce, "Woman, 67, still sexually active, seeks..." You are far from alone.

I've always been quite highly sexed but I realize I don't want sex so often now that I'm 65. Will there come a time when I won't want sex at all?
As age slows down your body you may find that you gradually become less energetic and your sex drive starts to decline. However, women who start off highly sexed, are likely to remain so, and provided you have a willing and interested partner, there is no reason why you can't continue to enjoy sex until the end of your life. One problem that can cause a decline in sexual activity as you get older is familiarity and boredom in long-term sexual relationships. This is why it is important to keep finding ways to inject variety into your sex life (see Chapter 5).

At 60 I feel I still ought to have an active sex life but the truth is I could quite happily go without sex now. Would it matter if I gave it up?
If you are currently without a partner, it wouldn't matter in the least. If celibacy is your preferred lifestyle, consider this a positive choice – many other women feel just the same. The choice becomes more complicated, however, if you are in a relationship. If your partner would be upset by a non-sexual relationship, it might be advisable to seek a compromise, such as mutual masturbation or sensual massage in place of intercourse. Apart from the physical release that comes with orgasm, sex fulfils other important functions, such as making your partner feel loved, needed and cared for. Make sure that you still find ways to demonstrate these things.

At 57 it seems to be getting harder to reach orgasm and, when I do, it's not as intense. Why is this?

It's probably due to a combination of factors. Reduced testosterone in the body means that sexual sensitivity is lessened so that it takes longer to get aroused, orgasm takes longer to reach and is less powerful when it happens. Also, lower oestrogen levels in your body means that your vagina, like your skin, gets dryer. Taking hormone replacement therapy (HRT) that includes testosterone can help to restore orgasmic intensity and vaginal suppleness.

Is there a female equivalent of sildenafil (Viagra)?

The makers of sildenafil – the "impotence drug" for men – are working hard on an equivalent pill for women. Women's sexual response works in a similar way to men's in that the genitals become engorged with blood, and the clitoral shaft – like the penis – becomes erect. Whether improving blood flow to the genitals boosts sexual ability and enjoyment in women as it does in men has yet to be resolved. One of the realities of aging is that sexual sensation does decrease to some extent. This is true of men as well as women.

Sex fact

Low oestrogen levels after the menopause make the genitals prone to thinness, dryness and cracking. For this reason, you should wash the genitals with a small amount of very mild soap or just use pure water. A local application of vitamin E cream can combat dryness and irritation.

casehistory

"I miss the intimacy of sex desperately."

Irene, 63

I've been married to Nate for 35 years and we've always made love. But in the past couple of years, Nate has slowed down. I know he's found it harder to get an erection and it's certainly taken him longer to climax, but now he seems to have given up the struggle. My friends seem to think I ought to be grateful but I'm not. I miss the intimacy of sex desperately. These days Nate hardly touches me, which is such a contrast to how we were in the past. Have I got to get used to this or is there something we could do?

Nate, 67

I always knew that men lost their ability to perform with age and, finally, it seems to have happened to me. It's a shame because I still fancy Irene. But I'm not far off 70 and we've had a great sex life together.

Anne responds:

"My first advice was that Nate should get a thorough medical check-up to find out what was happening to his body and hormones. Once Nate and Irene were in possession of this information they would be able to take action.

It turned out that Nate had a mild form of adult-onset diabetes which becomes more common in both sexes with age. Amongst other things, diabetes can make it difficult to get an erection. Careful diet combined with medication brought the diabetes under control and Nate began to feel more energetic. However, sexual experimentation showed that he still had erection problems. Nate was prescribed sildenafil (Viagra) and he and Irene were encouraged to try out a programme of mutual massage sessions. Nate didn't enjoy taking medication much since he said that he couldn't feel much difference between the before and after of orgasm. But the sildenafil/massage combination did get the couple's sex life going again. Irene was delighted to have regained their lost intimacy and when Nate stopped using sildenafil but continued having sex, they both learned to cope with Nate's slightly floppy erection. Irene managed to see this as a positive challenge."

What illnesses of old age are likely to affect my sex life?

The following illnesses can all have an impact on your sex life but you can use self-help measures to overcome difficulties.

- Arthritis attacks the joints and can affect mobility and comfort during sex. Hot baths and taking painkilling medication before sex can help. You may find that the spoons position is helpful – you lie on your side and your partner penetrates you from behind.
- Heart attack sufferers often feel anxious that sex will precipitate another attack. Evidence suggests that this is unlikely, especially in couples in long-term relationships. There is some evidence from Japanese research that sudden death from a heart attack during sex is more likely to occur during an extra-marital sexual encounter. Presumably this is because stress is heightened. Even this is rare.

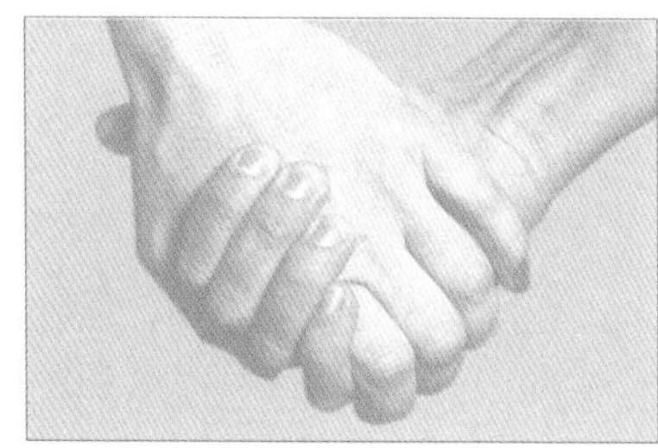

- Diabetes can cause yeast infections of the vagina and vulva, but only if it is not managed properly. The effect of diabetes on sex is most noticeable in men (it can cause impotence).
- Some gynaecological problems such as uterine prolapse and uterine cancer become more common in older women. Uterine prolapse can prevent deep penetration during intercourse because the cervix starts to descend into the vagina. One possible warning sign of uterine cancer is vaginal bleeding after intercourse (or any unusual bleeding). Any gynaecological symptoms such as these should be reported to your doctor straight away.

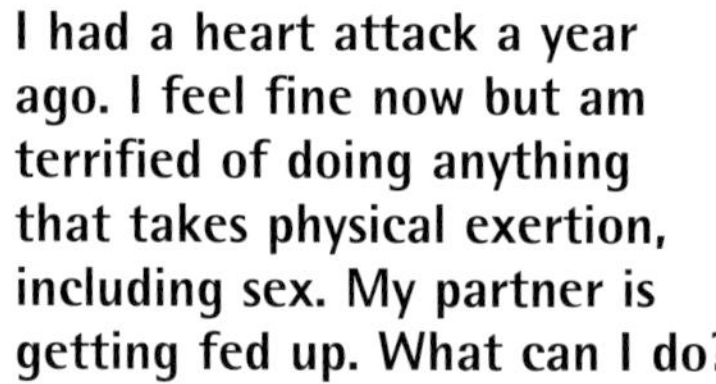

I had a heart attack a year ago. I feel fine now but am terrified of doing anything that takes physical exertion, including sex. My partner is getting fed up. What can I do?

Test yourself by walking up at least 20 stairs at a moderate pace. If you are still breathing normally when you reach the top, you are easily fit enough to make love (in fact, this is probably far more physical exertion than you would experience during intercourse). To alleviate your anxiety, resume your sex life gently by asking your partner to use man-on-top positions or oral sex. If stair-climbing makes you feel unfit, consult your doctor about a suitable exercise programme that will help you to build up stamina. Walking, swimming and the Pilates method may all be good. And ask your doctor for specific recommendations about sex – the chances are it's fine to go ahead.

sextips

Improving sex and intimacy in later life

Some sexual and emotional problems become more common in later life. These include lack of vaginal lubrication, slow arousal times and a breakdown in intimacy and affection between partners. The following tips can help:

- Improve vaginal lubrication by using good quality lubricants. They are available in the form of jellies and pessaries. Some products have specially designed applicators.
- Improve sensation during sex by spending much longer on mutual stimulation and foreplay.
- Improve erotic stimulation – try getting absorbed in a sex film. Good erotica can often begin the process of desire and arousal and be a genuine sex aid. Sexy literature can do the same thing. You can also try using sex toys and surfing sex sites on the Internet.
- Improve your body's physical responses. Consider taking HRT or testosterone.
- Make a date for intimacy and give each other the present of a massage session.
- Cuddle, stroke and hug several times a day.
- Tell each other "I love you" often.
- Say how attractive, handsome, beautiful the other looks. Take care of your appearance so that you still appear all of these things.
- Be romantic. Hold hands when walking and when watching a film together.
- Kiss each other on the lips.

My husband doesn't seem to want to have sex these days. He says that he doesn't get erections any more. Is this a natural part of the aging process or is there something wrong with him?

It's quite possible that there is an underlying physical cause for your husband's lack of sex drive. Some medications, such as those that treat depression or high blood pressure, can cause sexual problems. So, too, can a number of illnesses including diabetes, high blood pressure and atherosclerosis (a thickening of the arteries). Surgery or drug treatment for prostate cancer can also result in sexual problems. Your husband should see his doctor for a health check or to discuss the effect of his medication on sex.

indetail

Hysterectomy and sex

Many older women have had a hysterectomy – it's one of the most common gynaecological operations, second only to episiotomy in the West. The operation consists of the removal of the uterus and sometimes also the cervix, fallopian tubes and ovaries. Some women have hysterectomies to treat intractable menstrual problems such as endometriosis. Hysterectomy in older women may be performed as a treatment for uterine prolapse or cancer.

Many women feel concerned about the impact that hysterectomy will have on sex. Although, your desire for sex may be low after the operation while your internal tissues are healing, your sex drive and sexual sensitivity should soon return to pre-surgery levels. Performing Kegel exercises (see page 67) is a good way to tone the muscles around your vagina and enhance sexual pleasure after a hysterectomy.

If you have your cervix removed, you may notice a loss of sensation during intercourse. If this affects you, try compensating by paying extra attention to the clitoris and G-spot (see page 66) during sex.

intimacy skills

Some women have natural intimacy skills such as saying "I love you" or showing affection with a kiss or a hug. Others prefer to hold back until they really know a partner emotionally and sexually.

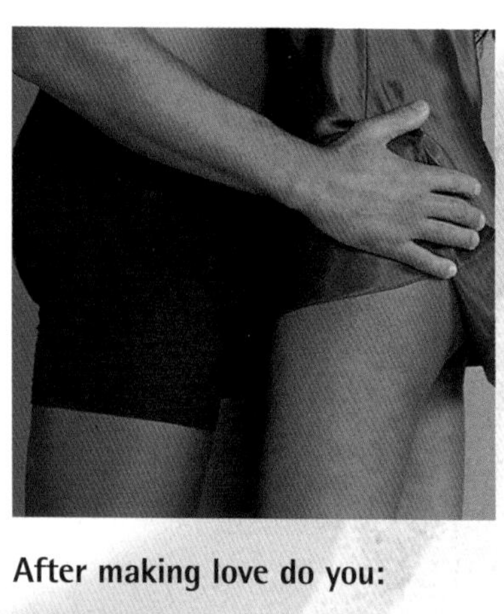

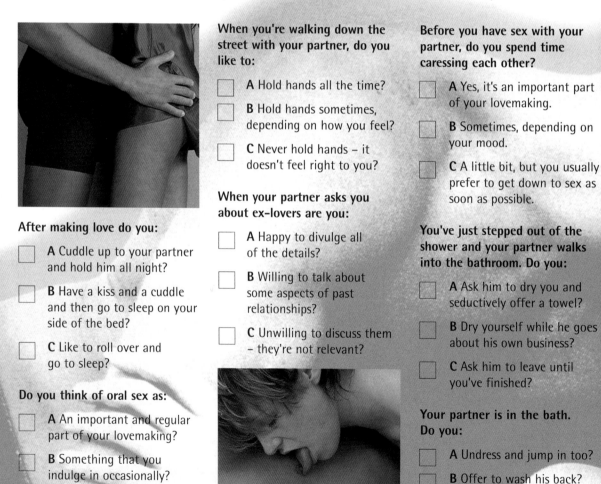

After making love do you:

- ☐ **A** Cuddle up to your partner and hold him all night?
- ☐ **B** Have a kiss and a cuddle and then go to sleep on your side of the bed?
- ☐ **C** Like to roll over and go to sleep?

Do you think of oral sex as:

- ☐ **A** An important and regular part of your lovemaking?
- ☐ **B** Something that you indulge in occasionally?
- ☐ **C** A rare part of your sex life?

When you're walking down the street with your partner, do you like to:

- ☐ **A** Hold hands all the time?
- ☐ **B** Hold hands sometimes, depending on how you feel?
- ☐ **C** Never hold hands – it doesn't feel right to you?

When your partner asks you about ex-lovers are you:

- ☐ **A** Happy to divulge all of the details?
- ☐ **B** Willing to talk about some aspects of past relationships?
- ☐ **C** Unwilling to discuss them – they're not relevant?

Before you have sex with your partner, do you spend time caressing each other?

- ☐ **A** Yes, it's an important part of your lovemaking.
- ☐ **B** Sometimes, depending on your mood.
- ☐ **C** A little bit, but you usually prefer to get down to sex as soon as possible.

You've just stepped out of the shower and your partner walks into the bathroom. Do you:

- ☐ **A** Ask him to dry you and seductively offer a towel?
- ☐ **B** Dry yourself while he goes about his own business?
- ☐ **C** Ask him to leave until you've finished?

Your partner is in the bath. Do you:

- ☐ **A** Undress and jump in too?
- ☐ **B** Offer to wash his back?
- ☐ **C** Wait until he's finished?

You want to try a new sexual position. Do you:

- ☐ **A** Suggest it to your partner the next time you speak?
- ☐ **B** Wait until you're in bed, then ask?
- ☐ **C** Try to steer him into it next time you have sex?

Your partner is wearing a new outfit which you find very sexy. Do you:

- ☐ **A** Tell him he looks fantastic?
- ☐ **B** Say his outfit suits him?
- ☐ **C** Don't say anything, your partner probably knows he looks good?

You think you're falling in love, with your new partner. Do you:

- ☐ **A** Tell him?
- ☐ **B** Wait until he says he loves you, then say it back?
- ☐ **C** Feel you don't need to say it?

Your partner is stressed out after a long day at the office. Do you:

- ☐ **A** Tell him to take his clothes off and give him a long, soothing massage?
- ☐ **B** Spend some time talking to him about his day?
- ☐ **C** Tell him to sit down and make him a cup of tea?

Your ideal night in with your partner is:

- ☐ **A** A long talk over dinner, followed by steamy sex?
- ☐ **B** Hiring a romantic movie and cuddling up on the sofa?
- ☐ **C** Watching TV, sharing a pizza and collapsing into bed?

You've been invited to a wedding next year. Do you:

- ☐ **A** Excitedly ask your partner to accompany you?
- ☐ **B** Tell your partner about it and see what he says?
- ☐ **C** Don't mention it to your partner yet – there's no guarantee that you'll be together next year?

You think your partner is unhappy. Do you:

- ☐ **A** Take him out for dinner and encourage him to talk?
- ☐ **B** Ask him what the problem is, hoping that it's not you?
- ☐ **C** Worry silently that it's about you and hope that he sorts things out?

ANSWERS

Mostly As You feel at ease with yourself physically and emotionally and this allows you to foster closeness with others. You're a giving person and are able to open up to a partner, confident that your relationship is a healthy one. Intimacy can create strong, balanced relationships – but beware of giving too much too soon to a new partner. Your affectionate nature and emotional candour could leave you open to heartache with the wrong partner.

Mostly Bs You enjoy intimacy and recognize that it's an important part of your relationship, but you do harbour niggling fears that, by allowing yourself to open up fully, you may get hurt. You need to build up a little more confidence and relax into your feelings. Take the lead more often and say what you really feel. You'll soon find that it gets easier. And try to express yourself through sex – after all it's one of the greatest languages of intimacy.

Mostly Cs You need to believe that your relationship is worth opening your heart for. Your reservations about getting close to somebody may be founded on past relationship failures or lack of affection as a child. Look at your existing relationship on its own merits and ask yourself whether it is a good one. If it is, you need to master your inhibitions and work with your partner to foster closeness. He needs to feel loved – try to take a risk and reveal your feelings.

sex when you're single

Being single is a positive lifestyle choice in the 21st century and one which more and more people are pursuing. Being single can include having casual sex, dating or actively seeking a long-term relationship. Or it can exclude sexual relationships entirely.

being single

I love being single but is it normal to be outside of a relationship for a long time?
Statistics show that many people are opting to live on their own. In the UK one in six households is single and this figure is increasing. Being single doesn't necessarily mean being celibate but it does mean having the time and space to concentrate on work, friends and other parts of life that you value. Enjoy this time and consider your lifestyle a luxury.

I don't want a relationship at the moment but I do miss having sex. What can I do?
The obvious solution to sexual frustration is masturbation. This aside, your other main option is to have casual sex (see pages 96–97). It's worth being clear about your motives for having casual sex, however. Casual sex can sometimes provide a way of avoiding intimacy if you have been hurt in the past. If you are still recovering from the aftermath of a painful break-up, it may be better for you to take some time off from sex until you feel strong again.

How often do single people masturbate? I worry in case I do it too much.
If you are young and have a high sex drive then it can be normal to masturbate once or even more a day. Masturbation only becomes a problem when you do it compulsively and it stops you from doing other things. Interestingly, in the 70s, New York model Viva tried the experiment of seeing how many orgasms she could have. After about two days she found that it was impossible to continue – her body had simply had enough.

How can I stop myself feeling lonely when I'm single?
In brief: stay active and look after yourself physically and emotionally. Find a form of exercise that you enjoy, whether a team sport such as football or something with a spiritual component such as yoga (exercise is a very good antidepressant). Nurture your relationships with your friends, family and colleagues. Embrace opportunities to meet new people. Don't wait for people to invite you out; be proactive and do the arranging and inviting yourself. And find a way to express yourself creatively in either your job, your leisure interests or both.

casual sex

How can I tell when someone is interested in casual sex?

Apart from the obvious tactic of asking them outright, you need to accept that it's not always easy to tell whether someone is interested in a sex-only relationship – people often send out mixed messages. The ground rules in the emotional tips box (see opposite) can help.

What's the best way to flirt with someone?

Ask people questions about themselves, show genuine interest, listen to what they are saying without interrupting and look at them when they are talking. We all enjoy receiving attention and most people respond warmly to genuine interest. One method of encouraging people to open up is to reveal things about yourself – this creates an atmosphere of equal exchange. Don't be afraid to use humour and banter in flirtation – laughter is a great aphrodisiac.

How can I show a person that I find them really attractive?

If you are genuinely attracted to someone, it will show in your eyes. The pupils dilate naturally when you feel attraction and the person looking into your eyes is likely to have an instinctive response to this. So don't be afraid to prolong your gaze for longer than usual. You can also convey feelings through other aspects of body language. Try smiling, nodding, standing in close proximity, leaning towards someone and touching their arm or shoulder. Keep your body language open and friendly – try not to cross your arms or legs or turn away.

Should I always carry condoms with me just in case?

It's always a sensible idea to anticipate the possibility of sex by carrying condoms – this certainly doesn't mean that you are compelled to use them. If you do make a habit of keeping condoms on you, don't forget to check the date stamp periodically.

I feel uncomfortable sleeping in someone's bed when I don't know them very well. Is it rude to get up and go home straight after sex?

Leaving straight after sex certainly sounds rather abrupt. Part of the joy of sex is the afterglow that comes in the wake of orgasm. Bear in mind, too, that your partner may feel used or rejected if you obviously can't wait to leave. As a compromise, you could stay for a short while after sex, perhaps until your partner has gone to sleep. Explain in advance that you won't stay the entire night. Say that this is because you find it difficult to relax in a new environment and that it's no reflection of how you feel about your partner.

I can have orgasms at the drop of a hat when I make love with a complete stranger. But once I find myself in a relationship it's impossible to climax. What's gone wrong?

There may be something about the intimacy of a relationship that makes you feel stressed and crowded. Sex with strangers, on the other hand, offers you freedom from responsibility, emotional obligation and commitment. I would suggest that this is an emotional problem that would benefit from sex therapy.

Since my divorce I've really discovered myself sexually through casual sex. But why do I feel so lonely?

Although casual sex has put you in touch with neglected aspects of your sexuality it has not been able to satisfy your need for intimacy and companionship. Listen to what your emotions are telling you – it sounds like it could be time to move on and cultivate a deeper relationship in which you can express yourself both sexually and emotionally.

emotionaltips

Casual sex

It's important to communicate carefully with casual sex partners so that you both know what to expect from each other.

- Give people time. Start off slow – if they don't respond to flirtation, back off and see what happens.
- Find out about someone's personality. Ask questions to see what you can discover, but steer clear of wild extrapolations.
- If you're already intimate with someone, ask them at each sexual stage if they like what you're doing/want to go further.
- Beware of people under the influence of alcohol. Whether people can have fully consensual sex when they are drunk is a contentious issue.

Are there any safety precautions that I should take when I have casual sex?

Yes – try to observe these guidelines:

- Always use a condom. Squeeze the tip and roll the condom all the way down the shaft of the penis.
- Go for regular sex check-ups at your local genito-urinary clinic.
- Avoid sex if you're drunk.
- Say a firm "no" to sex if you change your mind.
- Learn to ask about a partner's sexual history, including questions such as "when did you last have an AIDS test?"
- Remember that sex does not have to be penetrative. Suggest mutual masturbation as an alternative.
- If you go back to a partner's house, make sure that someone knows where you are, especially if you are a woman.

starting again

I recently split up with my long-term partner and wonder how long it would be sensible to wait before looking out for a new lover?
Everyone has different reactions to breaking up. Some people are anxious to feel they are still attractive and look for new sexual partners immediately. Paradoxically, once this type of person gains reassurance through sex, they may go on to manage very well without a partner. Other people are so bereft they can't even think about dating. Some people think they ought to be dating because they see this as part of their recovery, but find it difficult to feel attracted to anyone new. It may take up to two years to get over the loss of an important relationship (and longer in some cases). I would say that, if you feel grief-stricken, you would be wise to wait. It's best not to give yourself a hard and fast deadline. See how you feel and play it by instinct. Sometimes feeling spontaneously attracted to a new person can be the first sign that grieving for a former partner is coming to an end.

I'm ready to move on but where am I most likely to meet a long-term partner?
Research shows that proximity is usually responsible for initiating relationships. This means that you are most likely to meet a partner in your local neighbourhood, workplace, at school or college, at friends' houses, at parties, on holiday or at your place of worship.

However, if you don't have time to socialize or if most of the people you know are already in couples, you also have a good chance of forming relationships through dating agencies or on the Internet. Contemporary agencies try to match people closely in terms of age, background, interests and tastes. Many hold outings, parties and activities that take the formality out of one-to-one dating.

I went through a difficult break-up with my boyfriend over a year ago. I think I'm ready for another relationship now but I don't feel very sure of myself. How can I learn to be more confident?
Low self-esteem is very common after a relationship break-up and it can take a while to get your confidence back. Try practising the "yes/no" exercise. It's a simple technique that's often used in assertiveness training. In the course of one week, try to say "yes" to three things that you really want to do and "no" to three things that you really don't want to do. This could be as simple as saying "yes" to eating a chocolate bar because you really want it, or "no" to eating a chocolate bar because you want to cut out sugar from your diet. Or it can be more life-changing in that you say "no" to a boring invitation and "yes" to striking up a conversation with a man whom you find attractive. This is such a simple exercise but it can be transformative.

I'm about to date for the first time after ending with my long-term partner. How quickly should I have sex? Should I go for it on the first date?
Some people feel sexy and confident enough to enjoy sex immediately but many people do not. Spending a few dates talking, getting to know each other, discovering shared interests and establishing mutual sexual attraction gives you a good starting point. If you rush into sex, it can go badly wrong. If you give sex time, it can flower into something amazing. Also, rightly or wrongly, your date may think that you are more interested in casual sex than a long-term relationship if you initiate sex very quickly. However, you could always overcome this problem through honesty and frank discussion.

What does it mean if...

I keep comparing potential lovers to my ex-partner?

When you have emerged from a relationship break-up – particularly a recent one – some amount of comparison between new partners and old is inevitable. But if you feel that comparisons are preventing you from moving on, it could mean one or more of the following:

- You are not yet through a natural mourning period for your ex-lover and you need more time before forming a new relationship.
- You have a sense of unfinished business with your ex-lover and would benefit from talking this through, either with your ex-lover or with a counsellor.
- You have got "stuck" in a prolonged mourning period and your feelings about your old lover are obsessive – ask a doctor or counsellor for advice.
- The people you have met recently really aren't a patch on your ex-lover.
- You are being unrealistic in what you are looking for in a new partner.

dating

First dates are always so awkward. Is there any way of making them easier?
If possible, get to know someone in the context of a group first. If this is difficult, go out to a specific event or venue, such as a concert, film, play, gallery or sporting event. This way you have something to talk about, which is less stressful than focusing exclusively on each other. You might also find it easier to meet for lunch rather than in the evening. If sex presents itself on your first date, try to go entirely with your instinct about this person. If he/she feels right, then fine. If not, try saying, "I'm not quite ready yet". This leaves room for sex should either of you want to try again in the future.

How important are looks and dress when it comes to dating?
Physical attributes shouldn't matter but the reality is that they do make an impression on potential partners. You don't need to be beautiful (research shows that most people prefer even, regular features) but you do need to look friendly, approachable, clean and well-groomed. Confidence is attractive in a potential partner and, if new clothes and an attractive haircut can make you feel good, it's worth spending some time and money on these things. Pay attention, also, to your body language – negative or defensive body language, such as habitually looking or turning away from the person you are speaking to can be perceived as rejecting. If you stand or sit face on, with your arms open, this gives a welcoming and honest impression.

Some research suggests that we all rate our own attractiveness and we consciously or unconsciously choose partners to whom we give a similar rating to ourselves.

I'm really bored with the game playing that people do on first dates. Is there anything wrong with being upfront and straightforward?
This may work well for you, but the problem often lies with other people. If you are dating someone who does not yet possess the life experience or

confidence to share your upfront approach, you risk coming across as overly direct, unsubtle or even intimidating. If, however, you date someone as experienced as you are, they may appreciate your candour. If you want a love affair as opposed to a lust affair, bear in mind that there must be some mystery – somewhere for the imagination to go and ruminate – so try not to be so candid that you lose all possibility of romance. Pick your lover carefully and tailor your approach.

As a 25-year-old woman I hate waiting for a phone call after a date. Is it too pushy to call a man the next day if I want to see him again?

Many men welcome the fact that they can share equal responsibility with women for initiating dates – assertiveness is often greatly appreciated. The only downside of a next-day phone call is that some men (and women in the opposite situation) may interpret it as a sign of over-eagerness. Use your assessment of your date's personality to decide on a course of action – if in doubt, wait a couple of days.

Sex fact

A British telephone company once carried out a survey in which they asked people how they would feel about a woman who calls a man to ask him out on a date. The female participants in the survey considered that the woman would be perceived disrespectfully. In contrast, the majority of the men polled thought it would be wonderful to receive such a call and wished that women would do this more often.

How can I tell if the person I'm dating really likes me?

When you first start dating someone it's natural to search for clues that your date likes you and wants to keep seeing you. Both parties need to feel attractive and desired, but neither want to risk rejection. For this reason, both of you may avoid making overt statements of affection. However, gut instinct should tell you when a relationship is progressing well. Simple things, such as getting on with each other, laughing, having plenty to talk about, feeling that the other person is genuinely interested in asking you questions – and listening to the answers – combined with lots of touching, smiling and eye contact are all healthy signs. Some people express liking through sex which is often why lovemaking is so intense at the beginning of a relationship.

When is it right to tell someone I really like them?

Since this is what everyone wants to hear about him/herself, the answer is as soon as you feel it. But you need to understand that, just because you like a person, it does not, unfortunately, guarantee that they will feel the same. They may need more time than you.

I always get so nervous when I have sex for the first time with someone new. How can I be more relaxed?

First of all, accept that there will always be some amount of fumbling and awkwardness when you make love with someone new. The following tips will also help:

- Spend lots of time on cuddling and caressing.
- Think of lovemaking as a whole body activity rather than just genital stimulation.
- Talk to each other and have a sense of humour if things aren't going right.
- Take it slowly and don't feel that because you've started, you've got to finish having sex.

emotionaltips

Saying you don't want to see someone again

Even if you've only been on a few dates, telling someone that you no longer want to see them can be difficult for you and painful for the other person. Try to talk face to face rather than on the phone or neglecting to get in touch:

- Be firm and direct, but not cruel.
- Give a reasonable explanation for your feelings.
- Be prepared to explain more than once and perhaps several times.
- Allow the person to express feelings of anger or sadness.
- Give the person time to understand – your news may take a while to sink in.
- Have answers ready for questions such as "can we still be friends?"
- Don't give mixed messages by saying "it's over" and then having sex. This simply gives the other person unrealistic hope.
- Present your decision as a change of heart on your part and no fault of theirs.

casehistory

"He keeps cancelling dates in favour of his ex-wife."

Penny, 28

I've recently started dating someone who is separated from his wife and two children – and has been for over two years. He's really special but he keeps cancelling dates in favour of his ex-wife. He often just drops a date with me because his wife summons him because of something to do with the children. If they were real emergencies I'd understand, but it's usually something fairly trivial. He never seems to put his time with me first and I'm beginning to feel invisible. I don't know if we should stay together.

Oliver, 35

Penny doesn't have children of her own and I don't think she understands how precious my two kids are to me. It's terrible for me that I no longer live under the same roof as them. My ex-wife knows this and she often uses it to make me jump. But until my divorce is finalized I feel as if I must jump. The children – not my ex-wife – are my priority and I can't afford to lose them. I really like Penny – we got on well together, we've got loads in common and I really think we could have a future together. I just need her to be patient with me until my divorce is finally resolved.

Anne responds:

"This is a case of neither individual getting their prime desires met. Penny needs to feel special and Oliver needs someone who can take a back seat for the first part of the relationship – and to some extent in the future – for the sake of his children. At first sight it doesn't seem as if these two needs are compatible, and it's also very early on in a relationship for problems to be showing up. However, Oliver seems certain about his feelings for Penny and this is a strong basis on which to build. Oliver can try to make Penny feel special in ways other than always keeping dates. He can also be more assertive with his wife. He could rehearse dealing with difficult calls from his wife (saying, for example, "I would love to come over and help the children with their homework. Let's make an appointment for that.") instead of automatically getting into his car and driving over. He could arrange special nights when he is available for his children and dedicate his weekends to Penny. In return, Penny could do her best to trust in Oliver's feelings for her and be as patient as possible."

- If your partner says "let's do this later", agree.
- Be truthful about your own hesitations but make sure you don't voice them as criticisms.
- If you feel extremely self-conscious or as though you are performing, stop. It probably means that you've started being sexual too soon.

I've been dating a woman for a while and we get on really well. I'd like to have sex but she's nervous. What can I do?
Being nervous about sex with a new partner is very common because it takes your relationship onto a new level – this can make some people feel vulnerable. Don't rush your partner. Take it slowly and try these relaxation techniques before you make love.

- Check out your partner's body language. If she is sitting rigid or huddled at the end of sofa, for example, don't pounce on her. Hug, cuddle and stroke her until she relaxes.
- If your partner is still tense, offer to give her a massage. Make it clear that you don't mind if this doesn't become sexual. Explain that all you want to do is give her sensual pleasure.
- Try lying in bed in the spoons position. Synchronize your breathing with your partner's and then slowly make your breaths longer. With luck, your partner will adapt her breathing rhythm to yours and begin to relax.

I've been seeing a man for about three months. We have a great sex life but he's really unreliable, rarely calls me and our dates are few and far between. What's going on?
There could be lots of reasons for your lover's apparent reticence. He may be

extremely busy and juggling lots of different commitments, he may be inexperienced at dating or he may lack the emotional skills to know how to conduct himself in a relationship. Alternatively, he may want a sex-only relationship that excludes emotional ties (and you should consider the possibility that he may be married or living with a partner). Find a way to ask him about his private life and attitudes towards dating and relationships. Rather than being critical or accusatory you could try explaining that you would be interested in taking your relationship a step further (if this is true) and seeing him on a more regular basis. This could pave the way for further questions and discussion.

I've dated lots of women but I can't reach orgasm with any of them, even though I can manage it easily on my own. I'm worried because one day I'd like to remarry. How can I overcome this problem?
Alfred Adler, the famous psychologist, believed that all behaviour has a purpose, even – or especially - negative behaviour. Perhaps the purpose of your lack of orgasm is to shield you from commitment – a way of, quite literally, withholding yourself. And the advantage of doing this is that no-one can reject you. Presumably you could ejaculate when you were married? Is it possible that you have unresolved feelings of fear, anger, resentment, loss, guilt or sadness that are spilling over into your new relationships and sabotaging your sexual responses? You may need to go through a cathartic process of facing up to underlying feelings about your past and present relationships.

new relationships

How often do people normally make love at the start of a relationship? My new girlfriend and I made love 11 times the other day.

In the first flush of a relationship, it's common for lovers to have sex several times a day as part of the bonding process – younger lovers, that is. Sex is shorthand for "I fancy you and I want to get you under my skin". Even so, it would be straining convention to describe 11 separate acts of intercourse as typical. Of course you might mean 11 orgasms during one act of sex (possible for a woman) or 11 episodes of lovemaking without orgasm at all. It would certainly be very difficult for a man to ejaculate 11 times during a 24-hour period, whatever his age. The greatest claim I have heard was from a teenage Hungarian couple who say they had sex 16 times on their wedding night, but who can prove what? Your question suggests that you are preoccupied with sexual frequency – you are likely to find that, as time goes by, you will learn not to count the number of times you have sex but to enjoy the bond.

In many ways my new man seems perfect. He takes me out to dinner, buys me flowers, kisses me passionately, is always in raptures about me and implies that we would sizzle together in bed. The only trouble is that he has never done anything beyond kissing me and we've never made love. I'm beginning to doubt the whole relationship. Should I confront him about this?

Since you are not receiving any voluntary explanations it sounds as though you should definitely take the initiative, especially if you have already tried to initiate sex and failed. The reasons for this man's sexual reticence could be many and varied: he may have a wife or partner; he may be afraid of sexually transmitted infections (STIs; see pages 156–159); he may already have a STI; he may be impotent; he may have spiritual or religious beliefs that preclude intercourse; he may be saving himself for the woman he intends to marry (which might still be you); he may have a psychological fear of sex; or he may be playing games. Whatever his reasons, your relationship is unlikely to develop until you both have a frank and honest discussion.

My new girlfriend is super fit. During intercourse she wants me to ram into her harder and faster than I am able. It either makes me come or makes me gasp. I'm not used to making love like this. What can I do?

Sex in a new relationship is different and surprising by nature. But however willing you are, you cannot produce sexual stamina out of a hat. The best idea is to tell your new girlfriend the score and then announce your intention to get fit. In the meantime, ask her if she would enjoy more oral sex, hand-held vibrator pleasure or mutual masturbation. Alternatively, you could ask her to get on top of you and do all the hard work of pelvic grinding during sex – meanwhile, you can concentrate on pacing your climax.

emotionaltips

Introducing children to a new partner

Try to introduce a new partner to your children as soon as you feel sure that the relationship is stable and ongoing or if your partner is staying overnight and is likely to meet your children anyway. You don't need to go into details about the sexual nature of your relationship but you do need to answer any questions that your children might raise. Try to be as honest as possible while giving information that is appropriate to a child's age.

- Don't keep your dating a secret. Mention a new partner in casual conversation. For example, "my new friend Paul said..."
- Ask your partner to call at your home prior to an outing so that the children can meet him/her fleetingly and get an idea of what he/she looks like. Make sure that you offer a formal introduction just as you would with any other friend.
- Don't kiss and smooch all over the place, at least not until a new partner is a permanent part of your life.
- Warn your children in advance if your new partner is staying over for the night (particularly on the first few occasions). Say, for example, "by the way, don't get a shock if you meet Paul in the morning, he's going to be staying here tonight".
- If children ask where your partner will sleep, be honest and say, "in my bed".

My new guy is much younger than my former husband and much more athletic – sex goes on for so long that I get sore. How can I speed him up?
There's always an adjustment period during which new lovers get used to each other's different sexual styles. In your case, you need to synchronize your sexual times a little better. Try the following techniques, used by courtesans through the ages and designed to make a man lose his cool:

- Stroke his testicles.
- Tickle his perineum (the sensitive zone between his testicles and anus).
- Insert a finger or other (safe) object into his rectal opening.
- Stroke or pinch his nipples.
- Lightly smack his buttocks.
- Whisper sexual fantasies you know he finds overwhelming.

Don't do all of these at once! Use trial and error to find out which actions work for him and which don't.

I've just started going out with an old friend who had marriage problems. We haven't had sex yet but when he first undressed in front of me, I got an inkling of the trouble - his penis is tiny. Am I right to feel concerned?
A short penis is no deterrent to wonderful lovemaking. A man with a sensitive mind and skilful fingers can drive almost any woman wild. It is also worth bearing in mind that small penises tend to become longer when erect than large ones. Try to suspend any judgments until you have experimented with different ways of making love.

It's ages since my wife died and yet I have a problem with my new girlfriend. I really desire her but every time we start to make love, images of my wife enter my head and my erection disappears. What can I do?
This problem appears in the sex therapy clinic from time to time and it usually means that things are moving a bit too fast with a new partner. You probably became habituated to a certain pattern of sex with your late wife and find that this same pattern doesn't feel quite right with your girlfriend. If the problem persists, I suggest that you and your new

girlfriend try out some sensate focus exercises (see page 77). This gives you the chance to relax and explore each other sexually without any pressure to have intercourse. It will also enable you to create your own special sex life that is unique to you as a couple.

What do you do when a woman compares you to someone else? My new partner was married to a great guy who died last year. I think she loves me but I'm finding it difficult to measure up to her husband who, apparently, was amazing in bed.

It's important to understand that many of the current feelings your partner is experiencing are difficult and painful for her through no fault of yours. Sex may well put her in touch with the times she used to make love with her husband. Whether previous partners are absent through death or divorce, it can be hard to form new sexual patterns. If you are used to "doing" sex in a particular way for years, having to learn new moves can be a shock. If your friend is actively blaming you for being less skilful than her husband, remind her that sex with him was honed over the years, and that you too need some time. Ask her to teach you what she needs but don't be afraid of pursuing your own sexual style as well. I suspect you may have to go through a rough patch as a kind of testing time. Your friend may be angry with her husband for dying and may be directing some of her resentment and grief at you. Provided you can hang on in there, you stand a good chance of creating a terrific relationship, but don't let yourself get walked all over. Be persistent and firm. And loving.

Should I tell my new lover that I have children? I'm scared that it will put him off.
It depends on how you want your relationship to progress. If you just want to date and have some fun, then it's not essential to disclose personal details. If, on the other hand, you want to invite your lover home and allow the relationship to develop, you need to be honest from the outset. By not revealing the fact that you have kids, you are limiting the future. Not only is your lover prevented from knowing the "whole you", he will also have a huge hurdle to leap if you change your mind and tell him the truth several weeks or months into your new relationship. My instinct is to be candid about your children. You don't have to make a formal announcement, just try to bring your kids up naturally in conversation.

Knowing my kids are in the next room, even though they are asleep, really puts me off lovemaking with my new partner. What can I do?
If it's possible, swap the rooms around in your house so the children are no longer next door to you. Otherwise, invest in sound proofing, door locks or more babysitters so that you can go to your partner's house sometimes. You owe yourself – and your kids – a normal life.

casehistory

"Our sex life went downhill when I moved in with him."

Wendy, 29

Things were fine between Michael and I for the first few months when we were dating and living separately. But our sex life went downhill when I moved in with him. We've barely had sex for weeks and I'm really upset. I love Michael but I find myself craving more physical intimacy. I've offered to move out but Michael says he doesn't want me to go now.

Michael, 38

Our relationship worked really well as long as Wendy visited. But then when she moved in it sort of took me by surprise. In one way I wanted her there, but in another I felt as if I'd lost my own space. Almost immediately I started to go off the idea of sex. I want to stay with Wendy and I don't want her to move out. I just don't know how to make things better.

Anne responds:

"In spite of their differences this couple seem to love each other. Their immediate problem is that they are literally getting out of touch. The first thing they should try is taking turns to stroke and caress each other's bodies for at least 20 minutes each (see the sensate focus exercises on page 77). This will allow them to be sensual with each other and to gradually revive their sex life. They also need to dedicate time to discussing their relationship – weaknesses in new relationships are often exposed at turning points such as moving in together (or sometimes just going on holiday). Michael needs to feel that he still retains some of his independence and Wendy needs to feel wanted and secure."

My new boyfriend is separated with custody of his two small sons. He is worried that if I stay overnight at his house, his sons will be upset and confused. As a result, I find myself driving home at two o'clock in the morning or – worse – made to stand outside the front door at six o'clock so that the children will think I've dropped in for breakfast! Should I give him up?
No, but you could work on making your new boyfriend feel so great about you that he feels comfortable introducing you to his kids. You could also explain that, although you understand his anxieties about his children, you are developing your own anxieties – say that you don't feel happy about behaving like this and you don't want this situation to continue indefinitely. Give the relationship as much time and patience as you possibly can and, if things don't show any sign of changing, then it may be right to question your boyfriend's commitment.

relationship skills

It takes experience, skill and enthusiasm to sustain a relationship. Find out whether you're a relationship "natural" or partner-phobic – afraid of getting too entangled just in case you can't escape again.

When you meet a prospective new partner are you:

- ☐ **A** Excited, you can't wait to include someone else in your life?
- ☐ **B** Happy, it'll be nice to get to know him/her?
- ☐ **C** Pleased but worried about the impact on your free time?

Have you had serious, long-term relationships in the past?

- ☐ **A** Yes – most of your relationships have been committed and long-term.
- ☐ **B** Some but not many.
- ☐ **C** No – all your relationships have been casual.

How often do you like to see your partner:

- ☐ **A** As much as possible?
- ☐ **B** Weekends and a couple of nights during the week?
- ☐ **C** Twice a week or less?

As your relationship continues do you think sex:

- ☐ **A** Gets better and better?
- ☐ **B** Reaches a pleasant plateau?
- ☐ **C** Can become a bit predictable after a while?

You're not particularly keen on some of your partner's friends. Do you:

- ☐ **A** Make the effort to try to like them?
- ☐ **B** Be civil to them when you see them, but hope that's not too often?
- ☐ **C** Avoid occasions where you know they'll be present?

You've arranged to go out to dinner with some friends, but your partner phones and says he/she really needs to see you. Do you:

- ☐ **A** Cancel dinner and go out with your partner?
- ☐ **B** Invite him/her along and say that you can be alone together after the meal?
- ☐ **C** Tell your partner you can't see him/her tonight and arrange to see him/her on another occasion?

You've been with your partner for two years and there's a new face at work that catches your eye. Do you:

- ☐ **A** Appreciate the scenery but do nothing about it?
- ☐ **B** Flirt a little, but harmlessly?
- ☐ **C** Flirt outrageously and hope for an assignation in the stationery cupboard?

When you have worries or problems outside your relationship do you:

- ☐ **A** Discuss your woes with your partner?
- ☐ **B** Mention them to your partner but deal with them yourself?
- ☐ **C** Handle them alone and leave your partner out of them?

You're very fond of your partner, but communication between you seems to be breaking down. Do you:

- ☐ **A** Set aside an evening to talk about your problems until you find a solution?
- ☐ **B** Ride it out and hope that things get better?
- ☐ **C** Take it as a sign that you are not right for each other?

Your partner is keen for the two of you to have dinner at his/her parents' house regularly. Are you:

- ☐ **A** Delighted?
- ☐ **B** Pleased, but you'd rather not see them too often?
- ☐ **C** Worried - you don't like this kind of routine?

Your partner has gone away for two weeks. Do you:

- ☐ **A** Live for phone calls, letters or e-mails?
- ☐ **B** Look forward to your reunion?
- ☐ **C** Make the most of your freedom?

As your relationship evolves do you and your partner:

- ☐ **A** Get ever more intimate?
- ☐ **B** Get closer but not much?
- ☐ **C** Still feel you don't know each other?

When you make plans for the future do you:

- ☐ **A** Include your partner?
- ☐ **B** Consider various options?
- ☐ **C** Exclude your partner?

ANSWERS

Mostly As You are good at looking at relationships in the long term and at keeping things fresh. You're not afraid to make a commitment to your partner and to put time and energy into developing the foundations for an enduring relationship. Your commitment to a relationship includes keeping your sex life exciting and varied. However, problems can arise if you completely sacrifice your personal life in favour of your partner. If things go wrong romantically, you have little else to fall back upon.

Mostly Bs You're open-minded when it comes to commitment, and positive about long-term relationships. With a little effort towards enhancing communication and bringing your partner into all areas of your life, your potential for sustaining a healthy and fulfilling relationship is great. When you feel you need your own space, though, make sure you take it. Why not spice up your sex life and arrange exciting dates together to keep the physical aspect of your love life fresh?

Mostly Cs You definitely need your own time and space. Your relationships are important to you but you are wary of them eating into other areas of your life. This fear makes you balk at commitment. Protect your independence by all means, but open up a bit too. It's also worth revising your attitude towards sex in relationships – rather than letting it become routine and boring, think about sex as a tool to increase intimacy and closeness.

spicing up your sex life

The sexiest relationships are those that keep the spark of passion alive. Instead of relying on old routines, try playing games, sharing fantasies, experimenting with new positions and techniques and teasing each other with sex toys.

props, tools and toys

Are there any aphrodisiacs that really work?

There is no magic potion that miraculously increases sexual desire, arousal, ability and sensation (if only there were!). Some traditional aphrodisiacs such as yohimbine or Spanish fly do have an effect on the genitals but this is slight or may be coupled with unpleasant side effects. Yohimbine (obtained from the bark of an African tree) has a minimal effect on arousal and may cause a dangerous drop in blood pressure. Spanish fly (made from the dried and crushed bodies of a type of beetle) works by irritating and inflaming the genitals, but it is also a poison and taking it can be fatal.

Alcohol is sometimes used as an aphrodisiac – although small doses do have an anti-inhibitory effect that allows you to let go and openly express sexual feelings, large doses have the opposite effect and impede sex by inducing a type of impotence.

The closest substances to aphrodisiacs that are endorsed by the medical profession are sildenafil (Viagra) for men (see pages 58–59) and testosterone for women (see page 74), both of which should only be taken under medical supervision.

I've heard that weird and wonderful substances such as tiger's penis, rhino's horn and mandrake root are supposed to increase your sexual prowess. Do they work?

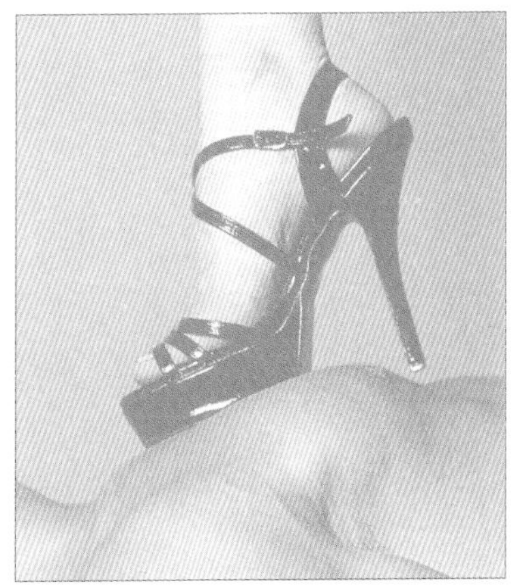

Only if you believe they will and, even then, not often! These substances have earned reputations as aphrodisiacs simply because they resemble or exaggerate the shape and size of the human genitals (some foods, such as oysters, mussels and figs, are perceived as sexy for the same reason). Some Asian cultures believe that consuming the penis of a tiger will confer the potency of this powerful creature on the user. The rhino, with its phallic horn, is associated with a similar mythology. Mandrake, a psychoactive plant root that figures heavily in witchcraft and magic, bears a slight resemblance to the human figure with all its bumps and lumps. As with ginseng root (another reputed aphrodisiac), mandrake contains ingredients that may offer increased alertness and energy. Be warned, however, that it also contains chemicals which can make you sick.

Can perfumes be aphrodisiacs?

Smell has a highly individual impact on men and women. Certain perfumes worn by one person may smell extremely exotic and will catch the attention of a partner, whereas the same perfume worn on someone else has no impact at all. Women are thought to be more sensitive to smell than men.

Sex fact

We all give out our own erotic musk in the form of fresh sweat. Sweat contains pheromones, invisible substances that trigger an emotional response. Animals signal their readiness to mate by secreting pheromones.

Do creams that claim to prolong erection really work?

Most of these creams are little more than mild anaesthetics, which work by dulling the sensitivity of the penis. If anything, they are likely to diminish desire rather than enhance it. However, the drug company that developed sildenafil (Viagra), is working on a cream that stimulates the local production of nitric oxide, a chemical used by the body to trigger blood vessel dilation. Research suggests that the cream has a 70 per cent chance of curing impotence and may also increase genital sensitivity in both men and women.

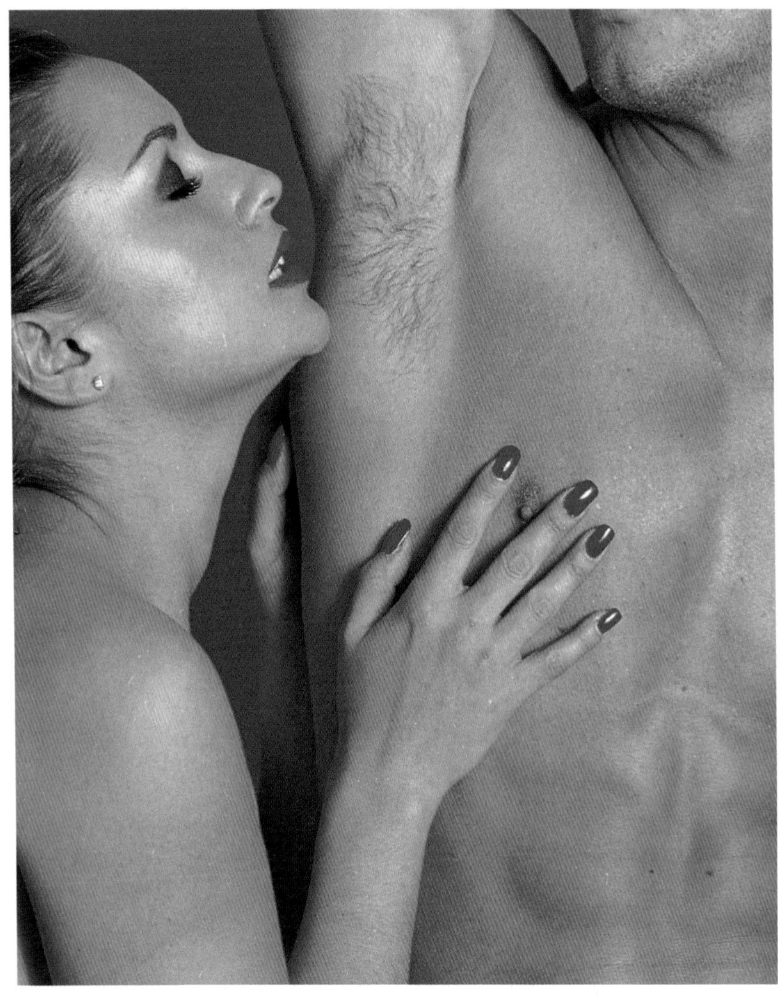

What are the best lubricants?

KY jelly is odourless, flavourless and slippery rather than sticky. Senselle is an excellent lubricant – aimed at older women – which possesses the exact texture of natural vaginal secretions. One of the best lubricants, in terms of both ease of use and lack of expense, is saliva. It works brilliantly and has the advantage of smelling of you or your partner. You can also buy fruit-scented lubricants.

There are so many different vibrators. Which are the best ones for clitoral stimulation?

A standard battery-operated, cigar-shaped vibrator is as good as any of the fancier specimens at providing clitoral stimulation and it costs a lot less. There is also a slim, pencil-shaped vibrator that is designed specifically for clitoral stimulation. The secret of getting good sensation out of any battery-operated vibrator is to equip it with long-life batteries and to renew these frequently. An alternative to the battery-operated vibrator is the giant mains-operated Japanese sort.

Where can I buy a vibrator?

You can buy vibrators and other sex toys directly from a sex shop or by mail order (see advertisements in the back of sex magazines) or there are many websites on the Internet that sell sex aids. For examples, checkout the useful addresses listed at the back of the book (see page 168).

Is an orgasm from a vibrator different to an orgasm experienced during sex?

No – all orgasms work in much the same way with the focal point being the clitoris. However, orgasms do differ in terms of subjective experience. An orgasm with a vibrator may feel more intense and last longer than a climax during normal sex. Despite this intensity, some women miss the range of other physical and emotional sensations that come from real-live body-to-body sex.

I've heard that some vibrators are specially designed to stimulate the G-spot. How do they work?

The G-spot area is high up on the front wall of the vagina and if you can exert steady or vibrating pressure on it you may be able to trigger a climax. In theory, any cylindrical vibrator could be used to do this but you may find that a specially designed vibrator with a long, slim body and a slight curve at the tip is useful. The curved tip helps you to target the G-spot from the right angle.

I've seen a vibrator shaped like an egg. What does it do?

This invention dates from the 70s. Attached to the egg is a lead that goes into a battery-operated control box. Once the egg has been inserted into the vagina, the control is turned on and the egg vibrates inside you. This can be pleasant at the vaginal entrance but the vibrations are unlikely to cause much sensation if the egg is inserted deep inside the vagina.

My boyfriend has suggested using a clitoral stimulator during sex. How does this work?

A clitoral stimulator is a device, usually worn by the man at the base of his penis, that is designed to rub across his partner's clitoris during intercourse. Stimulators are made of soft rubber and can be helpful if the penis makes virtually no contact with the clitoris during sex. The drawback is that they won't necessarily provide the depth of pressure or the rhythm that you need to reach orgasm. They cannot compare to the sensitivity of the fingers or tongue, for example. Another drawback is that, if the stimulator and clitoris are not lubricated, your clitoris can be battered into an anaesthetized state which means you won't feel anything!

What do duo-balls do?

Duo-balls are two small weighted balls that, when inserted in the vagina, roll around each other. This creates different sensations depending on what angle you are sitting or lying at and it's supposed to keep the wearer in a permanent state of sexual arousal.

sextips

Sex toys for men and women

There is a huge variety of sex toys available on the market today. Here's a selection of some of the most popular ones.

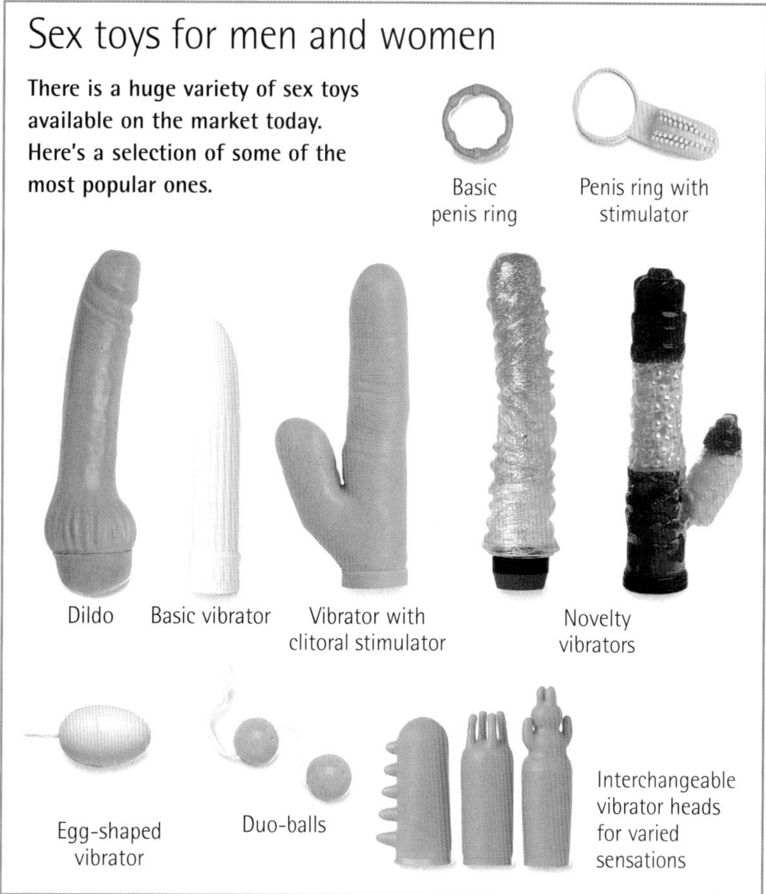

Basic penis ring

Penis ring with stimulator

Dildo

Basic vibrator

Vibrator with clitoral stimulator

Novelty vibrators

Egg-shaped vibrator

Duo-balls

Interchangeable vibrator heads for varied sensations

I suspect that duo-balls would work only if you are exceptionally sensitive – the interior of the vagina is not equipped with many nerve endings.

Are there vibrators for men?

There are two main sorts of vibrator especially designed for men. One is in the shape of a ring fitted around the base of the penis (a battery-powered control box is switched on to make the ring vibrate). It can be used during masturbation or sex with a partner. The other sort of male vibrator, which can also be used on a woman, is a short, slightly curved device designed to be inserted anally. A special hilt prevents the vibrator from slipping inside the anus and getting lost in the rectum. When inserted, the curved part of the vibrator massages the prostate gland, an area of extreme sensitivity, and this can result in rapid orgasm.

What does it mean if...

my partner needs porn to get aroused?

For most men pornography is a sexual "extra" with no emotions attached. Using it could be compared to eating a slightly different type of food or pursuing a pleasant hobby. However, a dependence on porn could mean any of the following:

- Your partner may have problems getting sexually excited. For example, men with mild impotence problems find porn can help; so do some women with arousal and orgasm problems. Porn provides the extra edge that's needed to make sex work.
- Your partner has unwittingly conditioned himself to become aroused in response to porn. Perhaps he got used to masturbating to porn when he was a teenager.
- In exceptional circumstances pornography is used as an alternative to sex with a partner. When this happens it indicates that there are relationship problems between the couple (not necessarily sex problems) that would benefit from help from an experienced counsellor.

What are penis rings and how do they work?

Penis rings are designed for men who have problems maintaining an erection. A common reason for this is that blood flow into the penis leaks away again due to organic damage. The penis ring, which is worn at the base of the shaft, grips the penis tightly enough to lock in blood, enabling the man to sustain the erection and enjoy a satisfactory experience of intercourse. Penis rings should only be worn for a limited time to avoid damage to the penis. Rubber bands should never be used as a substitute device (they are too tight).

Do shaped condoms make a difference to sex?

Shaped condoms are designed to provide extra sensation for women. Special ribbing or projections on the outside of the condom are meant to stimulate the inside of the vagina. This sounds good in principle, but the trouble is that, with the exception of the vaginal entrance, the vagina is not richly endowed with nerve endings and most women don't have a great deal of sensation inside their vagina. So, the truth is that shaped and speciality condoms make little difference to sensation during sex. Thickly ribbed condoms may also blunt sensation for the man (useful, however, if he suffers from premature ejaculation). In addition, shaped and speciality condoms may not carry a safety kitemark, which means that they cannot be relied upon for protection against sexually transmitted infections and pregnancy. Also, protuberances on some condoms may increase the chances of them splitting during sex.

How can black leather and rubber improve sex?

Leather and rubber have both a visual and an olfactory impact. Men and women clad in glistening black look slick and sexy and their outline leaves little to the imagination. Both leather and rubber possess very distinctive smells and many people associate such scents with sexual arousal. If you are male, you may like to invest in a can of spray designed especially for rubber and massage your partner's latex cat suit so that she glistens all over. If you are female, you may like to don super-tight-fitting black leather trousers and high-heeled shoes so that you are the epitome of wicked femininity. And, of course, you can buy all manner of strap, harness and binding equipment that fits around or inside the buttocks, the thighs and even on each side of your genitals. The pressure from these heightens sexual tension while the appearance can instantly arouse a susceptible partner.

Sex fact

Edible lubricants are gelatine-covered capsules that contain flavoured gel. You pop one in your mouth before oral sex and then bite into it to drench your partner with tasty, exotic juices.

My friend says that she has amazing sex when blindfolded. What difference could a blindfold make?
A blindfold offers a sense of helplessness and allows you to feel vulnerable. Your mind is likely to start racing as your imagination fills in the gaps created by sight deprivation. Your anxiety levels may also go up. An astute sexual partner will pick up on these swirling emotions and exploit them erotically. Another advantage of sex while blindfolded is that you are forced to pay more attention to the physical sensations you are giving and receiving. From your partner's point of view, the sight of you naked and blindfolded is likely to be extremely arousing because it confers dominance and power. The best sort of turn-on is one that works on both partners – and blindfolds manage that.

I am thinking of getting my penis pierced. I'm told piercing could enhance my sexual sensation. Is this true?
The reverse is more likely to be true. Any damage to the penis will cause the development of scar tissue which by nature lacks sensitivity. The main appeal of piercing lies in the fact that a partner may find it titillating. Penis piercings may offer slightly different vaginal sensations to a partner during intercourse but are unlikely to make a major sensual difference.

How could looking at porn affect our relationship?
Many people find occasional glimpses of pornography erotic since it offers them the opportunity to be a voyeur. Even though you would never consider spying on other people in reality, porn allows you to do precisely this within safe and legal boundaries. Porn can kick-start or enhance sexual arousal so that you feel deliciously horny and ready to go. Women may find that looking at porn makes the path to orgasm quicker and easier. However, this is mostly true of soft porn – hard porn tends to evoke disgust in many women. Avoid porn if it makes you feel insecure, especially if you believe that your partner is more turned on by porn than by you.

sex games

I like the idea of playing games in bed but where do I start?

A sex game can be anything you want it to be – simple or elaborate, funny or serious. It can involve playing with food or water, role playing, enacting sexual fantasies or experimenting with sex toys, such as vibrators, dildos and S&M gear. The important thing is that you and your partner tailor sex games to your own needs and preferences. You could start by experimenting with dominance and submission during sex, which many people find erotic. Take an item of clothing such as a scarf or a tie and use it to pull your partner gently closer. Use the same piece of clothing to gently bind the wrists together. This simple act can dramatically increase your partner's sense of sexual anticipation. Now teasingly caress the length of your partner's body. Don't give away what you are going to do next – this will heighten suspense and tactile response. Manipulate your partner into positions that show how powerless he/she is. If you are the bound partner, struggle and protest a fair bit – this makes the scenario much more exciting for your mate.

I like the idea of subjecting my man to lots of different tactile experiences. Can you suggest an erotic game we can play?

You could give your partner a wonderful all-over massage with oils that culminates in a genital massage. You could also play a sensual touch game in which you blindfold him and ask him to identify a number of unusual materials and textures that you use to caress his body. These could include silk, satin, fur, feathers, ice, toothpaste and lubricating jelly. If you enjoy spanking games, you could test your partner's ability to identify different spanking tools, such as your hand, a piece of lightweight bamboo, a soft cat-o'-nine tails or a fur mitt. If he guesses wrong, his punishment is an extra spanking!

I want to plan a special event for my boyfriend's birthday – some kind of sexual treat that he won't be expecting. Can you give me a suggestion?

Plan a private celebration in which you indulge your boyfriend's every wish. Greet him at the door with a bottle of champagne and then feed him a light birthday supper. When he has finished eating, say that you will treat him to the best thing on earth to help him digest his meal. Lead him to an armchair, take off his shoes and give him a soothing foot massage using warm massage oil with a few drops of essential oil added (choose peppermint for zest). While you are massaging one foot, wrap the other in a warm towel then, at the end, wrap both feet in a warm towel. Make sure that he keeps his eyes closed during the massage and that he doesn't help you by moving his limbs – all manipulation is your responsibility. The experience you are trying to create is one of complete helplessness, luxury and trust (similar to the experience of babyhood). When your boyfriend is completely relaxed, lead him into the bedroom. Now try out some grown-up sexual techniques on him (see pages 78–81). The idea is that this time is devoted entirely to him – your needs can be looked after at another time.

I find the sensation of water in the shower wonderfully sensual. How can I turn the experience of having a shower into an erotic game?

The shower is a natural sex toy: it combines heat, pressure, moisture and friction all in one device. According to *The Hite Report*, water massage using the shower is even a favourite method for some women to reach orgasm. You and your partner could try any of the following in the shower:

- Cover each other in liquid soap and take turns to give each other an erotic massage.
- Use the shower in mild S&M games. You can give pleasure by directing warm water at the genitals and punishment by blasting cold water on your partner's back.
- Have a combined bath and shower. Lie back in the bath and use the flow of water from the shower (at a slightly higher temperature than the bath water) to massage different parts of the body, such as the perineum, the genitals, the toes, the lips, the soles of the feet and the backs of the knees.
- See if you can masturbate each other to orgasm using only the jets of water from the shower head on each other's genitals.
- Surprise your partner with an impromptu oral sex session in the middle of a shower.
- Have shower sex – the best position is one in which the woman leans forward and the man penetrates her from behind. The man can also lift up the woman so that she grips his waist with her thighs – be careful though, it's easy to slip in this position.

Which sex games use the sense of smell?

Try subjecting your partner to a series of scent tests. First, blindfold your partner, then line up an array of unusual, exotic or erotic scents, such as massage oil, ylang ylang essential oil, the rubber of a condom, your favourite perfume or aftershave, vaginal juices or seminal fluid and fresh sweat from your armpit. Devise a system of rewards and punishments for right and wrong answers. A reward could be 20 seconds of genital stimulation, a punishment could be 20 seconds of spanking.

I want to play a fantasy game with my partner. Can you suggest one?

Here are two games, the first is orchestrated by the man and the second by the woman:

- Blindfold your woman and tell her you are taking her into the harem of a Turkish sultan. Since the sultan is a man of extreme ugliness she is not allowed to set eyes on him – should she even be caught peeping, she will be sentenced to a caning. In the harem she will be attended by eunuchs whose sole duty is to prepare her for the sultan. This preparation consists of oiling and anointing her body and then stimulating her genitals so that she is ready for the great man. Your job is to play the roles of eunuchs and sultan, ensuring that your lover's blindfold remains securely in place throughout.
- Blindfold your man and tell him that you are taking him into a harem of exotic women who are allowed to use him for sex in any way that they desire. Because they are never allowed out of the harem they all are hungry for sexual contact. Tell your lover that since the women care only for their own satisfaction, he must not expect much sexual attention for himself. Now play the parts of different women in the harem. Manipulate his body or parts of his body with your hands to place him in whatever position you want. End by sitting astride him to have sex and as you ride him, forbid him to climax. Don't let him take the blindfold off.

My partner has bought a huge mirror which she has put next to our bed. What are some good games that involve watching ourselves?

Mirrors are an excellent way of turning up the sexual temperature because of the intense satisfaction that visual stimulation can bring. You are effectively watching your own private, live porn show. There are lots of games that involve mirrors – try experimenting with any of the following:

• Order your partner to do something specifically provocative in front of the mirror while you watch. This could be undressing, drying him- or herself after a bath or shower, rubbing his or her body with massage oil or stimulating his or her genitals.

• Give your partner fellatio or cunnilingus in front of the mirror.

• Have sex in different positions, such as sex from behind, or sex on a chair positioned in front of the mirror. Alternatively, adjust the position of the mirror so that you can see the penis moving in and out of the vagina. You could even try straddling the mirror if it's a long thin one.

• Play a fantasy game in which you pretend that the mirror is a window into a next-door room. In that room are two lovers who are performing especially for you.

• Play sexual anatomy lessons by telling your lover to expose certain areas – such as the clitoris or the anus – in front of the mirror. Your lover should then demonstrate, for your education, just what happens when these areas are stimulated. As the pupil, you are compelled to watch the demonstration in the mirror.

• Experiment with one partner wearing a blindfold. This encourages the other partner who is watching the sexual action in the mirror to be completely uninhibited.

Sex fact

One of the most common sex games that couples play is telephone sex. Each partner takes it in turn to give the other a sexy description of what he/she is wearing, feeling and doing. As the erotic tempo increases each partner can listen to the other stimulating themselves to orgasm.

I love food and would like to combine it with sex. What games can my partner and I play?

What about taking your partner on a hanky-panky picnic? You could do this on a summer's day, making sure that

indetail

Going on a sexy picnic

If you're planning a picnic that ends in sex, choose the following luscious, sensual foods and pack them into a hamper together with a rug that's large enough to lie in and cover you:

• Chilled wine.
• Bite-sized sandwiches.
• Prepared fruit, such as melon slices, or soft red berries, such as strawberries, cherries or plums.
• Some frozen grapes in a thermos flask.
• A supply of cylindrical-shaped foods such as carrots, cucumbers, chocolate bars and lollipops – these can be eaten suggestively or used to stimulate your partner's erogenous zones.
• Condoms – fruit flavoured.

sextips

Sexy food games

Eating is a sensual activity that can go hand-in-hand with sex. Foods that lend themselves to sexy games tend to be sweet, sticky, creamy or juicy. Try the following games or make up your own:

• Ask your partner to hide a dab of honey on his body. Your job is to find it with your tongue.
• Use a new paintbrush to paint the body with runny foods such as cream, ice-cream, syrup, yoghurt or custard.
• Have a food fight. Smother each other in whipped cream, crush fruit into his hair and pour custard all over her.
• Eat a whole meal from your partner's body. Arrange the starter on the chest, the main course on the belly and the dessert on the abdomen and genitals.

you find a secluded spot for your gourmet goings-on. Or, if you can't wait for the sunshine, try turning your bedroom into a picnic spot – play birdsong music in the background and spread a checkered tablecloth on the floor. Eat the food (see box on page 119) as provocatively as possible. Provide bite-sized sandwiches and feed them to each other. Put a frozen grape between your teeth and offer it to your partner (or drop it down his/her top by "accident"). Share the same piece of watermelon and then kiss the juice off each other. Demonstrate on a chocolate bar how you would give oral sex and then do the real thing. And to ensure you really get into the mood, start the entire proceedings with a glass or two of chilled wine.

My partner likes putting whipped cream on me during sex. What other things can we do with food?

You can have a sexual banquet. This is a unique type of banquet in that there are no tables, chairs, knives or forks – your partner's naked body is the plate upon which the food is served and you are the sole diner. Essential ingredients are a can of whipped cream, a pot of honey or syrup and a selection of soft, juicy fruits. Use the food to stimulate your partner's body. Aim for subtle stimulation at first – slowly drip honey from a spoon into the navel, squeeze fresh orange juice onto the skin, run an ice-cube over the nipples, lick chocolate sauce from the neck or, using a can of cream, make a pattern on the body and then lick it off. As your partner gets aroused, start to stimulate the genitals in an indirect way. For example, dribble champagne between her legs or place a bagel around his penis and nibble it. As the sexual tension mounts, start to concentrate on the genitals directly: decorate them with cream, ice-cream or yoghurt and then suck it off. Or you can use food, such as carrots and cucumbers, as natural dildos (make sure you wash them first though).

sextips

Fantasy swapping

Revealing fantasies takes courage. We may fear shocking our partner or being the object of humour, ridicule or even disgust.

- Make a pact – agree to take it in turns to swap fantasies. No opting out is permitted!
- Start in a mild way and hot your fantasies up progressively.
- Make sure that your respective fantasies are of equal "value". For instance, if your partner describes a wild fantasy, then yours must be equally exotic.
- Don't make your partner feel bad or guilty about any of his or her fantasies and, equally important, don't bring up fantasies that you know will make your partner feel insecure or inadequate.

I've heard of role-playing in sex but what does it involve?

Role-playing games are a bit like sexual charades. They involve acting out a scenario with an explicitly sexual theme. You and your partner take on agreed roles and stay in character as you interact. Roles might include: priest and virgin, teacher and schoolgirl, dominatrix and victim. Sexual role-plays can be planned and elaborate – involving costumes, props and storylines – or they can be spontaneous in which you and your partner rely solely on your imaginative powers. The aim of role-playing is to build up slowly – sometimes agonizingly so – to a sexual crescendo. Effective role-playing involves a lot of temptation, tantalization and sexual frustration – all ingredients that promote arousal.

I like the idea of submission and domination but I'm not sure what to do. Is there a "safe" way to start?

Games of submission and domination only work well when there is a solid sense of trust between both partners, so one of your prime concerns should be to establish this from the outset. It's also important to agree on a specific safety word that means "stop". Either partner can use this word at any stage to withdraw from the game. This is a necessity because games of submission frequently involve crying out "no, no, stop, stop!" when you're actually quite enjoying yourself. The minute your code word is uttered both of you must stop immediately and trust each other to do so. If you feel that you can't trust a partner, don't start games that involve any element of psychological or physical humiliation.

I get the impression that my man would love me to give him "discipline" or "correction" and I like the idea of doing this. Can you give me some tips?
Start by dressing for the part. Wear clothes made of black leather or PVC (perhaps combined with black lace or other see-through materials), tight and shiny garments, stockings or thigh-high black riding boots which reveal the tops of your naked thighs. And remember to keep in role. If you are the dominatrix, your lover needs to be shown who is boss. Since he is bound to misbehave (because he wants to be punished) you are going to have to be firm and punish him as you see fit. Stand over him as he lies naked on the ground. Press his face against your thighs and order him to kiss or lick you there. Use props, such as a light cane, which you can flick against his naked skin so that he gets a hint of what will follow if he is disobedient. You can increase your lover's vulnerability by making him wear a blindfold, tying his wrists behind his back and pushing him over onto all fours so that his head is resting on the ground. Test your cane out on his buttocks in this position so that he knows what to expect. And say that you will relent and stop caning him, provided he makes wild, passionate love to you. Expect him to be difficult and to need a lot of punishment – it's all part of the game!

I like feeling overpowered during sex. How can I get my boyfriend to be more dominant?
Tell him that you want to play at being a bride or a virgin and that you'd like him to be in charge. Resist his advances slightly and appear reluctant throughout, thus allowing him to overcome you. Pretend that this is your first sexual experience. Let your boyfriend undress you and then cover your breasts as if you are shy about revealing your body. You can even wear white to emphasize the virginal role you are playing, but make sure that the fabric is extremely tactile. Respond lovingly to your boyfriend but don't take the lead in any way. Stay in role, allowing yourself to become more and more aroused. Let him see, very clearly, just how turned on this game makes you.

I love being tied up by my girlfriend, but I also like doing the tying. Can you give me an idea for a bondage game?
Try acting out the following scenario. The room is dark except for a single candle burning in the corner. There is a black sheet draped across the bed (which should have a bedhead for tying purposes!). You are a slave master and your girlfriend is a slave

emotionaltips

Rules for playing sex games

Before you embark on a sex game, it's worth agreeing on a few basic ground rules with your partner:

- Don't do anything that makes your partner upset or afraid.
- Go slowly and gently, especially if you're playing games that involve dominance and submission and have the potential to humiliate.
- Agree on what you will and won't do beforehand.
- Agree on a special code word that means "stop". This is because people often use the word "stop" when they don't actually mean it.
- Make sure that you trust each other and don't agree to anything you feel unsure about.

girl. Lead her into the room and order her to take off all her clothes. Explain that she has been a bad slave girl and must be punished for her wrongdoing. Tell her to lie face down on the bed and then tie her hands with soft ties (use scarves or neck ties) to the bedhead. This position exposes her naked buttocks and makes her feel vulnerable. Tell her to remain absolutely still and then leave the room for a minute or two. Just when she thinks you have forgotten about her, re-enter and "discover" that she has moved slightly. Since this is totally forbidden, she must be punished. Punishment can take the form of a light spanking or you can invent your own mild torture techniques. Keep leaving the room and, every time you come back, continue with the punishment. Finally, order her to make love to you in any way that you command. You can also play this game by handcuffing your partner to a table and leaving her standing naked!

My partner enjoys S&M games and finds pain erotic. I don't mind playing games but I don't understand the pain – how can it be sexy?

Some people have an extremely high tolerance for pain. This may partly be due to a "practice" effect – having participated in lots of sadomasochistic games, for example – but it may also be due to a strong motivation to gain pleasure from punishment. Those who suffer acute sexual guilt can find that their guilt is appeased or relieved by punishment. Some people also have an irresistible desire to swap power-roles, for example, the mighty judge who is temporarily absolved of all responsibility when he is humiliated

during sex with a dominatrix. Other people have strong psychological associations between pain and pleasure that were formed in childhood. For example, corporal punishment at school may have established a connection between caning and arousal. An interest in S&M can also come from the desire to experiment with the more dramatic, taboo or forbidden aspects of sex.

I like the idea of spanking and being spanked but I've never done it. Are there any right or wrong ways of spanking someone?

Spanking for sexual purposes should be firm enough to make the skin tingle but not so hard that it hurts. (Unless you enjoy pain, it can be a major disincentive to have sex!) A light slap of the hand or a playful thwack with a carpet beater brings the blood to the surface of the skin and creates a warm, tingling sensation that can be a pleasant precursor to sexual arousal. This degree of spanking might sting but it definitely does not hurt – if it does, stop. Safe spanking implements include carpet beaters, paddles, spatulas, fly whisks and soft flails. If you are using hardcore S&M toys such as whips, canes, rulers or riding crops, approach with caution as these can do serious damage. Try using them to symbolize rather than actually deliver punishment.

Is there a spanking game that I could play with my girlfriend?

Ask your girlfriend where on her body she would like to be spanked and then spank her somewhere else. When she protests spank her somewhere else again. Sometimes of course, you can spank in the desired place – the idea is

casehistory

"Our sex life needs an overhaul."

Jerry, 44

Sue and I have lived together for 10 years. Sex was OK at first but it has tailed off in recent years. Basically our sex life needs an overhaul. I don't know where to start as I've always had quite a conventional approach to sex and believed that as long as you love someone, the physical side of things will fall into place. Sue is much more adventurous than I am and I suppose that I'm afraid that if I can't satisfy her she might start looking elsewhere for sex.

Sue, 40

I've been very happy with Jerry but he's quite straight when it comes to sex – we usually make love in the missionary position with the lights off. I'd quite like to try some more sexy stuff such as dressing up in high heels and having Jerry take advantage of me. I've got this fantasy of myself dressed up in kinky underwear and Jerry finding me so irresistible that he forces me onto the floor and makes love to me there and then. But we've never had that kind of passion or spontaneity in our relationship and I wouldn't know where to start.

Anne responds:

“Because Jerry's and Sue's sexual relationship had more or less ground to a halt they decided to go to counselling together. During the course of their counselling sessions, Sue admitted that she enjoyed a rich fantasy life when she masturbated on her own and that she would like to share and act out some of her fantasies with Jerry. Initially, Jerry felt excluded by the fact that Sue masturbated and fantasized without him. Then, after some discussion, he started feeling flattered that he was the object of so many of Sue's fantasies. He also agreed that it would be a good idea to be more experimental in bed. Although enacting sexual fantasies didn't come naturally to Jerry he found that he enjoyed Sue's response in bed – he noticed that she seemed more aroused and keen to have sex than she had done for ages. This, in turn, made him feel reassured that his relationship was strong and that he wasn't about to lose Sue to another man. Sue, meanwhile, lost her inhibitions and felt able to express the extrovert side of her sexuality in a way that she hadn't before. Both Sue and Jerry feel they have rediscovered their sex life and their relationship is stronger as a result.”

to tease, tantalize and frustrate. Frustration increases arousal levels and is a turn-on in itself.

How can my lover and I bring sexual fantasies into our sex games?
Start by discussing the fantasies that you enjoy, the ones you're ambivalent about and the ones that you dislike. This helps to establish the ground rules for game-playing. Be completely honest – if a particular fantasy doesn't appeal to you, say so, but make sure that you do it in a non-judgmental way that doesn't make your partner feel criticized. And be sensitive if your fantasies focus on someone who is not your lover – although you may know that you have no intention of sleeping with your new colleague at work, you can easily make your lover feel insecure. Start off by choosing a favourite fantasy or even a sex scene from a film (such as the food scene in *9½ Weeks*), and enact it by dressing up and using props. Alternatively, you could write down different fantasy roles or characters on pieces of paper. For example, slave, dominatrix, teacher, virgin, schoolgirl, porn star or prisoner. You can also use names of famous people (but, again, beware of making your lover feel inadequate). Mix up the pieces of paper and get your partner to pull one out of a hat. Now you must both behave as if he/she is that character.

I know my partner would like to enact her sexual fantasies but she feels embarrassed about it. How can I encourage her to express herself?
Talk openly about your own fantasies and encourage her to talk about hers (follow the rules for fantasy swapping in the box on page 121). Then gently enact aspects of her fantasies the next time you make love – see what effect this has and take your cues from her responses. Alternatively, you can make an educated guess about what your partner's fantasies might consist of and experiment with various themes.

My partner and I feel silly enacting our fantasies. How can we get over this?
You could start by reading a book of fantasies together. Try Nancy Friday's classic compilation of women's sexual fantasies *My Secret Garden*. Take it in turns to read a fantasy aloud to each other at bedtime. Once you're familiar with other people's fantasies you'll feel less silly expressing your own.

My boyfriend fantasizes about public sex. How far can we go without upsetting people or breaking the law?
Sex outdoors is fine as long as complete privacy is guaranteed, for example, on a deserted stretch of sand dunes, or in a remote corner of a park or wood. However, sex in openly public places is entirely different because, as you say, you risk not only offending others but also breaking the law. This is where compromise comes in handy.

The following ideas incorporate exhibitionism and danger without putting you at risk:

- Start foreplay in public places and then rush home to have sex. Play footsie under a restaurant table, kiss in the street, sit on his lap and whisper provocative suggestions.
- Be opportunistic. Have sex in the bathroom at a party. Fondle each other in a lift.
- Make love in a dark room looking out onto a bright street. You can see people outside but they can't see you.

Should I tell my boyfriend about my fantasy to paint his face and dress him in my underwear? It turns me on every time I think about it.
Consider your boyfriend's likely reaction. Would he go rigid with horror or is he flexible in his approach to sex? Is he someone who always sticks to masculine conventions or is he comfortable with the feminine side of his personality? Approach the matter playfully and with a sense of fun. See if he likes being stroked with your silky undergarments for starters.

What does it mean if...
my partner enjoys pain during sex?

It means that your partner is a masochist, someone who likes to be submissive and to have pain inflicted as an integral part of sex. The ideal partner for a masochist is a sadist, someone who likes to dominate and inflict punishment. The crucial question for partners who play sadomasochistic games is what level of pain is safe and acceptable? I consider it advisable to stop at the kind of stinging pain that comes from spanking with your hand or a cat-o'-nine tails made out of felt strips. Of course there are some people who prefer their pain stronger than this but, for your own wellbeing, I consider it wise to go no further.

How do you play doctors and patients in bed?
Decide who is to be the doctor and who is to be the patient. If you want to don a white coat as doctor, feel free. Ask your patient to hop up on to a table having removed all underwear first. If the patient is female, tell her to open her legs and then start to examine her genitals – surgical gloves can add authenticity! Press gently on different areas around the clitoris and vagina and ask the patient how this feels – if she starts getting really aroused tell her that you need to do an internal examination and gently insert your finger into her vagina. Keep asking her to report back on different sensations. Next ask the patient to get on her hands and knees so that you can do an inspection from the rear. Using a new pair of surgical gloves, examine her rear and, again, ask her to rate different sites for sensation. If the patient is male, lift up his penis and inspect it from all angles. Slide his foreskin down and measure his penis size. Slide your finger around the head of the penis. Hold and measure the weight of his testicles (guess). Using lubricating jelly stroke your finger from the tip of his penis right down underneath his testicles and along his perineum. Ask him how this feels. To make the game work really well, ensure that, in your role as doctor, you stay cool and professional and don't show any signs of arousal yourself.

sextips

Kissing games

A deep and passionate kiss can make sex extremely erotic. The lips are one of the most sensitive parts of the body and a sensual kissing game is one of the fastest ways to turn each other on.

- Feed each other soft, juicy fruits, such as plums, peaches or nectarines, with your fingers. Let the juice run over your lips and then indulge in a delicious kiss.
- Exchange a frozen grape between your mouths until it defrosts, then bite into it and share the taste.
- Change your kissing style. Try gently sucking or biting your partner's lips. If you normally exchange soft, slow kisses, try hard, urgent kisses.
- Apply shiny lip gloss to your partner's lips and then kiss it off.
- Read the *Kama Sutra* and try out the different types of kiss. One passionate kiss that's recommended is the "bent kiss" in which the lovers' heads are angled slightly to one side – this permits maximum lip contact and tongue penetration.

advanced sex

indetail

The three-handed massage

Invented by massage-master Ray Stubbs, the three-handed massage combines a special full-body massage with intercourse. Partners should take it in turns to indulge each other.

- For her: ask your partner to lie on her front. Sit astride her thighs and rub massage oil into her back, buttocks and legs. Now, for maximum slipperiness, apply oil to your abdomen, genitals and thighs. Massage her back with your hands and, at the same time, let your body glide backwards and forwards over her thighs and buttocks. Your penis is in contact with her skin and forms part of the massage (hence "three-handed"). Aim for flowing, sensual movements. As you both become more aroused, let your penis find its slippery way between your partner's legs. Allow yourself to penetrate her exceptionally slowly – the slower you are, the more tantalizing your touch will be. Let your hands and penis slowly massage her simultaneously, so that all the movements blend.
- For him: ask your partner to lie on his back and sit astride him. Follow the instructions above but use your breasts as well as your hands and genitals to massage his body. When he is aroused let your vagina gradually slip against his penis. Keep doing this in an exceptionally slow rubbing movement before finally letting him inside you. Continue to massage your partner with your hands.

How should we go about having anal sex? And can women have an orgasm from anal penetration?

The anus requires plenty of lubrication before you attempt anal sex. Unlike the vagina it doesn't secrete its own lubrication – so, to prevent painful friction, use lots of water-based lubricating jelly, both on the anus and penis. Relaxing the anus can also facilitate penetration. It's important to use a strong condom to prevent the transmission of infection – the condom should be changed if anal sex is followed by vaginal sex.

Since anal penetration does not stimulate the clitoris, women are unlikely to reach orgasm without additional stimulation. It can help if the man reaches his hand around the woman during penetration and rubs her clitoris. Having said this, some women find anal sex so erotic that they can reach orgasm without extra help. Men who receive anal penetration are likely to reach orgasm very easily because the highly sensitive prostate gland is directly stimulated. Prostate massage, of any sort, usually results in rapid and easy climax.

I have read about something called auto-fellatio. What is it and how do you do it?

Auto-fellatio refers to the extremely difficult practice of a man stimulating his own penis using his mouth and tongue. Needless to say, you would need the skills of an acrobat plus bones of india rubber. Auto-fellatio is most definitely not for the overweight. Warning: even attempting auto-fellatio is liable to give you a stiff neck!

sextips

Advanced sex positions

If you are quite flexible, it can be fun to try some unusual or athletic sex positions. These four come from ancient erotic texts such as the *Kama Sutra*.

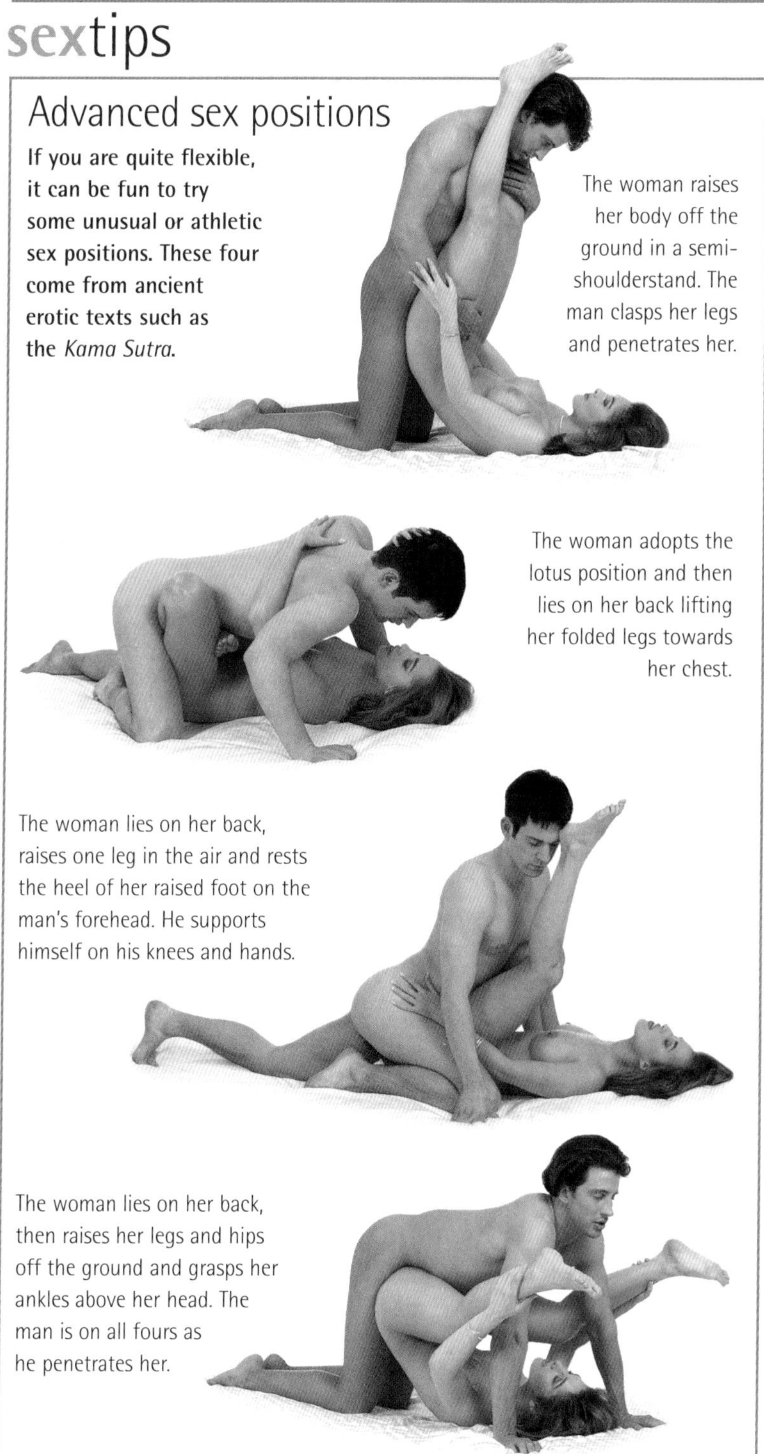

The woman raises her body off the ground in a semi-shoulderstand. The man clasps her legs and penetrates her.

The woman adopts the lotus position and then lies on her back lifting her folded legs towards her chest.

The woman lies on her back, raises one leg in the air and rests the heel of her raised foot on the man's forehead. He supports himself on his knees and hands.

The woman lies on her back, then raises her legs and hips off the ground and grasps her ankles above her head. The man is on all fours as he penetrates her.

What is tantric sex and how does it improve lovemaking?

The Indian art of tantric sex focuses on building a spiritual bond between lovers and enhancing intercourse by greatly prolonging it. Done properly, it can lift you into a state of timelessness and spiritual ecstasy through sex and orgasm. A tantric sex programme usually takes place over two or three days (often many more) and is not something that can be learned quickly. Couples are encouraged to foster intimacy by spending hours caressing each other's body and passing relaxed time together. Sexual arousal builds slowly over a passage of time, meaning that both mind and body grow alive with sexual energy. Climax, when it eventually happens at the end of a long and pleasurable exercise, is also drawn-out.

I am curious about threesomes. How do they normally work?

A threesome at its simplest means three people making love together. This can be stimulating for its novelty value, or for the extra physical sensation provided by two sets of hands, lips, bodies and genitals being close to yours. Lovemaking can mean doing everything together or taking it in turns so that one person is always watching. Doing everything together may include intercourse if there are two men and one woman – one man penetrates the woman vaginally while the other one penetrates her anally. If there are two women and one man, one woman can have intercourse with the man while the other woman adds to either partner's sensation by giving hand or tongue stimulation. The various possibilities are limited only by the imagination of the participants.

are you adventurous?

The secret of a steamy and satisfying love life is a spirit of adventure – being willing to try something new, break down inhibitions and taboos and accept a sexual challenge.

You are at a dinner party and someone suggests a post-prandial game of strip poker. Do you:

- [ ] A Enthusiastically agree and hope for a losing streak?
- [ ] B Agree, but hope for good hands?
- [ ] C Opt out and watch?

What are your views on anal sex:

- [ ] A You're a seasoned pro?
- [ ] B You have to be in the right mood?
- [ ] C You've never done it?

You're at a restaurant and your partner takes a shine to the sexily clad waiter/waitress. Do you:

- [ ] A Invest in a similar costume and give your lover a thrilling role-playing evening?
- [ ] B Serve dinner to your partner the next evening with a glint in your eye?
- [ ] C Feel jealous?

You are taking a drive and your partner suddenly decides that he/she is feeling horny. Do you:

- [ ] A Pull over at the next secluded spot and test the car's suspension?
- [ ] B Pull over and give your partner a steamy kiss to drive him/her crazy?
- [ ] C Say you can't wait to get home?

Your partner has brought round a tub of your favourite expensive ice cream. Do you:

- [ ] A Smear it all over your partner's chest and lick it off slowly?
- [ ] B Get a spoon and ask your partner to feed you?
- [ ] C Get two spoons and enjoy it in front of the TV?

You're on holiday and snuggling up with your partner on an almost deserted beach. Do you:

- [ ] A Peel off your partner's swimming costume and make love in the sand?
- [ ] B Fool around a little in some secluded sand dunes?
- [ ] C Get into the sea and fool around below the waves, where no one can see what you're doing?

A couple of acquaintances ask you if you are interested in joining them for an "adult evening" at home. Do you:

- ☐ A Accept immediately – the invitation sounds tantalizing?
- ☐ B Accept out of curiosity and see what develops?
- ☐ C Decline politely?

You are at a friend's party and someone puts on a racy porn video. Do you:

- ☐ A Instantly sit down on the sofa to watch closely, discussing the action with fellow viewers?
- ☐ B Watch with interest out of the corner of your eye?
- ☐ C Move into the other room to party with other guests?

You are taking a walk in the woods with your partner and you feel sexy. Do you:

- ☐ A Pin your partner up against the nearest tree?
- ☐ B Find a shady grove and have a bit of fun in the undergrowth?
- ☐ C Enjoy a heady kiss and start walking home where you can take things further?

You're having an affair with a colleague. Do you:

- ☐ A Regularly have sex in the stationery cupboard?
- ☐ B Decamp to a friend's flat in the lunch hour for sex?
- ☐ C Maintain a professional relationship during working hours but make the most of the evenings?

Your partner is cooking you dinner and asks you to turn up wearing something sexy. Do you:

- ☐ A Arrive wearing a long coat – with nothing underneath?
- ☐ B Wear your sexiest outfit – and no underwear?
- ☐ C Wear your sexiest outfit and your sexiest underwear?

You are having a romantic evening in a restaurant and you want to show your partner just how much you fancy him/her. Do you:

- ☐ A Slip your shoe off and use your foot to stimulate him/her underneath the tablecloth?
- ☐ B Whisper naughty suggestions?
- ☐ C Play footsie underneath the table?

ANSWERS

Mostly As Wow! You're very sexually outgoing and open-minded. You probably have a high sex drive and great sex is an important part of your relationship. You're not afraid to express yourself sensually, wherever you may be, and you're also up for experimentation. Be warned though – not everyone is as keen on such free expression of sexuality as you are. Your confidence and sense of adventure are great, but your sexual self-possession may be slightly intimidating for a less uninhibited partner.

Mostly Bs You keep your sex life exciting and unpredictable by enjoying passionate encounters but you believe that keeping something back can sometimes be a good thing and will make those erotic moments all the more meaningful. Be confident enough to continue enjoying your sex life exactly as you do at the moment. And don't be afraid to indulge your curiosity.

Mostly Cs Although you are open to suggestion, you tend to be cautious and careful when it comes to spontaneous sexual expression. It could be that the thought of sex outdoors or in a busy restaurant just doesn't turn you on, but it may also be that you have picked up some inhibitions along the way and have grown conservative in your approach to sex. If you feel that inhibitions hamper your sex life, try to loosen up a bit and do things that are a little more experimental.

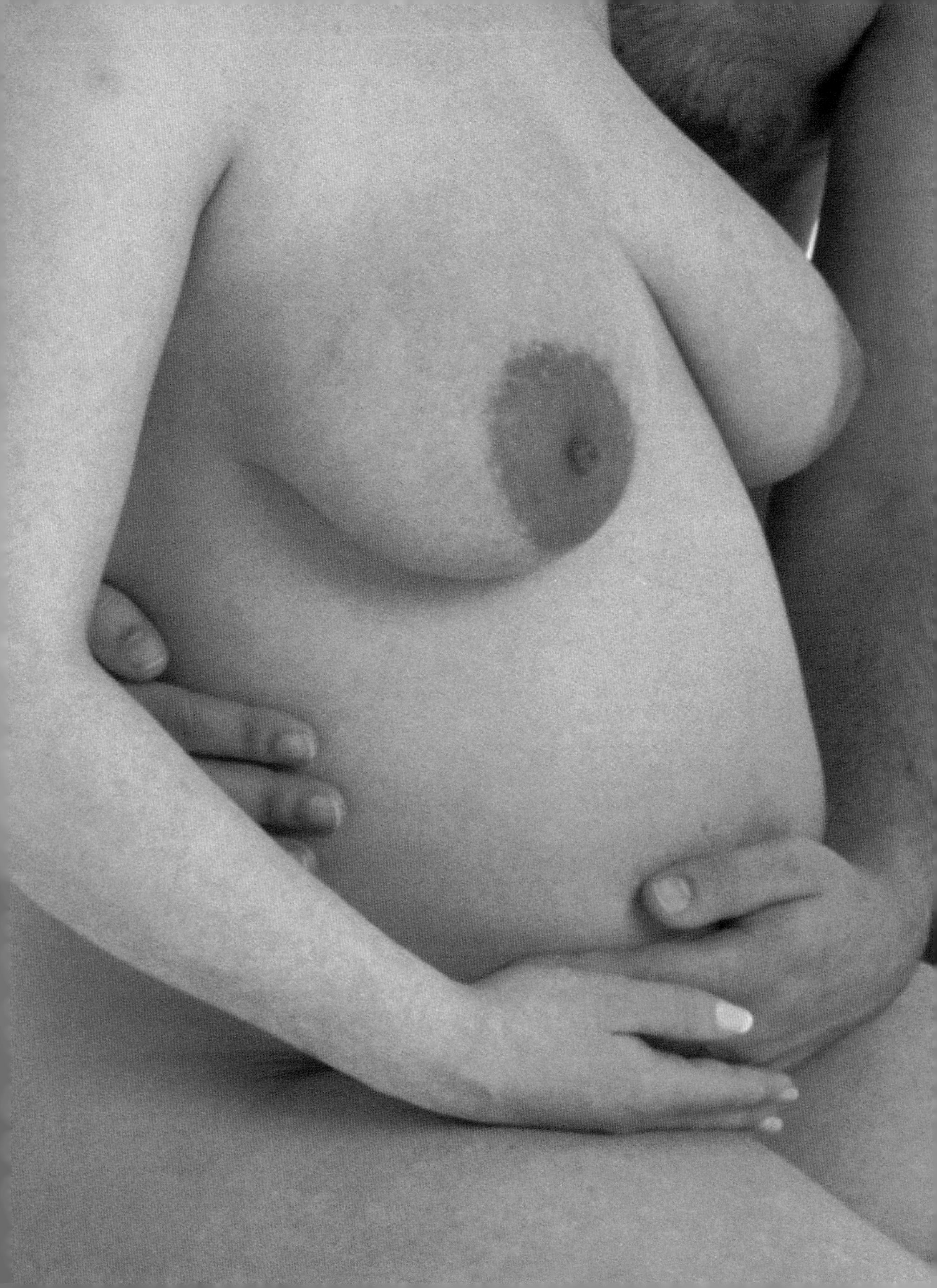

pregnancy and beyond

Your sex life may need to adapt to the changes of pregnancy and the practicalities of childcare but it shouldn't have to grind to a halt. In fact, the more intimate and connected you and your partner feel, the better this will be for your baby.

early pregnancy

What sort of sex drive is normal in the first few months of pregnancy?

Every woman and every pregnancy is different but, generally speaking, the first three months can be immensely tiring and this together with morning sickness can diminish your desire for sex. However, most women find that their libido and energy levels return during the second trimester of pregnancy. Some women feel sexy and sensual throughout pregnancy – and there is the added bonus that you don't have to bother with contraception or worry about periods and premenstrual syndrome.

What if I just don't feel like having sex?

Even if you don't feel like sex it's good to stay physically intimate with your partner. This doesn't have to mean intercourse – it can mean back rubs, foot massages, cuddles, mutual masturbation and oral sex. Although

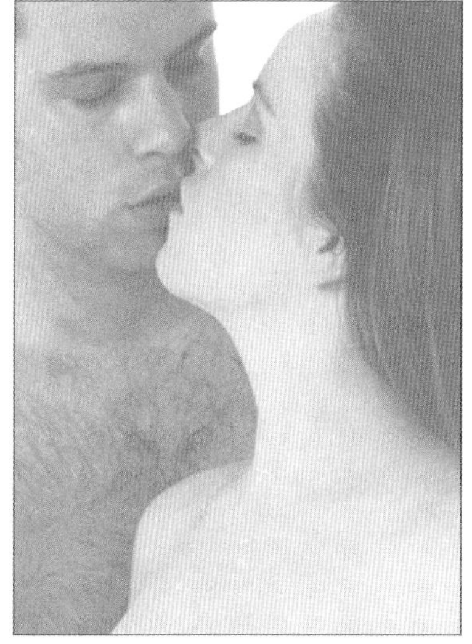

oral sex is perfectly safe during pregnancy a man should avoid blowing air into the vagina.

Can having sex during the first trimester harm the baby?

Some men believe that their penis will hurt the unborn baby during sex – it can't. Some men even unconsciously fear that the baby will damage the penis. Again, this cannot happen. Sex and orgasm are perfectly safe during early pregnancy. The exception to this is when a woman is suffering from a threatened miscarriage – always have any vaginal bleeding or spotting checked out by a doctor. Women who have experienced recurrent miscarriages in the first trimester should also consult a doctor about guidelines for making love.

I'm seven weeks pregnant and I can't stand having my breasts touched during sex. Is this normal?

Yes. The breasts often become painful and tender during the first trimester. This is a result of all the pregnancy hormones that are flooding your body. Explain this to your partner so that he can concentrate on stimulating other erogenous zones of your body. The breasts usually become less tender during the second trimester.

middle and late pregnancy

I'm 12 weeks pregnant and have had no desire for sex during the last three months. Will things get better in the second and third trimesters?
They should do – energy and libido usually return in the second trimester and some women feel sexier now than at any other time in their life. The last three months are more complicated because your increased bulk can make you feel tired, and mobility during sex is limited. Despite this, you may desire sexual stimulation because your genitals are engorged with blood and feel sensitive. If intercourse is difficult, masturbation is a great alternative.

I've noticed that my orgasms are more intense now that I am pregnant. Is this normal?
It's normal to experience increased levels of sexual tension in the genitals from around the fourth month onwards. The hormonal changes of pregnancy cause blood flow to the pelvic area to increase – this makes the vulva and vagina swollen and extra-sensitive. In some women this heightened sensitivity results in more intense orgasms or even first-time multiple orgasms. On the other hand, since blood does not drain away from the genitals after orgasm (as it does when you're not pregnant), some women are left feeling unsatisfied by orgasm, as though they haven't quite "made it".

Should I avoid using sex toys when I am pregnant?
It's OK to use sex toys on the outside of the body but it's advisable not to insert them into the vagina during pregnancy because of the risk of introducing infection.

I feel fat and unattractive and I don't think my husband can possibly desire me. I'm very reluctant to make love because it means undressing in front of him. My husband tries to reassure me but it doesn't help. What can I do?
It can be hard to accept the newer, larger version of yourself, especially if you associate being big with being unattractive. You need to work on establishing a more positive body image. One way of doing this would be to talk about your feelings at your antenatal classes and find out what other pregnant women think and feel – this can be extremely reassuring and can help to give you an alternative perspective. Talk to your husband as well – it sounds as though he is being very supportive. Give him the chance to express the fact that he loves your new curves. If you cut him off sexually now, you may find that it is hard to revive your sex life once your baby is born and your body is back to normal. And don't get stuck with the myth that intercourse is the only way to have sex. This just isn't true. Pregnancy is an ideal time to spoil each other with oral sex, mutual masturbation and massage.

emotionaltips

Advice for men

Do:

- Be tender, romantic, patient and understanding.
- If she doesn't feel very sexy, suggest alternatives to intercourse such as a whole-body massage.
- Reassure her that you find her new shape attractive.
- Take your time when lovemaking.
- Use lots of pillows for comfort.

Don't:

- Expect her to concentrate on lovemaking if the baby is moving energetically inside her.
- Be upset if she doesn't have an orgasm every time.
- Expect, or try for, simultaneous orgasm.
- Put anything inside her vagina except your penis.

indetail

Your hormones

Major hormonal changes take place in the body during pregnancy with extra quantities of the female sex hormones oestriol (a type of oestrogen) and progesterone being produced. Oestrogens are associated with a sense of wellbeing, while studies suggest that progesterone is associated with discomfort and menstrual-type symptoms. Levels of testosterone fall slightly in pregnancy, which may account for decreased sexual interest and response in some pregnant women.

Pregnancy hormones cause increased blood flow to the genitals, which become engorged with blood and the vagina swells as a result. Although this can provide a snug sensation for the man during sex, it can make some women feel orgasmic contractions less strongly.

Are some men especially attracted to pregnant women?
Some men are attracted to the wellbeing, wonderful complexion, radiance and fecundity of the gently swelling curves of the pregnant form. However, other men say that they don't find pregnancy attractive at all. It seems to be a matter of entirely personal taste.

I am devastated to find that my husband has had a brief affair while I've been pregnant. Why should he do this? He's never had an affair before.
Unfortunately, this situation is not uncommon. If a man feels threatened or dismayed by pregnancy, one possible reaction is to seek escape in the form of sex with someone else. Your husband may have felt any or all of the following:

- Threatened by pregnancy in that most of the attention is now focused on the woman and her dominant role in reproduction.
- Dismayed by the physical changes of pregnancy. Deep down a man may feel "cheated" of his partner's sexy pre-pregnancy body.
- Frightened about sharing a partner with the new baby.
- Anxious about the responsibilities associated with fatherhood (including financial worries).

Talk to your husband about his reasons for having an affair and, if possible, try to gradually pick up the pieces. Don't hide your emotions – vent your feelings and see whether you can both learn from this period of hurt and sorrow (see pages 24–27).

I've had a very romantic affair during each of my two pregnancies but have gone off these men straight after the birth. Why should I behave in this bizarre way?
"Pregnancy sexuality" – a combination of physical arousal and emotional abandon – may have been the driving force behind your affairs. Or did your regular partner go off sex during your pregnancy? The reversal of these situations, plus fatigue, might account for your withdrawal from your lovers after the birth of your children.

sextips

Sex positions during pregnancy

You may need to be more inventive during sex as your bump gets bigger. Experiment with different positions and depths of penetration and see what feels best. Avoid taking any weight on your breasts and belly.

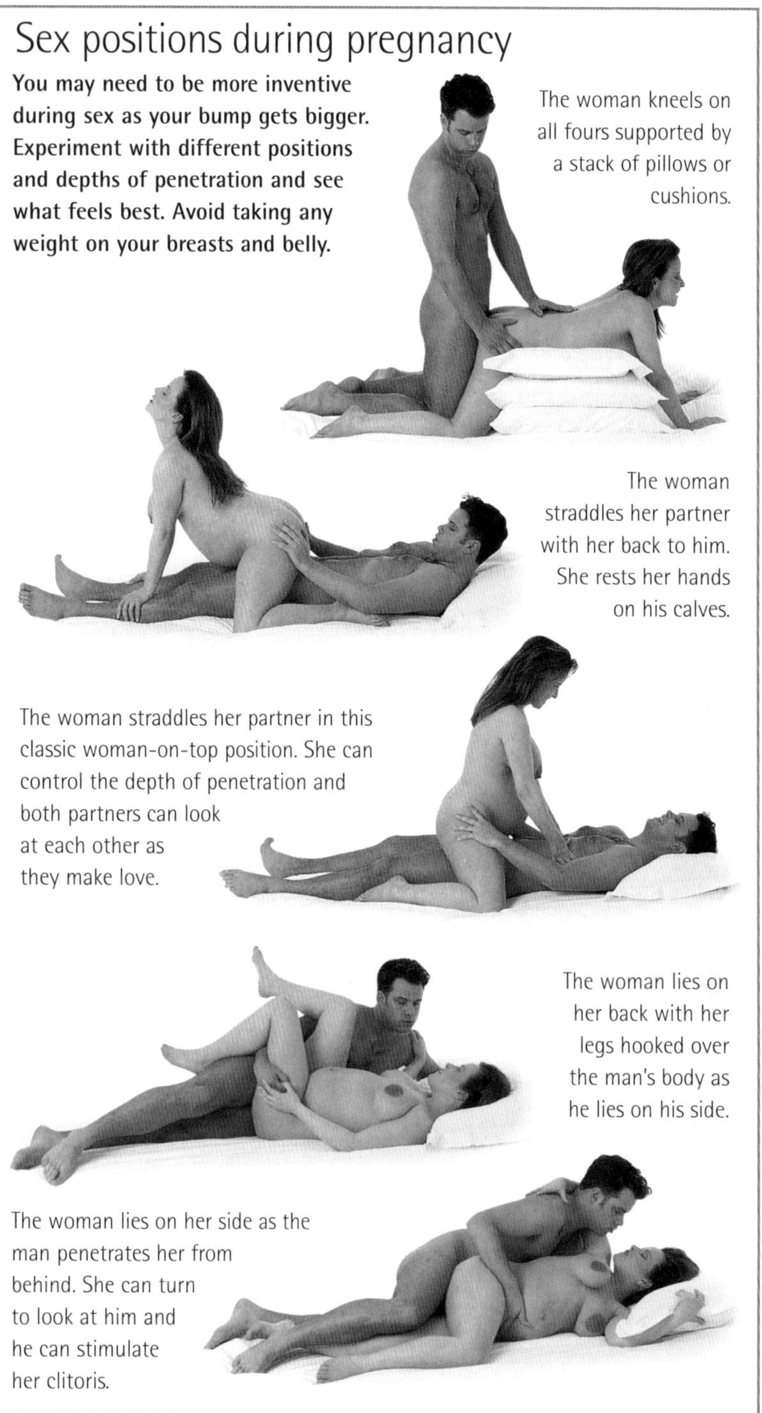

The woman kneels on all fours supported by a stack of pillows or cushions.

The woman straddles her partner with her back to him. She rests her hands on his calves.

The woman straddles her partner in this classic woman-on-top position. She can control the depth of penetration and both partners can look at each other as they make love.

The woman lies on her back with her legs hooked over the man's body as he lies on his side.

The woman lies on her side as the man penetrates her from behind. She can turn to look at him and he can stimulate her clitoris.

My pregnant partner and I have a sex problem but we have been advised that there is no point going for sex therapy until quite a long time after the birth. Why is this?

It would be very difficult to carry out sexual homework properly in the late stages of pregnancy and the early stages of new parenthood. In addition, a woman's body is in an altered hormonal state during pregnancy which means that her sexual and emotional responses are altered too. For this reason, it's better to wait until your partner feels more like her old self again and the two of you have established a routine with the baby.

I am now very pregnant and really don't want sex for a while. Is it OK to say this to my husband?

It's fine provided you say it with thoughtfulness and sympathy. The last thing your husband will want at this sensitive time is to feel rejected. Try to stay intimate in ways apart from intercourse – be romantic together, kiss, cuddle, hold hands, pay each other compliments and share your hopes and fears. Be understanding if your partner wants to masturbate and, if you feel like it, offer to stimulate him to orgasm using your hands or mouth.

Is it safe to continue having sex right up to the end of pregnancy?

As is the case throughout pregnancy, the baby is cushioned and protected within the foetal sac and sex is not dangerous for either woman or baby (although you should avoid having sex after your water has broken). A very large bump can make it difficult to manoeuvre during sex and some women may prefer mutual masturbation to intercourse for the simple reason that it's easier. If the man is heavy, he should avoid lying on his partner's abdomen during sex.

Are there any sex positions to make intercourse easier towards the end of pregnancy?
Missionary position sex can become difficult from about the fourth month onwards and rear-entry, side-by-side and woman-on-top positions (if the woman has enough energy) may be more comfortable. An excellent sex position for middle pregnancy is the scissors position. The woman lies on her back and the man lies in a slanting position on top of her with one leg between hers and one leg outside of hers (hence the scissors appearance). This angles his body so that he is lying across her hips with less pressure on her abdomen. This position also makes it easy for the man to stimulate the clitoris with his fingers.

Is it true that sex at the end of pregnancy can trigger labour?
There are substances found naturally in semen that can cause uterine contractions. They are called prostaglandins, and if your partner ejaculates inside you near the end of your pregnancy it's possible that they may help to trigger labour. This will only happen, however, if your baby is almost ready to be born anyway.

casehistory

"He wants to have sex all the time – far more than he did before I was pregnant."

Jane, 26

I'm in the sixth month of pregnancy and I'm very happy about it. I love my husband Nick just as I've always done, but he isn't contented with our sex life any more. He wants to have sex all the time – far more than he did before I was pregnant. He seems very anxious and he won't take into account that my body is changing in ways I can't control. I don't have the sex drive that I did before and Nick doesn't understand this.

Nick, 26

I've always relied heavily on Jane for emotional support. I was quite depressed when we first met and our relationship has helped me get over that. As a result of this pregnancy I think Jane seems less loving than she used to be and this really upsets me. Now that she's lost interest in sex I feel as if my life is falling apart. If she doesn't love me any more I don't know what I'll do.

Anne responds:

"Nick comes from a single-parent family. His father left when he was six and Nick has had problems with low self-esteem and depression since his teens. The unborn baby feels like a rival to Nick and as a result he is very anxious – this manifests itself as a constant desire for sex. Nick needs to work on the idea that love can be shown in many ways and not just through sex. Jane, meanwhile, needs to understand the underlying motives for Nick's sexual demands and step up the amount of love, affection and reassurance that she gives him. Perhaps Nick and Jane could come to a sexual compromise that includes occasional oral sex and mutual masturbation. If Nick continues to suffer from extreme anxiety, he could ask his doctor about the possibility of taking antianxiety medication."

Will I lose my libido once I've had my baby? Pregnancy has made sex wonderful.
Every woman is different but there seems to be a natural period following childbirth, and particularly during breastfeeding, when sexual desire becomes subsumed in motherhood. It's also common to feel exhausted by the demands of caring for a small baby and this can force sex down your list of priorities. This doesn't mean that you won't want to be physically intimate with your partner but it may mean that, for a while, you just won't be so interested in sex. I believe that it takes the female body at least a year to get back to anything approaching "normal" and this includes sexual desire. Try to stay intimate with non-penetrative sex and massage.

new parenthood

How soon do most couples resume their sex life after having a baby?

The official advice in the UK is to wait for six weeks after the birth to avoid the risk of infection and allow your cervix and vagina time to heal, especially if you had an episiotomy (a cut made from the edge of the vagina to prevent tearing during delivery). Guidelines vary from country to country, however, and in France couples are advised to wait for just three weeks after childbirth before making love. You can ask your doctor for an individual recommendation, but you should definitely avoid intercourse until the flow of lochia (the vaginal discharge that occurs after delivery) has stopped.

When do I need to start using contraception again?

You should start using contraception as soon as you resume your sex life. Even if your periods haven't yet returned, you may be ovulating and this means that it's possible for you to conceive. Breastfeeding confers contraceptive protection but it isn't 100 per cent reliable, especially if you aren't breastfeeding full-time.

What sort of contraceptive should I use?

Discuss with your doctor the best type of contraceptive for you. Your choice will be influenced by factors such as whether you would like to have more children in the future and whether you are breastfeeding. While you are breastfeeding, barrier methods of contraception, such as the condom, or intrauterine methods, such as the IUD (see pages 151–153), are preferable to hormonal methods, such as the combined pill, which can interfere with milk production.

I am worried that my vagina will be slack now that I've had two children. I'm concerned about the effect this will have on sex. What can I do?

The best way to increase vaginal muscle tone is to start doing Kegel exercises (see page 67) shortly after you give birth. These strengthen the vaginal musculature so that it becomes more supple and able to hug the penis during intercourse and contract with vigour during orgasm. You simply need to isolate your pelvic floor muscles and then practise a sequence of contraction and relaxation exercises. The joy of Kegel exercises is that nobody can see you doing them. This means that you can practise them while standing at the bus stop, at work or simply at home while you are cooking.

My partner's vagina feels too tight after childbirth. I get the feeling that she is trying to "shut me out" although she insists this is not true. What's happening?

If your partner had any surgical intervention during delivery, she may have been sutured (stitched) inexpertly, thus creating problems. This is the simplest explanation, so ask your partner to have a check-up with her doctor. An alternative explanation is that your partner may indeed be too tense to allow easy sexual penetration. You could help her to overcome this by easing back into sex very gently, giving her plenty of reassurance and sympathy, and experimenting to find the most comfortable way of making love. Being supportive in other ways, such as helping at home, can relieve pressure on your partner – it's very common for women to feel over-burdened and stressed during the early months of looking after a new baby. Absolutely sperm-tight contraception will help your partner overcome anxieties about sex if she is worried about getting pregnant again.

Sex fact

The hormone oxytocin is produced during both suckling and orgasm. During breastfeeding it helps mother bond with child, and during orgasm, it helps woman bond with man.

I am embarrassed about the fact that I get turned on when I breastfeed. Is this abnormal?

No it isn't and, instead of feeling embarrassed, try owning up to your feelings so that you and your partner can have some fun and enjoyment from them. Why not incorporate a bit of "breastfeeding" into your love play? If this doesn't appeal to you, try to arrange things so that you and your partner are sometimes able to make love shortly after feeding times. It would be a great shame to give up breastfeeding simply because you couldn't accept the odd extra orgasm!

The minute I get sexually aroused, my breasts start to leak. What should I do?

Since there's not a great deal you can do to prevent this, your best option is

to accept it and incorporate it into your lovemaking. On a practical level, try dispensing with nightclothes and cover your bed with towels. If you are worried about your partner's reaction, voice your anxiety. This will give him the opportunity of saying that he doesn't mind – which he's highly likely to do. Try not to avoid lovemaking as a result of milk leakage – your partner may feel, rightly or wrongly, that he is being rejected. It's important to foster intimacy with your partner now as this can pave the way for a happy sexual relationship in the future when you have stopped breastfeeding and are less preoccupied with the immediate demands of babycare. Bear in mind that milk leakage doesn't last for ever. It occurs most commonly in the early days of breastfeeding.

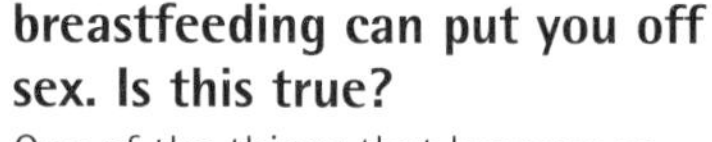

I have been breastfeeding for six months and during this time I haven't felt a shred of sexual desire. I've heard that breastfeeding can put you off sex. Is this true?

One of the things that happens as a result of breastfeeding is the generation of a hormone called prolactin, a side effect of which is reduced sexual desire. You can rest assured that when you are ready to stop breastfeeding your hormones and sex drive will get back to normal. Incidentally, although your libido may be low you are still able to experience sexual pleasure and have an orgasm – you just need more time and patience.

My sex drive hasn't returned even now I've stopped breastfeeding. What's wrong?

It's possible that you still have high prolactin levels after breastfeeding (prolactin can reduce sex drive). Consult your doctor about a blood test to assess your hormone levels. If high prolactin is confirmed you can be treated with a drug called bromocryptine which restores sex drive and hormone levels to normal.

Could our baby be adversely affected by the sound of our lovemaking? She shares our bedroom.

It's unlikely that your baby will interpret your noises as distressing. It's even possible that she might derive comfort from the routine cries and murmurs of lovemaking. Alternatively, she may perceive them as "aural wallpaper" or background static. You would be unlikely to worry in the same way about your baby hearing you snore or sneeze, so why single out sex for unnecessary concern? Also, bear in mind that some babies can sleep through any kind of noise, especially in the first deep-sleep hours of the night. If you remain concerned or inhibited by your baby's presence, try simply putting her cot in an adjacent room for the duration of your lovemaking.

My partner hasn't touched me since our baby was born. Previously he couldn't have sex often enough. What's happened?
Men, as well as women, can experience a range of emotions in response to the birth of a child. For example, your partner may be worried that life has stopped being fun or that he now has lots of responsibilities to face up to. His lack of interest in sex may reflect stress or depression. Or maybe becoming a parent has distorted his view of you and him as sexual beings? He may associate himself with his father and you with his mother – this alone could affect his sexual identity. Try parking the baby with your mother one weekend and taking him off for a child-free break. Help him confront the feelings behind his sexual denial. There's a lot going on inside him that needs to be expressed. It's in your interest to allow him to be honest about any feelings of doubt or hostility since this would allow you both to move forward.

I can't get properly aroused with my partner unless I fantasize that she is a prostitute instead of a mum. What's my problem?
What is so wrong with using fantasy to enjoy sex with your partner? You are actually coping in a very practical way with the erotic difficulties presented by your partner's new maternal status. It's not as if she is going to breastfeed and dandle babies for the rest of her days.

sextips

Sex after you've had a baby

You'll need to accept that there may be some temporary changes and disruptions to your sex life soon after the birth of your child. These tips can help you to ease back into sex:

- If you find you don't produce much natural lubricant during sexual arousal, use a jelly or cream.
- If you and your partner are exhausted from too many sleepless nights don't expect to have a normal appetite for sex. Don't be self-critical if you simply don't feel sexy.
- Rely on kissing and cuddling for intimacy.
- Have a sense of humour about sex especially when it doesn't go as planned.
- If you feel discomfort when you have intercourse, accept that it will go in time (but always consult a doctor about severe pain).
- Don't worry if you don't have an orgasm during sex. Just enjoy the sensual pleasure of making love.
- Make appointments to have sex when the baby is taking a nap. Don't believe the myth that sex has to be spontaneous to be enjoyable.
- Having a child can powerfully enhance the bond between couples – trust the fact that love will resurface later in the form of sexual connection.

My partner has suddenly started demanding sex all the time since our baby was born. I'm finding it very stressful. What can I do?
It's possible that your partner sees your baby as a demanding rival who is taking up all of your time and attention. This kind of reaction is particularly common in men who suffered from parental deprivation or had to compete hard for attention in infancy and childhood. Although jealous responses in adulthood may seem inappropriate they are deeply ingrained and hard to shake off. Your partner needs your reassurance – the first thing you can do is show him lots of attention in ways other than sex. Cuddle him and tell him how much you love him. Second, be firm about inconsiderate demands for sex. You could say: "I'd love to, but not right now – shall we make a date for later?" Third, help him develop a relationship with his baby. The more he treats the baby as a person instead of as a symbol of his own deprivation, the sooner he will stop seeing it as a rival.

Now we're parents it's rare to find the time or opportunity to make love. What can we do?
Many other parents will sympathize with you. Try following the advice for overworked couples on page 14.

are you supportive?

Having children can take relationships into a new dimension – one in which support skills are vital. Some people are naturally good at anticipating and caring for a partner's needs. Others have to work at it.

Your partner is feeling self-conscious in bed because he/she has put on weight. Do you:

- [ ] A Kiss him/her from head to toe to reassure him/her?
- [ ] B Say you still find him/her as sexy as ever?
- [ ] C Say you don't mind the extra weight?

Your partner has problems at work and comes home stressed and tense. Do you:

- [ ] A Run a hot bath and wash his/her back while he/she tells you all about it?
- [ ] B Offer to discuss the problems?
- [ ] C Leave him/her alone?

You don't enjoy your partner's favourite sex position. Do you:

- [ ] A Indulge him/her anyway?
- [ ] B Give your partner what he/she wants sometimes?
- [ ] C Rule out that position except on rare occasions?

You partner is having difficulties giving up smoking. Do you:

- [ ] A Give him/her a treat at the end of every successful week of quitting?
- [ ] B Keep asking him/her how it's going?
- [ ] C Stay detached – this is his/her personal struggle of willpower?

Your partner says that he/she is worried that you fancy a mutual friend. Do you:

- [ ] A Be reassuring and insist that your partner is the only person for you?
- [ ] B Tell him/her not to be ridiculous, there's nothing to be worried about?
- [ ] C Secretly enjoy his/her anxiety - it's flattering?

Your partner has had a low sex drive of late. Do you:

- [ ] A Demonstrate your love with soft, sensual caresses and see how your partner responds over time?
- [ ] B Gently broach the subject of sex and see if your partner wants to talk about it?
- [ ] C Feel rejected and tell your partner how upset you are?

Your partner is physically exhausted but you're in the mood for going out. Do you:

☐ A Give him/her a long and soothing massage and suggest an early night – going out can wait?

☐ B Stay in with your partner but feel disappointed?

☐ C Phone round to see if any one else is free to go out?

Your partner likes to celebrate your anniversary but how often do you remember the day?

☐ A Always – you like to arrange a surprise.

☐ B Most of the time – you usually have dinner together.

☐ C Rarely – you usually need a reminder.

Your partner is having problems reaching orgasm. Do you:

☐ A Find solutions together – physically and emotionally?

☐ B Tell your partner you'll be patient and hope that things work out?

☐ C Find it difficult to talk about?

Your partner has been withdrawn recently. Do you:

☐ A Be extra attentive and make time to listen to him/her?

☐ B Ask him/her what the problem is?

☐ C Ignore it and hope he/she snaps out of it?

Your partner has had a big family argument. Do you:

☐ A Listen sympathetically and suggest practical ways in which you can help?

☐ B Listen impartially?

☐ C Keep out of it?

Your partner rushes through foreplay too quickly for you. Do you:

☐ A Lead by example by spending a long time stimulating and caressing various parts of his/her body?

☐ B Ask him/her to slow down a bit?

☐ C Complain that he/she is too quick for you?

If you want sex but your partner doesn't, do you:

☐ A Cuddle up and enjoy an early night just holding each other?

☐ B Cuddle up but encourage your partner to change his/her mind?

☐ C Lie on your side of the bed feeling a bit put out?

ANSWERS

Mostly As You are a very supportive lover. You have a healthy overview of your relationship and are there for your partner when he/she needs it. You express your caring attitude both sexually and verbally. This makes for a happy relationship in which your partner can feel safe, secure and confident. Just one word of caution – although it's great to be so supportive, make sure that your own needs don't get neglected.

Mostly Bs You care a great deal about your partner and take an interest in any problem that your partner may be experiencing. You are ready and willing to show your support, although sometimes your partner might appreciate it if you went a bit further with your actions. A little extra effort would prove to him/her that your relationship matters a great deal to you and that difficulties can be overcome together.

Mostly Cs Although I've no doubt that you love your partner, you may not be as tapped into his/her needs as you could be. Try to be sensitive to any problems that your partner is experiencing. It may be that you are reluctant to acknowledge that there are problems, or you lack confidence in your abilities to deal with them. Or maybe you don't realize that your occasional non-committal behaviour can be construed as apathy or indifference. Don't be afraid to show your partner how much you care – your relationship will be the stronger for it.

questioning your sexuality

Some people feel sure of their sexuality – gay or straight – from childhood or adolescence. Others take longer and may not come to terms with their sexual orientation until later on in life. Some people need a period of experimentation to discover themselves.

exploring sexuality

Is it true that no-one is 100 per cent gay or straight?
The famous sex researcher Alfred Kinsey suggested that, on his Kinsey scale of sex orientation, sexuality could be gauged at anything ranging from pure heterosexuality through bisexuality to pure homosexuality. By this reckoning, then, there are indeed people who are 100 per cent homosexual or heterosexual.

Is it OK to experiment with both sexes before I make up my mind about my sexuality?
Yes, but before you embark on serious sexual experimentation it's worth analyzing your feelings so that you can avoid hurting other people or getting hurt yourself. Are you intrigued by the idea of gay sex? Do you feel like you're missing out on a sexual trend? Does gay sex seem like a tempting escape route from unsuccessful straight relationships? Or do you have genuine and long-standing feelings of attraction to members of your own sex? Be clear about your motives before you start and bear in mind that there are some times of life, such as adolescence or relationship breakdown, when your sexual motives can be muddled.

How do you know if you're gay?
Some people say that they just know instinctively that they are gay. These people usually have overwhelming feelings of sexual attraction to the same gender while being sexually indifferent to or put off by the idea of sex with the opposite gender. Other people find out that they are gay by a process of trial and error.

How does gay sex differ from straight sex apart from the fact that there's no penis/vagina intercourse?
Obviously, sex acts between gay men are likely to be very penis oriented and lesbian sex acts are likely to focus on the clitoris. However, in the course of their research, sex therapists Masters and Johnson noticed another major difference between gay and straight sex. Gay men were observed to spend hours stimulating many different areas of the body with a special emphasis on the nipples. As a result of this long, sensual build up, their orgasmic experience appeared to be powerful and intense. In comparison, straight couples were more perfunctory when it came to all-over body attention and, as a result, orgasm was thought to be less intense.

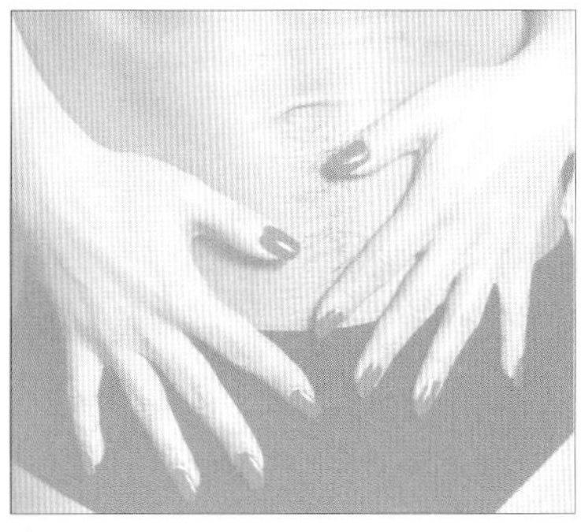

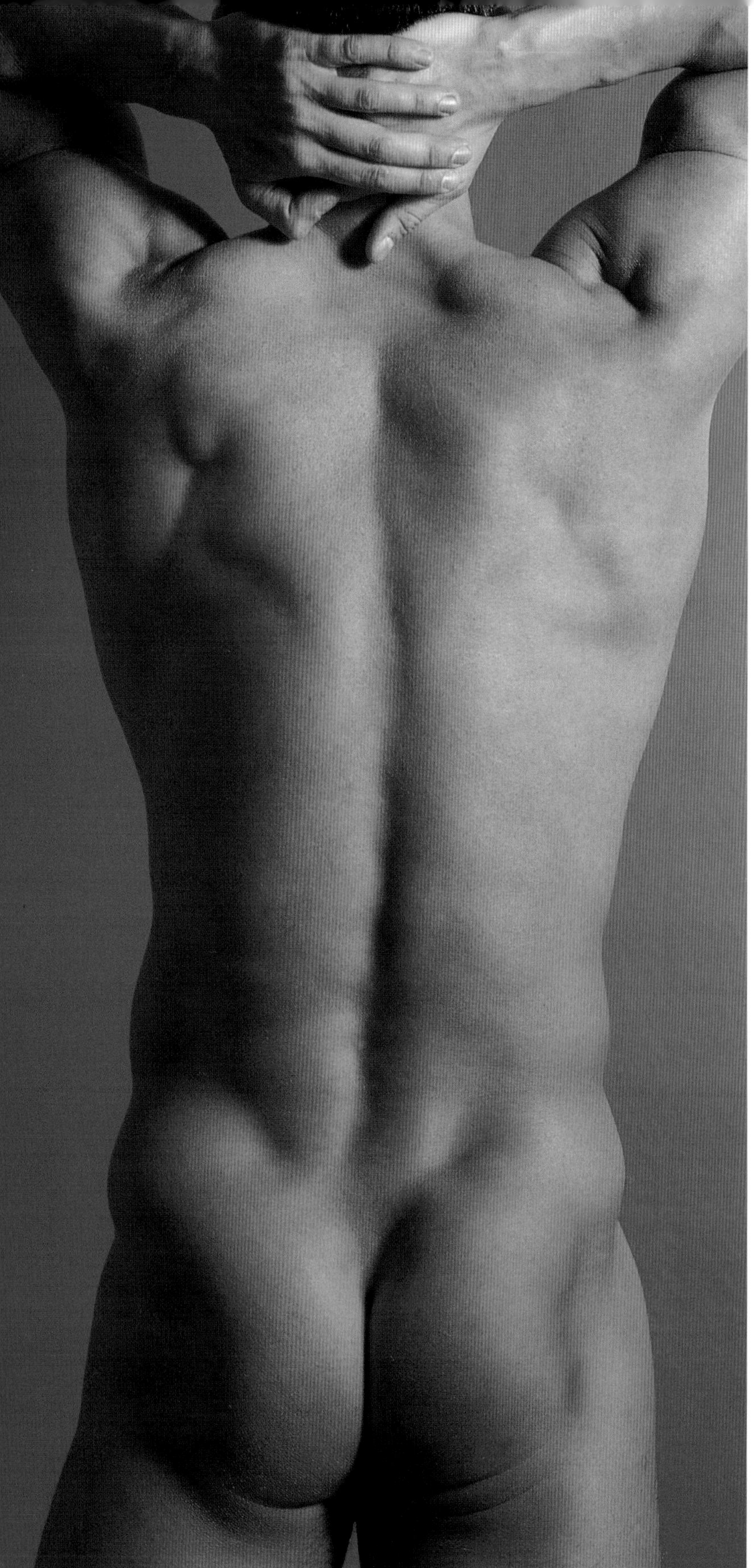

I have fantasies about same-sex friends. Does this mean that I'm gay or bisexual?
It may do, but it could also mean that you have an active sexual imagination. You can have fantasies about anyone without this necessarily being a reflection on your real sexual desires or gender preferences. The research of sex therapists Masters and Johnson revealed that some gay men fantasize about relationships with heterosexual women. Despite their fantasies, these men remained firmly homosexual.

I'm depressed because I think I might be gay. What can I do?
You can tackle your depression using a combination of talking therapy and drug treatment – consult your doctor about both. What you cannot do, however, is eliminate the possibility of homosexuality – just as some of us are straight, some of us are gay. There is no "cure" for homosexuality because, quite simply, it isn't something that needs to be cured. The passage of time will reveal whether you really are gay. If you are, the best thing that you can do is to embrace your sexuality as a positive part of your identity. Talk things through with a gay counsellor to find out what is right for you.

I am 29 and a happily married mother of two but I've recently become extremely attracted to another woman. What does this mean?
It could mean any number of things ranging from a temporary infatuation to the desire to be intimate with someone you respect and admire, to the discovery of your true bisexual or lesbian sexuality. Not all women discover their true sexual identity as teenagers. There are many married

women for whom time and the security of marriage permit the gradual discovery of lesbian feelings. Until you understand your feelings better it might be a good idea to wait before you make any major lifestyle changes.

I believe that I'm a bisexual man but my gay friends say that I'm just sitting on the fence. Could they be right?
Research shows that, rather than being a sexual compromise, bisexuality is a genuine and legitimate sexual choice. Sex therapists Masters' and Johnson's research on homosexuality reveals a distinct group of bisexuals, many of whom are rated as absolutely 50/50 in their sexual orientation. In my opinion, anyone with an active sexual interest in both sexes could be considered bisexual.

I think that I might be gay but I've never had a relationship. How do I go about finding one?
If you live in an isolated country community or a small town this can be difficult. One way of making contact with other gay people is to respond to classified advertisements in magazines and newspapers (or advertise yourself). Alternatively, you could look at gay websites on the Internet or seek advice from a gay telephone helpline. Many gay men and women choose to live in cities because this makes socializing so much easier. Most cities have an active gay scene consisting of clubs, bars and cafes.

If a man enjoys wearing female clothes, does it make him gay?
No. Many transvestites (cross-dressers) are heterosexual men who are happy with their sexuality but who have a fetish for women's clothing. Transvestite men are often motivated by a powerful erotic association made in childhood between feminine clothing and sexual arousal. Some transvestites get comfort and relaxation from cross-dressing because they shed the perceived burdens and responsibilities of manhood along with male attire. Some transvestite men cross-dress openly in front of their wife or girlfriend, others do it in secret.

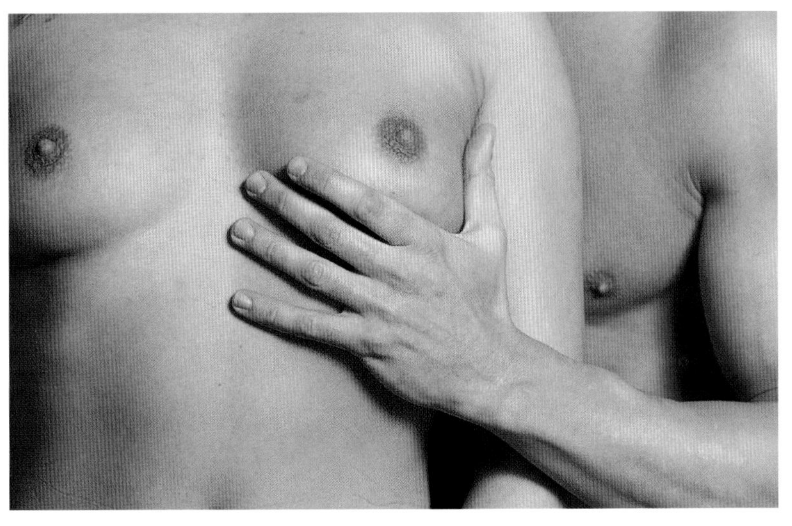

What does it mean if...
my partner has had a homosexual experience in the past?

- He or she was going through a period of sexual experimentation – as many people do – and has now chosen to live a heterosexual lifestyle and have straight relationships.
- He or she has bisexual tendencies but has a far greater preference for the opposite sex and is perfectly able to settle down in a straight relationship.
- He or she is bisexual and can be equally attracted to both sexes. Again, this doesn't preclude a committed sexual relationship with you.

I've been a closet cross-dresser for several years. Should I tell my wife?
You need to consider the following three things:

- Is your compulsion to cross-dress getting unavoidably stronger so that it's likely that your wife could find out by accident?
- Is your wife in any way receptive to conversation on the subject?
- What do you stand to lose if you tell her and things go wrong?

If you decide to go ahead and confess, you will need to reassure your wife that you remain heterosexual and that you still find her sexually attractive (presuming this is true). She will definitely need this kind of reassurance. Please also bear in mind that, in the event of separation and divorce, the courts are likely to be prejudiced against a cross-dresser when it comes to deciding on the custody of any children you have.

are you heterosexual?

Many people have natural feelings of curiosity about sex with a person of the same gender – but some feel more inclined to act upon this curiosity than others.

Have you ever had a same-sex kiss?

- A Yes.
- B Once, but only for a laugh.
- C Never.

Did you ever have a crush on a teacher of your own sex?

- A Yes, definitely.
- B Possibly, but you are not sure whether or not your feelings were sexual.
- C Certainly not.

Your partner suggests having a threesome with someone of your sex. Do you:

- A Jump at the chance?
- B Think it might be interesting?
- C Think it's a bad idea and say no?

On a slightly drunken night out a friend bets you that you won't snog your best (same-sex) friend. Do you:

- A Enjoy the snog and take the money?
- B Snog your friend, but feel a bit weird about it?
- C Lose the bet?

There is a sexy actor (of your own sex) in a film on TV. Do you:

- A Wait eagerly for the sex scenes?
- B Enjoy the film a bit more as a result?
- C Admire him/her dispassionately?

A hen/stag party enters the pub you're in and there's a stripper of your sex. Do you:

- A Enjoy the act and appreciate the stripper's body?
- B Watch with curiosity?
- C Feel embarrassed or look away?

You find a new same-sex work colleague attractive. Do you:

- ☐ A Flirt openly?
- ☐ B Admire from afar?
- ☐ C Feel sure that your feelings are non-sexual?

A gay/lesbian sex scene pops up on TV. Do you:

- ☐ A Suddenly pay attention?
- ☐ B Watch with some interest?
- ☐ C Switch channels?

In a club, a person of the same sex flirts with you. Do you feel:

- ☐ A Interested and open to suggestion?
- ☐ B Flattered but nervous?
- ☐ C Unnerved?

When you think of gay sex do you think:

- ☐ A It's perfectly natural?
- ☐ B It works for some people?
- ☐ C It's difficult to understand why two people of the same sex would be attracted to one another?

A same-sex friend is very tactile with you. Do you:

- ☐ A Respond to the touch and wonder whether it's intended to be provocative?
- ☐ B Enjoy his/her friendly style?
- ☐ C Wish he/she would stop?

A same-sex friend is wearing a sexy new outfit. Do you:

- ☐ A Openly admire him/her?
- ☐ B Admire him/her without saying anything?
- ☐ C Not really notice?

A same-sex friend has had a sexy dream about you. Do you:

- ☐ A Feel very excited?
- ☐ B Avoid reading too much into it?
- ☐ C Find this off-putting?

When you are in the showers at the gym, do you:

- ☐ A Peek at the naked bodies with appreciation?
- ☐ B Notice the nudity, but don't linger?
- ☐ C Not really notice – nudity is no big deal?

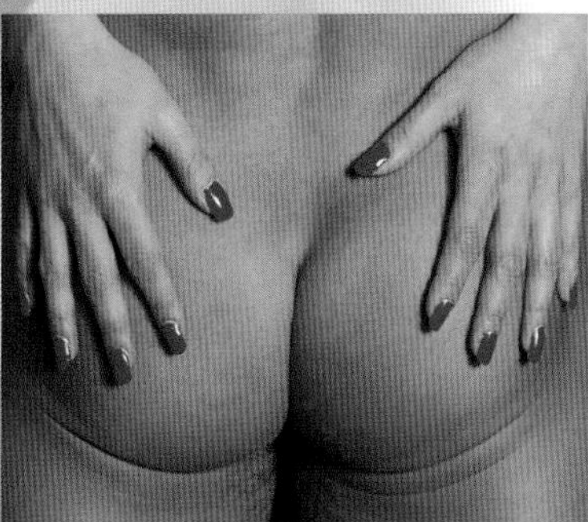

ANSWERS

Mostly As You are uninhibited about your sexuality and when you fancy someone of the same sex you don't mind showing it. You may already have decided that you are bisexual or you may be one of those people who don't feel the need to label your sexuality in any formal way – sometimes you fancy your own sex and sometimes you don't. Carry on enjoying this open approach to sex but take care not to get hurt – not everyone is as sexually liberated as you are.

Mostly Bs Like many people you probably have a latent curiosity about gay sex that isn't quite compelling enough to act upon. If a situation presented itself and you were in the mood, you might consider experimenting, but gay sexual experiences aren't something that you'd actively seek out. You probably find it stimulating enough to have the occasional gay fantasy. On the other hand, if you want to explore your sexuality more actively, you should feel free to do so.

Mostly Cs You have a very clear view of your sexuality and homosexual encounters don't have a role to play in your sex life. Perhaps you have questioned your sexuality in the past and made up your mind that you are very definitely straight or perhaps same-sex sex has never even occurred to you. It's fine to be so resolved about your sexuality – you're simply making the choices that are right for you while respecting the choices of others.

your sexual health

As individuals we now have greater knowledge than ever about fertility and sexual health. This means we can all take responsibility for preventing both unwanted pregnancy and sexually transmitted infections (STIs).

contraception

Which contraceptive is most likely to prevent pregnancy?
Hormonal methods of contraception, such as the combined pill, are the most effective forms of birth control. Assuming it is used correctly, the combined pill is 99 per cent effective. It contains the hormones oestrogen and progestogen (a synthetic version of the natural hormone progesterone) and works by preventing ovulation in each menstrual cycle. Other hormonal methods of contraception include implants and injections that are nearly 100 per cent effective (consult your doctor about the availability and suitability of these methods). The intrauterine device (IUD) is also very effective (98 to 99 per cent). It works by preventing the implantation of a fertilized egg into the wall of the uterus. Another type of IUD, known as the intrauterine system (IUS), is even more effective (nearly 100 per cent) as it is impregnated with progestogen, which makes fertilization less likely in the first place. One disadvantage of hormonal methods of contraception is that, although they are effective at preventing pregnancy, they don't protect you from STIs.

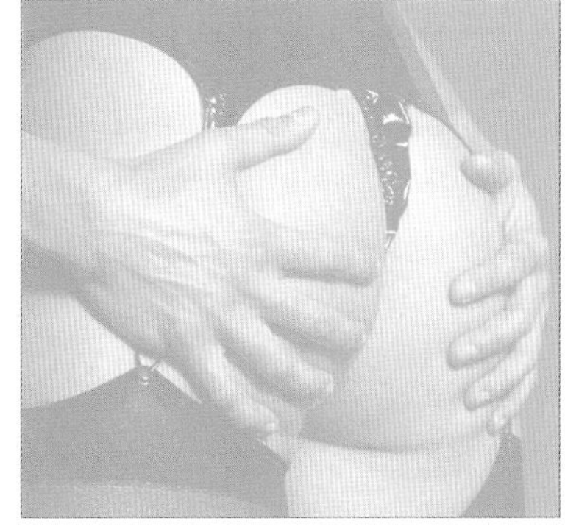

I've been taking the pill for years and I'm getting tired of taking hormones every day. What are my other options, bearing in mind that my partner doesn't like condoms?
A good alternative to hormonal contraceptives are barrier methods such as the diaphragm and female condom. The advantages of a diaphragm are that you insert it only when you want to have sex; neither you or your partner are aware of it during lovemaking; and it poses few long-term risks to health. Initially a diaphragm must be fitted by a medical professional so that you get the right size for your body. You should always use spermicide with a diaphragm.

The advantages of the female condom are that you can buy it over the counter, you can insert it any time prior to sex and remove it any time afterwards. The female condom is more expensive than other types of contraception and it's important that you use it correctly, making sure, for example, that the man's penis enters the condom and doesn't slip between the condom and vagina.

Other contraceptive options include the IUD and natural family planning, but the suitability of both of these should be discussed with your doctor.

A friend told me that I can't take the pill because I'm over 35 and I smoke cigarettes. Is this true?

The combined effect of smoking, taking the pill and being over 35 is to increase your risk of thrombosis (blood clotting) and high blood pressure, both of which can seriously endanger your health. However, this only applies to the combined pill and not to the progestogen-only pill (POP). If you would like to take the POP, you should discuss it, together with other options, with your doctor.

I don't have a regular sexual partner and when I do sleep with someone it's essential that I don't get pregnant. What contraceptive should I use?

If you have casual sex it's important that you protect yourself against sexually transmitted infections as well as against pregnancy. For this reason you should use a male or female condom every time you have intercourse. Condoms are a reliable form of contraceptive but if you want to make absolutely sure that you don't become pregnant, you could consider

sextips

The main types of contraception

The main types of contraception are barrier methods such as condoms, caps and diaphragms, hormonal methods such as pills, implants and injections, and mechanical methods such as the intrauterine device. Discuss with a doctor or family planning specialist which method is best suited to your needs and lifestyle:

- Male condom – this is the most popular method of contraception and consists of a sheath made of latex or polyurethane that is unrolled along the man's penis before intercourse and disposed of afterwards. Used correctly, condoms are 98 per cent effective.

- Female condom – this is a loose tube-shaped device that is inserted into the woman's vagina before intercourse and disposed of afterwards. It is 95 per cent effective.

- Combined pill – this is the main type of contraceptive pill and it contains the hormones progestogen and oestrogen. Taken correctly it is 99 per cent effective.

- Progestogen-only pill or "mini-pill" – this is suitable for smokers, women over 40 and those who cannot take oestrogen. It is slightly less effective than the combined pill.

- Intrauterine device (IUD) – this is a small plastic device wrapped in thin copper wire that is inserted into the uterus by a doctor and provides contraceptive protection (99 per cent effectiveness) for several years. One type of IUD, known as the intrauterine system (IUS), releases progestogen into a woman's body and is almost 100 per cent effective.

- Diaphragm and cap – rubber devices that cover a woman's cervix. They are filled with spermicide and inserted prior to intercourse then extracted several hours afterwards. Used correctly they are 92–96 per cent effective.

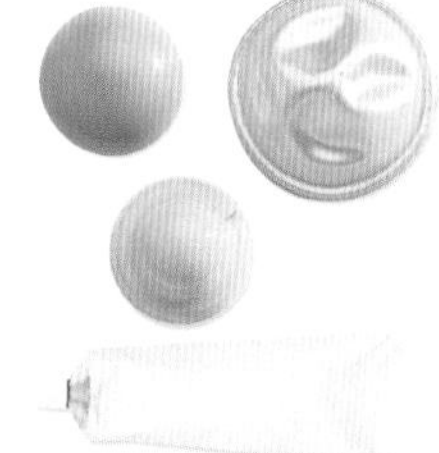

- Other hormonal methods – injections and implants are extremely effective contraceptive methods (over 99 per cent) but they are less popular than hormones taken in pill form. They must be administered by a doctor.

also using a back-up contraceptive such as the pill. Weigh up the advantages and disadvantages of this with your doctor.

I'm having my third child soon and I'm pretty sure I don't want any more. What's the best method of contraception for after my baby is born?
Many women who have completed their families choose to use the IUD or IUS because it offers a long-term contraceptive method that can be virtually forgotten about once it is in place. Some women choose sterilization as a permanent method of contraception but, since this is difficult or impossible to reverse, you need to be absolutely sure that you don't want any more children. Bear in mind that, if you are breastfeeding, some methods of contraception, such as the combined pill, are not suitable.

I like the idea of controlling my fertility naturally but how reliable is this and which are the best methods?
Natural birth control has a much higher failure rate than any other contraceptive method. This failure rate varies according to which method is used but it can be as high as 30 per cent. The most ineffective method is the withdrawal method (also known as coitus interruptus) in which the man pulls out of the woman's vagina just before he ejaculates. The key to successful natural birth control is a high level of familiarity with your menstrual cycle so that you can identify ovulation. Then you abstain from sex for several days before and after ovulation (alternatively, you can use a barrier contraceptive, such as a condom, during this time). Drug companies have created devices to make ovulation detection easier. One such device consists of an electronic monitor that reads the hormone levels in your urine and tells you the days on which you are fertile. Each day the monitor shows a green or a red light indicating whether or not it is safe to have unprotected sex.

How does the morning-after pill work?
The morning-after or "post-coital" pill is a form of emergency contraception that can be taken at any time up to 72 hours after you have had unprotected sex. It introduces a large dose of hormones into the woman's body, and this prevents the implantation of a fertilized egg in her uterus should conception have taken place.

Another form of emergency contraception is the IUD, which can be fitted by a doctor up to five days after unprotected sex. Again, this works by preventing the implantation of a fertilized egg in the uterus.

casehistory

"I'm afraid to let my husband come near me."

Aileen, 33

I seem to be one of those women who gets pregnant by just being breathed upon. You name it, I've tried it when it comes to contraception. I've managed to get pregnant once when using the diaphragm, twice using condoms and once with an IUD fitted. As a result, I've now got four children and a huge complex about having sex. I'm afraid to let my husband come near me. This is very hard on him and I'm afraid that he will become resentful and turn away from me. On the few occasions when we do make love I am so uptight and tense that I never enjoy it or get anywhere close to orgasm.

Anne responds:

"Anxiety about conceiving can be one of the biggest killers of sexual desire and enjoyment. Often a problem concerning birth control surfaces disguised as a sex problem – typically the woman is anxious and can no longer get aroused but can't clearly isolate the underlying reason for this. In Aileen's case the solution seems relatively easy. Either her partner could opt for a vasectomy or she could get a sterilization. The operation involves microsurgery (which leaves minimal scarring) and then the surgeon will cauterize or use clips or rings to block the fallopian tubes. Once the tubes are blocked ova can no longer travel along them and conception cannot therefore take place."

safer sex

What are the main dangers of unprotected sex?

If you don't practise safer sex, the main dangers are catching HIV (human immunodeficiency virus) and other sexually transmitted infections (STIs) such as genital warts, herpes, gonorrhoea, syphilis, chlamydia, trichomoniasis and hepatitis B. Viral STIs such as HIV and herpes can only be managed rather than cured. Some STIs can cause long-term damage to your health – chlamydia, for example, can result in complications that lead to infertility. There is also the danger that unprotected sex will lead to unwanted pregnancy.

What does safer sex involve?

The term "safer sex" refers to sexual practises that carry a relatively low risk of transmitting HIV. Safer sex also minimizes your risk of catching other STIs. Safer sex is designed to prevent the exchange of partners' body fluids during sex – this is the main way in which HIV is transmitted. Two of the most important safer sex practices are using a condom during penetrative sex (anal or vaginal) and having sex that is non-penetrative.

What are safe alternatives to intercourse?

Fantasy and masturbation are two safe forms of non-penetrative sex – you and your partner can take it in turns to describe your sexual fantasies while you both masturbate each other. You can use vibrators on each other, providing you don't share them. You can also have oral sex using a condom or a latex barrier. Whole body massage is another safe form of sexual intimacy providing you avoid any exchange of bodily fluids – for example, you should avoid ejaculating onto an area of broken skin.

I know I should have safer sex by wearing a condom but I find I don't get enough stimulation on my penis. What should I do?

First, try experimenting with different brands of condoms. If traditional latex condoms don't work for you, try polyurethane condoms which are much finer. You could also discuss with your partner the option of using female condoms. Another tip is to make sure that you have enough erotic foreplay so that you are very aroused before you put a condom on.

My partner's penis goes a bit limp when I put a condom on him. What am I doing wrong?

This is quite common – the best way to overcome it is to make condoms sexy. Start with a genital massage that turns into masturbation. Then, while masturbating your partner's penis with one hand, slip the rolled-up condom onto the top of the penis with the other (remember to squeeze air out of the tip). Continue to masturbate him as you roll the condom down the shaft of his penis. Alternatively, pop the condom in your mouth and put it on him as you give him oral sex – a trick used by Thai prostitutes.

If my partner and I are both virgins we don't need to use condoms, do we?

If you're sure that you have not been exposed to HIV in ways other than sex, then condoms may not

sextips

Putting on a condom

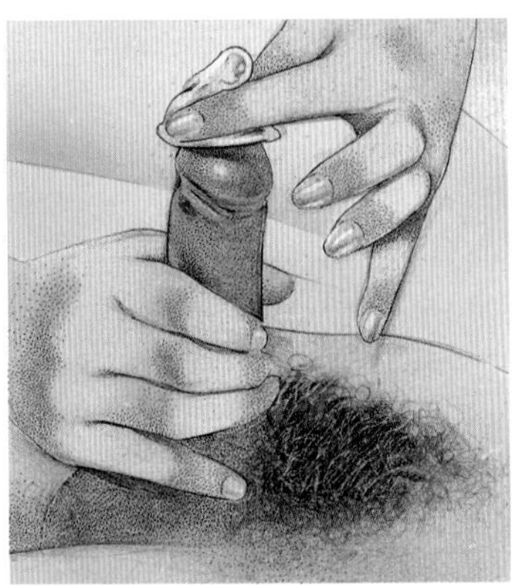

1. Rest the unrolled condom on the tip of the penis. Pinch the top of the condom to squeeze the air out.

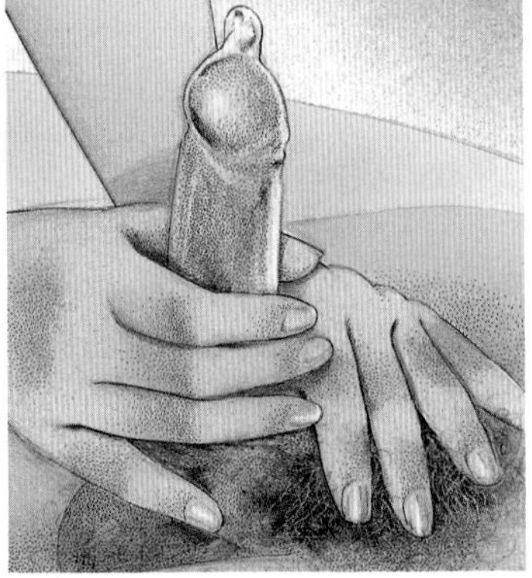

2. Unroll the condom down the length of the shaft so that the rim sits near the base of the penis.

be essential. Non-sexual ways of being infected with HIV include receiving an infected blood transfusion or being injected with a contaminated needle (perhaps through intravenous drug use). Babies may be infected by an HIV-positive mother before or during birth or as a result of breastfeeding. Assuming that neither of you is infected with HIV, you still need to consider the risk of unwanted pregnancy and discuss your birth control options with your doctor. And you also need to make sure that both of you are going to be completely monogamous.

How do I broach the subject of condoms with a new partner?

You could say something along these lines: "I really only feel safe having sex if we use a condom. How about you?" If, after a carefully worded discussion, your new partner refuses to use condoms, you could say: "I like you and I'd love to go to bed with you, but I feel so strongly about safer sex that I'm going to have to call it a day. But why don't we try to stay friends?"

How safe is oral sex?

It's not entirely safe because semen and vaginal fluids come into contact with the skin and mucous membranes of the mouth. If these mucous membranes are broken or ulcerated in some way (by cold sores or bleeding gums, for example), HIV can enter the body via infected semen or vaginal fluid. You can make oral sex safer by using a condom during fellatio and a latex barrier during cunnilingus.

Is mutual masturbation safe?

This should be risk free providing all of the following apply:

- Neither of you have cuts, sores or abrasions on your hands and fingers.
- Neither of you have cuts, sores or abrasions on your genitals.
- No vaginal fluids or semen come into contact with broken skin anywhere on your body.

Isn't it just gay men who get infected with HIV?

Not at all. This idea arose in Western countries because the first cases of HIV and AIDS to be diagnosed in the early 1980s were among homosexual men in the United States. Since then HIV has affected both the heterosexual and homosexual community. In Africa, where millions of people are infected, the majority of sufferers are heterosexual.

indetail

Sex and HIV transmission

Different sexual acts involve different degrees of risk. To be completely safe you need to avoid any exchange of body fluids.

Practices that involve risk:

- Vaginal sexual intercourse without a condom.
- Anal intercourse with or without a suitable condom.
- Any sexual activity that draws blood, whether accidentally or deliberately.
- Sharing penetrative sex aids such as vibrators.
- Unprotected fellatio, especially to climax.
- Anal licking or kissing.
- Inserting fingers or hands into the anus.
- Mouth-to-mouth kissing if either partner has bleeding gums/cold sores.

Less risky practices:

- Vaginal intercourse with a condom.
- Sexual activities that include urination.
- Cunnilingus using a latex barrier.
- Fellatio using a condom.

No risk practices:

- Dry kissing.
- Semen or vaginal fluids coming into contact with intact skin.
- Self-masturbation.
- Cuddling and caressing.

sexually transmitted infections (STIs)

I'm very nervous about catching a sexual disease. How can I protect myself?

The only fail-safe method of protection is to refrain from sexual contact, but most people find this less than ideal. Your best bet is to stick to sex with a single partner who, to the best of your knowledge, is free from infection. Or you should have safer sex (see pages 154–155), which means using condoms every time you have sex (or having non-penetrative sex). You should be vigilant about any warning signs of infection in a partner, such as an unusual discharge or odour, or genital sores, bumps or rashes – if you have any doubts, don't have sex. Of course, you can also tackle the subject directly by asking questions of a potential partner.

How can I raise the subject of sexual health with my new boyfriend?

One way of getting a partner to reveal their sexual health history is to reveal your own. For example, you could say: "I feel I ought to mention that I suffer from vaginal thrush from time to time. I'm fine at the moment and it's not likely to affect you." Then you could go on to say: "How about you?" Hopefully, a candid approach will allow an equally candid response.

How will I know if I've caught a sexually transmitted infection?

Signs of common STIs include a discharge from the vagina or penis; lumps, sores, ulcers or growths anywhere around the genitals, perineum and anus; painful urination; and sometimes fever. Some STIs, such as chlamydia and gonorrhoea, are difficult to detect because they may cause very mild symptoms or no symptoms at all. This is why sexual health screening can be important even when you don't have any obvious signs of a STI.

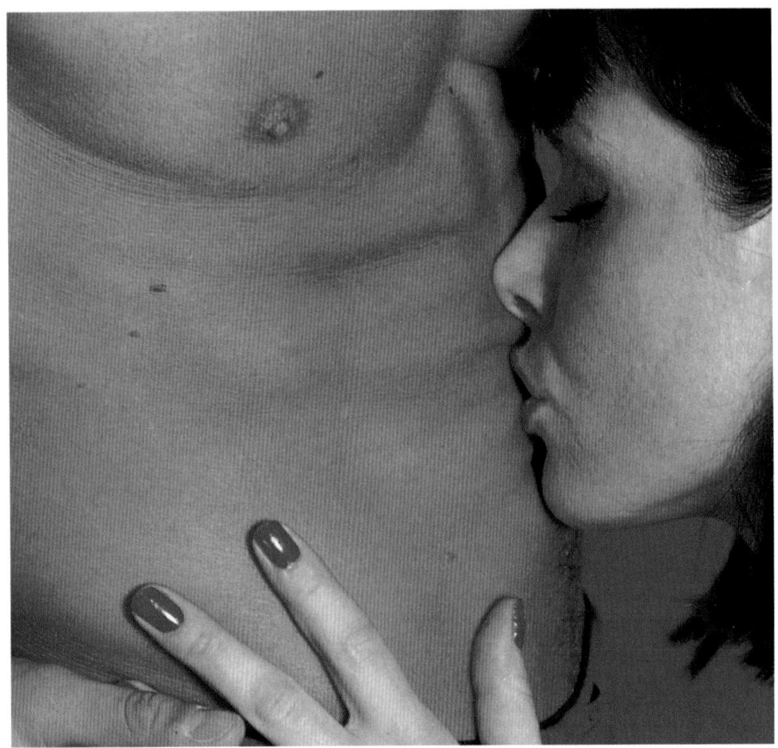

What should I do if I've slept with someone who I think has a STI?

You should seek medical help from a doctor or you can go to the STI or genito-urinary clinic of your nearest hospital. It's very important to be checked out, even if it turns that you haven't been infected. Undiagnosed and untreated STIs can be passed on to other sexual partners and can result in health complications for both you and others. To give just one example, some types of genital wart virus are associated with an increased risk of cervical cancer (it is recommended that any woman who has been infected with the genital wart virus should have an annual smear test).

Can STIs get better without medical help?

Most don't. And it would be very unwise to leave a STI untreated because it may lead to further illness. For example, untreated chlamydia in women can sometimes result in an infection of the fallopian tubes that leads to infertility problems.

What happens at a STI clinic?

You will be offered sexual health screening that will involve a variety of tests. You will be treated with complete discretion and your visit can remain confidential if you choose. The tests that you are offered may include an examination of the genital, pubic and anal areas, taking swabs from the genitals, and blood tests. All the doctors in a STI clinic are specialists in sexual medicine – as a result they can make an accurate diagnosis and offer you the latest treatments and advice. You may have to wait for the results of some tests and you should be prepared to return to the clinic for a follow-up check.

Can you get a STI without actually having sex?

Occasionally. Intimate body contact without actual intercourse can be enough to transmit some STIs, such as pubic lice. Gonorrhoea is sometimes passed on by deep kissing, but this is very rare.

Can you catch STIs from towels or toilet seats?

Trichomoniasis can sometimes be transmitted via moist objects such as towels and flannels. This is because *Trichomonas vaginalis* is a single-celled organism or parasite that can survive outside the body in moist places for several hours. If you have trichomoniasis, don't share towels and flannels and do your laundry regularly. Pubic lice can survive in environments such as bedding and clothing for up to 24 hours, so, again, if you are infected make sure your personal and domestic hygiene is thorough. Most STIs, however, are not passed on by casual, non-sexual contact. The usual routes of transmission are oral, anal or vaginal sex, kissing or skin-to-skin contact with an infected person. Some STIs, such as hepatitis B and HIV, can be passed on by blood transfusions, contaminated medical instruments or needles used by intravenous drug users.

indetail

Common sexually transmitted infections

These are some of the most common STIs:

HIV – this is the virus that leads to AIDS (acquired immunodeficiency syndrome). Untreated, HIV attacks the immune system to the point where the body becomes vulnerable to a range of possibly fatal opportunistic infections. Although there is no absolute cure for HIV, combinations of drugs have been developed that help sufferers to manage the virus.

Genital warts – these start as tiny hard lumps in or around the genitals and anus. They can grow rapidly and become cauliflower-like in appearance. A doctor can "burn off" the warts using acid preparations, laser therapy or other techniques.

Genital herpes – these are similar to the cold sores that some people get on the mouth and lips. The first attack of genital herpes is generally the worst and may be accompanied by fever and swollen lymph glands. Although there is no complete cure herpes symptoms can be managed with the prescription drug acyclovir.

Gonorrhoea – in men the signs are a thick, milky discharge and a burning sensation while urinating. Women may have a yellow discharge or remain symptomless. Treatment is with a high dose of penicillin.

Syphilis – the first symptom is a painless sore or ulcer, usually around the genital area. This disappears and then the disease moves into a secondary and tertiary phase, both of which can affect the health of the entire body. This is why it is very important to catch syphilis in its early stages when it can easily be treated with penicillin.

Chlamydia – in women this is usually symptomless (although it can go on to cause pelvic inflammatory disease). Men may have a burning pain when urinating, and a discharge from this penis. This is also known as non-specific urethritis (NSU). Treatment is with antibiotics.

Trichomoniasis – this is caused by a parasite and the main symptom in women is a foul-smelling, greenish-yellow discharge. Men may not have any symptoms beyond mild irritation of the urethra. Treatment is with antibiotics.

Pubic lice – these tiny insects infest the pubic area where they lay their eggs. Lice bites cause intense itching. Treatment is with special shampoos and lotions.

Bacterial vaginosis or vaginitis – this is a common infection in women – it is usually caused by *Gardnerella* bacteria and can result from poor personal hygiene. The main symptom is a thin, grey, fishy-smelling discharge. Treatment is with an antibiotic called metronidazole.

emotionaltips

Telling a partner that you've got a STI

There is no easy way to tell a current sexual partner that you've caught a STI, but it's better to be straightforward and honest from the outset.

- Pave the way to disclosure by saying: "I feel really bad about having to say this" or "I've been really worried about something and I think I should tell you what it is".
- When possible, stress that the problem can be cleared up or alleviated with only a couple of visits to a clinic.
- Don't expect to receive sympathy for your own condition.
- Make sure you are as informed as possible. Be prepared to answer lots of questions both about the sexual activities that led to the STI and the STI itself.
- If your partner wants to deny the possibility that he/she may be infected, gently point out that the best way to feel confident about sexual health is to have proof of it. Say that STIs are sometimes symptomless and can become more serious if they are left untreated.
- Offer reassurance that STI clinics respect confidentiality.
- Don't have sex with your partner until you have both been properly diagnosed and treated.

I have a vaginal discharge. How do I know if this is normal or a sign that something's wrong?
Normal vaginal secretions tend to fluctuate with the menstrual cycle. On most days the secretion is whitish and smells fresh and slightly sweet. Around the time of ovulation, it becomes transparent and looks a little like raw egg white. Towards the beginning of a period it may become slightly yellow and smell strong (but not unpleasant). Women who are pregnant or take the contraceptive pill may notice an increase in their vaginal secretions – this is also normal.

An abnormal vaginal discharge is discoloured, foul-smelling, unusual in texture or accompanied by itchiness, soreness or pain. In particular, look out for a discharge that is greenish-yellow, frothy and smells appalling – this may be a sign of trichomoniasis.

I'm suffering from a discharge and intense itchiness around my vagina. Have I caught a sexual illness?
You probably have vaginal thrush (candidiasis) especially if your discharge is thick, creamy in colour and smells yeasty. Thrush is a common yeast growth that can cause extreme soreness and itchiness. It can be passed between sex partners but you can also get it spontaneously, perhaps as a result of taking antibiotics or using highly perfumed soap on your genitals. You need to cut sugar out of your diet, stop wearing synthetic or tight clothing across the crotch, stop using perfumed products on your genitals and apply a fungicidal cream or pessary (ask your pharmacist or doctor) to the vagina. Plain live yogurt applied to the vagina also helps. If none of these measures help, or you

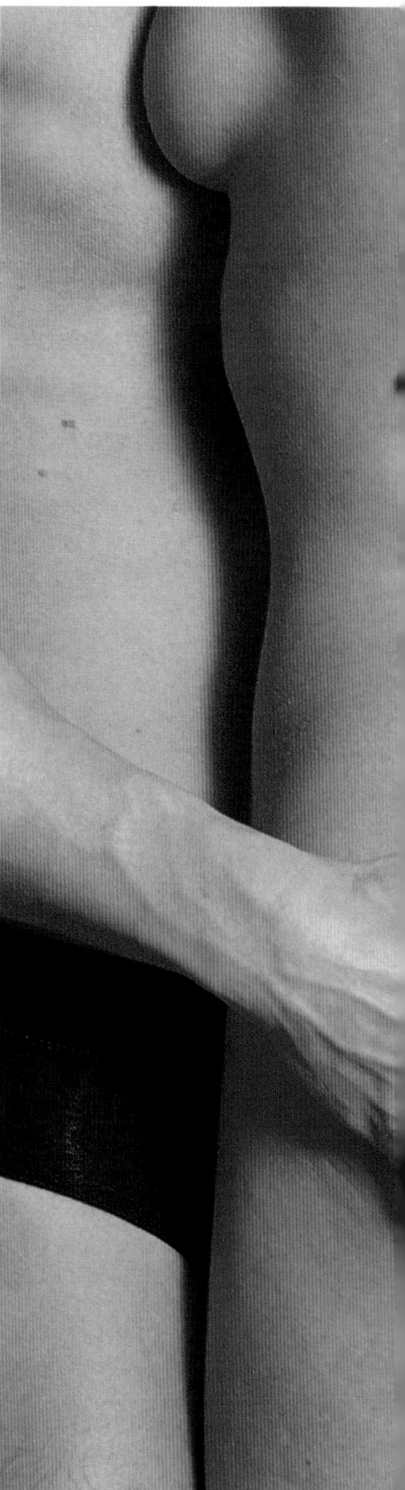

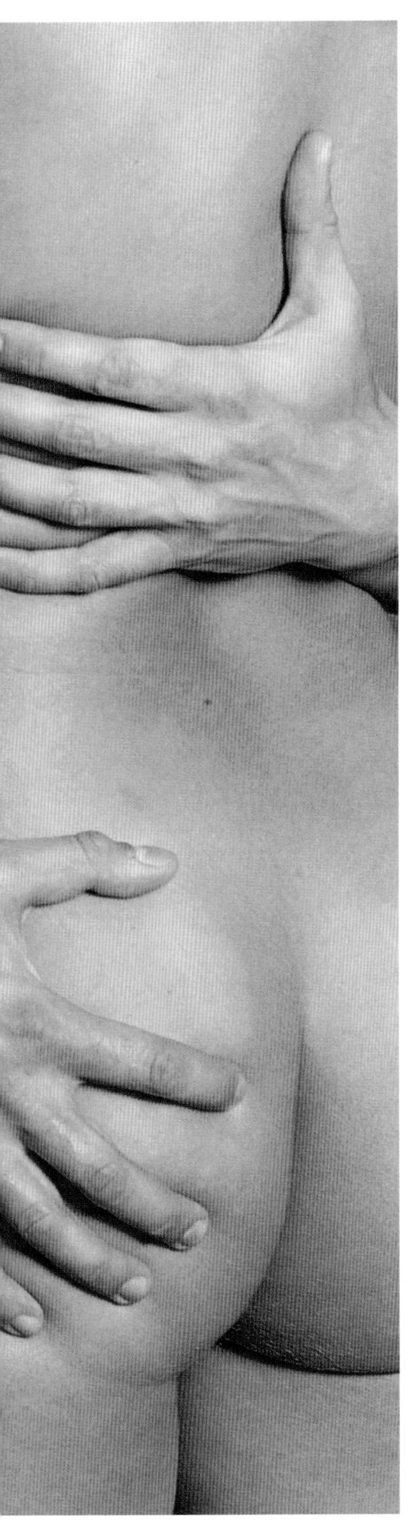

suspect you have an infection other than thrush, seek medical advice. Because thrush can be passed on to a sexual partner – causing inflammation and soreness around the head of the penis – you should avoid having intercourse until your thrush has been completely treated.

I think I've caught a venereal disease. I'm a teenage male and I've got a rash under my pubic hair. What could it be?
These are probably perfectly normal hair follicles that have become enlarged as a result of hormonal development and have now become tiny sebaceous cysts. Such a rash usually clears up of its own accord. But if you have any reason to think you might have caught a STI, it is always wise to consult your doctor.

I am horrified to find I have got genital herpes. It's so painful and unsightly – how will I ever be able to have sex again?
Genital herpes can feel very disabling the first time you experience it – both physically and emotionally. Although herpes is a virus that, once contracted, remains within your system, the first few outbreaks tend to be the worst. After this, eruptions usually decline in frequency and severity. In other words, it won't be quite so bad later on. There is also an extremely effective anti-viral medication (acyclovir) available in the form of a cream and tablets. Although it doesn't prevent herpes outbreaks, acyclovir can be used as soon as you are aware of an attack starting (many sufferers say that attacks are heralded by a specific tingling sensation). Early treatment will diminish the severity of the attack and help prevent frequent recurrences. As for lovemaking, although you should avoid sex for the duration of a herpes attack, there will be lots of times when you don't have an active outbreak and sex will be safer and more comfortable – consult your doctor about this.

I have found out that I have gonorrhoea. Should I tell my girlfriend?
You certainly should. Since gonorrhoea is sexually transmitted you may have caught it from your girlfriend. Alternatively, if you caught it from someone else, you may pass it on to your girlfriend (if you haven't already done so). Gonorrhoea can sometimes be symptomless in women, so even if your girlfriend doesn't have symptoms she may still be infected. In addition, if you get treated and your girlfriend doesn't, then future intercourse is likely to re-infect you. Untreated gonorrhoea can lead to complications such as prostate gland infection in men and an infection of the pelvic organs known as pelvic inflammatory disease in women (this can lead to scarred fallopian tubes and fertility problems). So, hard as it is, you must talk to your girlfriend.

sex and drugs

I've heard that some prescribed drugs can damage your sex life. Which ones are they?
The following can all have an adverse effect on sexual function:

- High blood pressure medication.
- Some antidepressants.
- Sedatives.
- Antianxiety and antipsychotic drugs.

Are there any drugs that a doctor can prescribe to improve sex?
There are no magical aphrodisiacs on the market but if you are suffering from chronic sexual difficulties then there are drugs that can help you. The most widely known of these drugs is sildenafil (Viagra; see pages 58–59) which helps impotent men by increasing blood flow to the penis thus enabling erection. Treatment with testosterone (see page 54) may help both men and women who are suffering from problems with sexual arousal and sensation. Hormone replacement therapy (see pages 86–87) after a woman's menopause can sometimes have a positive effect on her sex life, partly because it helps to resolve problems such as vaginal dryness and mood swings that can put women off having sex.

If you have a specific problem such as severe premature ejaculation a doctor may prescribe a drug such as clomipramine (an antidepressant) which can help you to last longer before ejaculating.

My husband has recently had to go on pills for high blood pressure. Now he's never interested in sex and finds it very hard to get an erection. What has happened? And what can we do?
High blood pressure pills are often responsible for a lack of sexual interest and the doctor should have warned your husband about this. Encourage your husband to speak to the doctor about taking an alternative medication that does the same job but has less of an inhibitory effect on sexual function. Your husband could also ask if it would be safe to take occasional holidays from the drug on the grounds that sex is one of the pursuits that makes life worthwhile!

Sex fact

Apomorphine (Uprima), a drug that has been used to treat Parkinson's disease, may be used an an alternative anti-impotence drug to sildenafil (Viagra). It works by stimulating parts of the brain involved in the erectile process.

I'm a 36-year-old woman and I've been taking antidepressants for a month. Now I'm having difficulties reaching orgasm. Why should this be when I've never had problems before?

One of the side effects of depression is that you lose interest in sex. So your sexual difficulty may have set in before you started taking the antidepressants. Alternatively, it may be your medication that is responsible. Different types of antidepressants vary greatly in their sexual side effects. Tricyclics, for example, often encourage sexual feelings to return as the depression lifts (although roughly 20 per cent of men and women continue to experience arousal problems while on the medication). Another popular antidepressant, fluoxetine hydrochloride (Prozac) results in impaired orgasmic ability for some women and ejaculation difficulties for some men. However, the good news about antidepressants is that once you have come off them, your sexual interest should be back up and functioning at 100 per cent.

What effect do recreational drugs have on sex?

Most recreational drugs have a negative effect on sex, either in the short or long term. Here's a summary:

- Nicotine inhaled by long-term smokers can lower fertility and cause circulatory problems that impede blood flow to the genitals and result in impotence in men.
- Cannabis enhances the user's state of mind. If you're feeling aroused, smoking a joint can increase sexy feelings, but if you're sleepy it will knock you out. As with cigarettes, long-term consumption has damaging consequences for your sexual abilities.
- Cocaine can cause retarded ejaculation and delayed orgasm. Long-term use can result in lack of sexual interest and desire.
- Heroin causes loss of sexual desire in the short term, while in the long term it can cause ejaculation, orgasm and fertility problems and impotence.
- Ecstasy causes warm emotional feelings but these may not translate into sexual ones.
- Amyl nitrate ("poppers") is used specifically to enhance the moment of orgasm but it can be dangerous, especially for people with heart problems. It also smells horrible!

I'm a former heroin user. While on the drug I lost all my sex drive. I'm now on a small dose of methadone but haven't got my sex drive back. Is this permanent?

Both heroin and methadone can have a negative effect on your sex drive, making you lose interest in sex and find it difficult to have an erection and ejaculate. When you manage to come off the methadone, give your body time to recover and you should see an improvement in sexual function.

I'm a 50-year-old man who has taken to using "poppers" (amyl nitrate) at the moment of orgasm. I find this increases the sensation of climax. The trouble is, orgasm without poppers now seems like a non-event. I fear that I'm addicted. What can I do?

I expect the reason you started using poppers in the first place was because of diminishing sensation during arousal and orgasm. This can be normal for both men and women as they get older. Your dependence on poppers is likely to result from this rather than from addiction. Some men find that a testosterone boost in gel or patch form helps to restore sexual sensation – ask your doctor to refer you for specialist advice. This would be a healthier option than using poppers, which may be dangerous if you have any kind of heart condition.

What does it mean if...

I need a drink before I have sex?

One woman I know used to get visions of her grandfather – a Methodist minister – looming over her every time she got close to orgasm! Not surprisingly, she found it very hard to relax during sex and almost impossible to climax. A little alcohol works on your brain just enough to remove a layer of inhibition – this is why many of us do daft things when we're under the influence. In the case of sex, once inhibition is removed we can let go and enjoy our natural sexuality. Having said this, alcohol is not the therapy drug of choice and it's important to note that, while a little aids relaxation, any more has the opposite effect of shutting down the sexual centres with a clang!

are you assertive?

Sexual health is an important part of all intimate relationships but one that many people find hard to broach. Do you take an assertive approach or do you wait for your partner to take the lead?

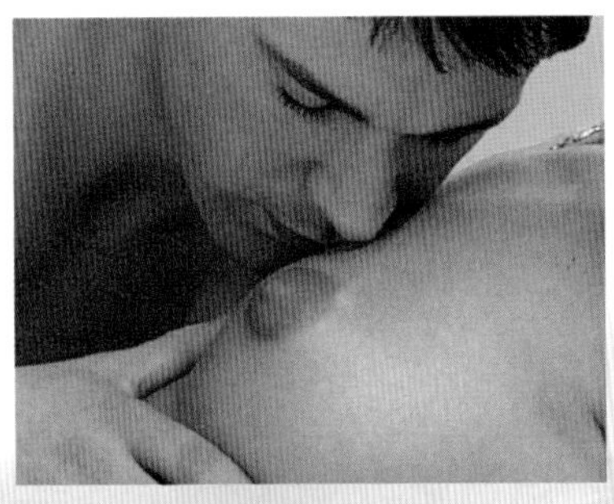

In a new relationship, how soon do you discuss sexual history?

- [ ] **A** Before you have sex for the first time.
- [ ] **B** After a while, when you get to know each other better.
- [ ] **C** When/if the subject arises – you don't want to pry.

You've just had sex with a new partner and you realize the condom has split. Do you:

- [ ] **A** Tell your partner immediately?
- [ ] **B** Pluck up courage, then tell your partner?
- [ ] **C** Hope he/she hasn't noticed?

Having found out about someone's sexual history you no longer want to have sex with him/her. Do you:

- [ ] **A** Be absolutely frank. He/she will respect your honesty?
- [ ] **B** Invent an alternative reason for your lack of sexual interest?
- [ ] **C** Back off with no explanation?

You're sexually active and, although you have safer sex, you occasionally worry about your sexual health. Do you:

- [ ] **A** Pay a regular visit to a genito-urinary clinic to get screened?
- [ ] **B** Go to a clinic to get checked out only when you feel extremely worried or think you may have symptoms?
- [ ] **C** Worry without doing anything?

You have a new partner, and you're just about to have sex together for the first time. Do you:

- [ ] **A** Stop and discuss contraception before things go too far?
- [ ] **B** Scrabble round for a condom at the last minute?
- [ ] **C** Let things go this time – you don't want to spoil the mood?

Your partner is really keen to have sex, but you've just realized you've forgotten to buy any condoms. Do you:

☐ **A** Insist on non-penetrative sex?

☐ **B** Discuss your options?

☐ **C** Go for it anyway – you'll be alright this once?

Your partner doesn't like using condoms, but they're your favourite contraceptive. Do you:

☐ **A** Insist that he/she gives them a go?

☐ **B** Ask if he/she will use them occasionally?

☐ **C** Take alternative precautions?

You're with a new partner and you want him/her to take an HIV test. Do you:

☐ **A** Ask him/her outright to take the test with you?

☐ **B** Ask him/her how he/she would feel about taking the test?

☐ **C** Discuss it hypothetically and gauge his/her reaction?

You are in a new relationship and you think that you may have given your partner a STI. Do you:

☐ **A** Tell your partner immediately?

☐ **B** Wait for the right time and ask your partner if he/she has had any symptoms?

☐ **C** Feel too embarrassed to broach the subject?

You think that your partner may have given you a STI. Do you:

☐ **A** Discuss it at the first possible opportunity?

☐ **B** Mull over the implications and broach the subject hesitantly?

☐ **C** Deal with it by yourself?

Your partner drinks too much and it's showing in his/her sexual performance. Do you:

☐ **A** Tell your partner that his/her drinking is getting out of control and it's time to do something?

☐ **B** Gently discourage him/her from drinking so much?

☐ **C** Put up with a situation you feel powerless to change?

Your doctor has prescribed some medication which you suspect is affecting your sex drive. Do you:

☐ **A** Go back to your doctor and discuss this in detail?

☐ **B** Privately check out the side effects of the medication?

☐ **C** Comfort yourself with the thought that you won't be on the medication forever?

ANSWERS

Mostly As It is always best to be upfront about important matters of sexual health and contraception, and you are certainly not backwards in coming forwards. This is great because it means that you are protecting your health and wellbeing and are not afraid to face problems head on. Occasionally, your forwardness may seem a little aggressive to a sensitive partner. Don't get assertiveness confused with aggression. Some matters of sexual health require delicacy. When it comes to lovemaking, it's always a great idea to stand up for your love rights, but don't forget that sex is a partnership.

Mostly Bs You know what's good for you and will discuss matters with your partner, although sometimes you may bide your time. This can be the best course of action in some circumstances. However, when it comes to protecting yourself against STIs, you may need to stand your ground a little bit more. You can adopt a style that combines sensitivity with assertiveness and both you and your partner will benefit.

Mostly Cs You are reticent about the more clinical sides of sexual relationships. This is common and may mean that you're not experienced at communicating frankly about sexual health. However, a proactive approach is important for your own wellbeing and can save you a lot of worry and angst in the future. If you practise being assertive in small ways, you will find that the bigger issues become easier to tackle.

index

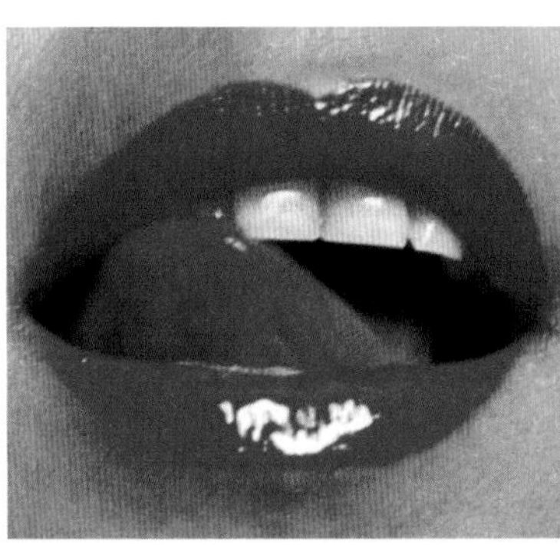

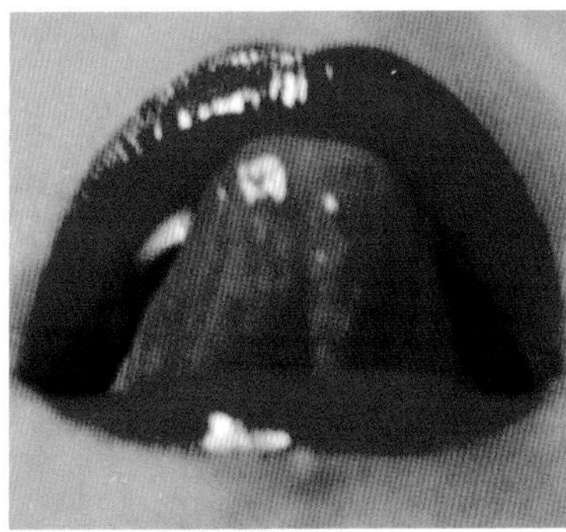

useful addresses

Advice and counselling

UK

Relate
Herbert Gray College
Little Church Street
Rugby, Warwickshire CV21 3AP
01788 573241
www.relate.org.uk
Counselling, sex therapy and relationship advice.

Samaritans
Freephone 08457 90 90 90
www.samaritans.org.uk
Free confidential service providing advice and support.

Brook Advisory Centres
65 Gray's Inn Road
London WC1X 8UD
020 7617 8000
www.brook.org.uk
Advice, help and information on sex, STDs, contraception, pregnancy and abortion.

British Pregnancy Advisory Service (BPAS)
Austy Manor, Wootton Wawen
Solihull
West Midlands B95 6BX
08457 304030
www.bpas.org

Rape Crisis Federation
7 Mansfield Road
Nottingham NG1 3FB
0115 934 8474
www.rapecrisis.co.uk
Provides details of local rape crisis centres.

National Aids Helpline
0800 567 123 (24 hours)
Free confidential service covering all issues related to HIV and AIDS.

London Lesbian and Gay Switchboard
PO Box 7324
London N1 9QS
020 7837 7324
www.llgs.org.uk
Information and counselling for homosexual men and women.

AUSTRALIA
Family Planning Associations Australia NSW Head Office:
328-336 Liverpool Rd
Ashfield, NSW 2131
Tel: (02) 9716 6099
Health Line: 1300 658 886
Call the Health Line for information and help from a registered nurse regarding sexual health issues. Check the directory for the nearest branch in your state.

Sydney Sexual Health Centre
PO Box 1614
Sydney, NSW 2001
Tel: (02) 9382 7440
Supplies information for local clinics

Relationships Australia
Tel: (02) 9418 8800
Offers counselling and mediation for couples and families, plus courses for relationsip education. Check directory for your local branch.

HIV/AIDS Information Line
Toll free: 1800 451 331
Provides information and referrals on any aspect of HIV/AIDs.

Rape Crisis Centre NSW
Tel: (02) 9819 6565 (all hours)
Toll free: 1800 424 017
Look in the directory for the Rape Crisis Centre in your state.

For good-quality sex aids try:

UK
Passion8, NES, PO Box 88, Hull HU5 5FW
Tel: 01482 873377

Ann Summers For your nearest shop, or to organize a party, phone 020 8645 8320 or visit the website: www.annsummers.com

Skin Two (for pvc and bondage equipment)
Tel: 020 7735 7195

Harmony 167 Charing Cross Road, London WC2H 0EN
and:
4 Walkers Court, London W1R 3FQ
www.harmonyxxx.com

AUSTRALIA
The Tool Shed Call (02) 9360 1100 or Toll Free on 1800 181 069 (outside Sydney) for your nearest shop in Sydney, or visit the website to view their selection of accessories, toys and clothing: www.thetoolshed.com.au

acknowledgments

Picture research Georgina Lowin

Picture credits
The publisher would like to thank the following for their kind permission to reproduce their photographs:
(Abbreviations key: t=top, b=bottom, r=right, l=left, c=centre)
Camera Press: David Roth 52. Gaze International: Hywel Williams 144. Alastair Hughes: 53. The Image Bank: Alain Daussin 4-5. Images Colour Library: 97; AGE Fotostock 17. Mother & Baby Picture Library/Emap Esprit: James Thomson 139.
Corbis Stock Market: Pete Saloutos 57. Getty Images: Dale Durfee 90bl; Joe Polillio 66; Kevin Mackintosh 60-61; Stuart McClymont 32-33; Uwe Krejci 9, 34. Superstock Ltd.: 84. Telegraph Colour Library: A Mo 135; Ian Sanderson 92-93; VCL/Paul Viant 108-109.

Jacket picture Credits
Front jacket The Image Bank
Back jacket Getty Images cr
Spine The Image Bank
All other images © Dorling Kindersley.
For further information see: www.dkimages.com

Index Dr Laurence Errington

Proofreading Constance Novis

Props
Ann Summers for the loan of lingerie.
Skin Two for the loan of pvc and rubber outfits.
Harmony for the loan of lingerie, pvc outfits and accessories.